MAR 2 9 2017

EAST MEADOW PUBLIC LIBRARY

3 1299 00958 1100

S0-CFG-564

East Meadow Public Library
1886 Front Street, East Meadow, NY 11554
(516) 794-2570
www.eastmeadow.info

MAR 2 9 2017

East Meadow Public Library

TAKE ME HOME

WALKING ON SACRED GROUND
IN THE LAST STAGE OF LIFE

Finding Meaning/Sharing Wisdom
Caring for Our Elders

Liza Catherine Johnson, L.M.F.T.

WingSpan Press

Copyright © 2011 by Liza Catherine Johnson
All rights reserved.

No part of this book may be used or reproduced in any manner
without written permission of the author,
except for brief quotations used in reviews and critiques.

Printed in the United States of America

Published by WingSpan Press, Livermore, CA
www.wingspanpress.com
The WingSpan name, logo and colophon
are the trademarks of WingSpan Publishing

Cover photo:
Pishkun sweat lodge by
Jim Wells, Great Falls, MT
photog@jimwellsphotography.com

Author photo:
Carolyn Karsten

First Edition 2011

ISBN 978-1-59594-441-2 (pbk)
ISBN 978-1-59594-758-1 (ebk)

Library of Congress Control Number: 2011928479

Contents

PART TWO

The Storytellers

The Last Stage of Life:
The Night Sea Journey and the Beacons of Light

Waking up to an elder's dependency

In this story, Enid Ikeda powerfully describes her experience of confronting her mother with the need to go into assisted living.

Waking up to choosing one's own life

Waking up to the dependency and the tremendous responsibility of a mentally ill elder can force one to make a choice as to whose life you are going to save. Here is Marsha Benoff's story.

Hostile dependency

Sometimes the caregiver tries to do everything possible to make facing dependency easier, but is met with hostility. Resentments and anger about becoming dependent can be directed toward the caregiver, consciously or unconsciously, making her or him the object of despised dependency. This storyteller wants to remain anonymous.

Interference from a spouse

Ruby Anastasia Sturcey's story describes a long painful process throughout which her efforts to face and deal effectively with her mother's dependency and approaching death are continually frustrated by her father who is in a state of denial.

Waking up to Mortality: The Caregiver's Call to Face Death

A time for healing family secrets
Emmelien Brouwers' story is a powerful portrayal of her mother who, at the end of her life, has a major revelation.

Great patience
This story takes us into the world of Parkinson's and shows how the caregiver reaches inward, finding unimaginable patience. This storyteller wishes to remain anonymous.

Finding love for a parent who has been abusive
Taking care of an elder can awaken childhood trauma. This is Colleen Donahue's story.

Unfinished business unresolved
Sometimes, no matter how hard we might try to resolve old wounds, nothing changes. This next story, by Roberta Rachel Omin, is a heartbreaker.

A surprise after death
Arlene Schofield's feelings change after her parents pass on. Here is her story.

instructed her to help her mother to the light. This is a powerful story for trust in oneself, especially in those realms that are often bewildering.

Miracles happen

Megan Burt's story takes us into the powerful world of prayer and a transformation that happens on the 'deathbed'.

Afterlife happening

Linda Moseley's story describes the tragic unexpected death of her mother and a mystical afterlife happening.

A deal for an afterlife experience

Roberta Rachel Omin's mother leaves her signs after she passes on.

Acknowledgments

This book would never have been written if it were not for my mother, Glady Isom Johnson. I honor her pioneer spirit and love of life and give great thanks to her even though she never had a chance to read this book.

I am deeply grateful for the enduring support of my mother-in-law, Ruth Ginsberg, who unfortunately died in 2008. She was the first person to read the beginning few pages of this book and that same day said it should be published. She was my editor and champion for three years.

I also give many thanks to Dr. Robert Bosnak, my dream teacher, who after reading my memoir suggested I make it a self-help book as well. I received many stories for the book from his Web site. He also taught me the techniques of embodied imagery and dream work that I have incorporated in some of the exercises in Part Three.

I am grateful to my meditation teachers, Dr. Richard and Bonney Schaub, for their wisdom and support that shine through in the Inner Home section.

I am indebted to the storytellers for their rich and heartfelt stories that offer so much wisdom and wide variety of circumstances.

I would never have been able to accomplish this daunting task without the talent and support of Paul Cash, my agent and editor, who helped me every step of the way.

I give thanks and appreciation for the members of my first professional writers' group, Talia Carner, Judy Epstein, Annie

Blachely, Linda Davies, and Adina Genn for help and their encouragement.

I am deeply grateful for the loving support and talent of Jean Brown, Joan Campagna and Dr. Andrea Gould, participants in my writers' group. We met for three years tweaking and inspiring each other's writing.

I am grateful for the love and support from my family, Dr. Alf Johnson, Claudia Dopkins, Linda Johanson, Elizabeth Galanakis, Cindy Bustamonte, Dr. Robert Ginsberg and friends, Chloe Heimbuch and Dr. Judi Musaro Lichter.

I am indebted to Tug Ikeda, my sixth grade teacher, who believed in me and instilled an enduring love for knowledge.

I want to thank The Jung Group: Sunny Holmes, Judy Tabak and Susan Kennedy for their support, love and advice.

I give much appreciation to Bridgette Nicolini who built my Web site.

I give thanks to Susan Harms, my cardio teacher at Body and Soul, who helped me strengthen my physical and mental stamina to finish the book.

Don Fish a Native from the Browning Blackfoot Indian Reservation in Montana, played a significant role as healer, guide and friend. In his quiet, yet powerful way he helped me reconnect to the spirit of the land and kindly offered his wisdom at various "stress points" on my journey with Mom. I will always remember him saying that his culture has no word for good-bye.

I will be eternally grateful to Peggy at the Goldstone for her unbelievable kindness and help and the great home she gave Mom in the last stage of Mom's life.

Bobbe Ann Thoeny, thank you for taking care of Mom's home every time there was an emergency.

My big black cat Bear died last year, at eighteen years old, just as I was finishing this book. He was my constant companion in the long lonely hours of writing. Thankfully, many times he helped me take breaks by jumping on top of my computer, demanding my undivided attention.

I don't know how Jeanne Ginsberg put up with me all of these years with the book as the main topic of my interest and conversation. Over and over again I asked her for help and advice and as always, she showed up with her shining light of wisdom

Introduction

*On September 12, 2000, I had a dream that woke
me up in the middle of the night. A voice, without
form, said, "Write the story of your mother's life." At
the time, I thought that would entail recounting the
unique adventures of her early life on a homestead
outside Calgary, Canada. Little did I know that her
story would instead begin with a stroke that marked
the beginning of her passage into the last stage of
life. I never imagined that Mom would have to deal
with the issues of assisted living and nursing homes,
broken hips, and strokes. She had always suffered
from high blood pressure and had weathered several
heart attacks years ago. I was certain that her
death, when it came, would be quick and clean.*

What lies ahead is the story of my journey with Mom through the
last stage of her life, a journey into assisted living and her eventual
death. I made a commitment to myself to join her in this as deeply as
possible. I had no idea how this decision would force me into depths
of my own character I never knew existed. My coping mechanisms
were often rendered useless. I had no road map for a journey ruled by
the unpredictable and offering no escape from the reality of death.

As time moved along, writing became my medicine and I
began to experience myself as the weaver of a sacred tapestry that
interweaved her life and mine. Stories from her childhood, as well as

personal accounts of her confrontation with Kronos, the God of Time and Aging, render visible golden threads of her pioneer soul—threads that seemed to shine through her as we made our way through the tangled forest at the end of her life. Other threads are colors of my soul. Everything she went through left its mark on me.

"Take me home" was something I heard Mom say again and again. Sometimes it was literal: Take me to the home I once occupied. But usually it was the wish to return to her former life where she felt a sense of belonging. "Take me home" resounded in me, the need to journey inward. The uncertainty of her health and well-being, which lasted over four years, forced me to find a way to feel peace on a dark night, to find something to guide me when I didn't know what to do, and to help me give comfort and advice to Mom about something I had not gone through myself.

I began to incorporate requests and prayers for help from my higher self and any higher being who could help me. I wrote down my thoughts and created places where I could be still in an atmosphere of candle light and silence. A relationship to my innermost self slowly emerged. I was deeply moved each time my requests for peace, comfort, or wisdom were answered when I walked out into the prairie, or slipped into a pine forest, or sat in candle lit contemplation. I began to feel accompanied, and my intense fear of death was softened. My "ordinary reality" began to shift: songs of birds, how the sun hit the waves, coincidences, intuitions, dreams—all became reminders of something watching over me, helping me along the way. This intrigued me and gave my life a renewed interest and purpose.

At the same time, there were many moments when nothing could relieve my anguish as I watched Mom suffer her physical, mental, and emotional breakdowns. I felt alone in the universe and, in this desperate aloneness, bit by bit, day by day I worked to recover my balance. The saving grace that became the "sun" in my world was the recognition of the preciousness of life. Each moment—no matter whether pain or frustration or love or tenderness or sadness or anger—became colored with, "This may be the last time." The feeling that life is a gift engendered gratitude and a deep regard for living, relating, and breathing in the present moment—noticing as though for the first time the shape of a rock, or the way a leaf falls to the ground, or a particular look on Mom's face. The blind one within could suddenly see, the deaf one could suddenly hear, the terrified one could suddenly breathe.

Upon completion of my memoir, I added stories from other caregivers to provide a wide range of perspectives on this time of life and help show how each phase of the aging process holds certain psychological and spiritual challenges for the caregiver. These stories are written from the heart, are psychologically astute, and contain many jewels of wisdom. I hope that sharing my and other caregivers' stories will be of comfort and make wisdom available to others on a similar journey.

The last section of the book is a guide to the Inner Home, a place I discovered for self-reflection, inner peace, and access to higher wisdom.

Part One

Take Me Home:

Walking on Sacred Ground in the Last Stage of Life

"Take me home is the universal longing of almost every living person as he/she gets older and can no longer take her or himself home. Home, the archetypal symbol of a safe place, of familiarity, of belonging looms as a beacon of light when the path in life begins to waver and fade into twilight." —Ruth Cowan Ginsberg

1: **The Dream**

A voice, feminine, compassionate, and strangely "other" awakens me out of a deep sleep, imploring me: "Write the story of your mother's life." I open my eyes and look around my bedroom, expecting to find some stranger. It is still dark out and I am seized by a feeling of awe, of fear. "Write the story of your mother's life" circulates through my mind and then echoes into every corner of my being: a mission, a calling from where? From whom?

I get out of bed and fumble around for my appointment book. I will have to wait until 2:30 p.m. to call Mom as I am booked with psychotherapy clients and there is a two-hour time difference. At 12:30 Montana time, I make a beeline for the phone. I get her answering machine. Unfazed, I begin to leave a long message about writing a book together, when all of a sudden she says "Hello?" in a strange, eerie tone. I say, "Oh, Mom, have you been on the phone?"

She says, "I don't know." To every question she responds, "I don't know." Fear begins to rise up in my chest as I suddenly realize something is very wrong. Struggling to orient myself to this 360-degree turn, I hold my breath as though to prolong each second.

I ask, "Mom where are you?"

She says, "On my bed."

I ask, "Did you read the newspaper this morning?"

Her voice becomes shaky and she starts to cry, again answering, "I don't know." I tell her that I'm going to call an ambulance. She says, "Please, no."

I say, "Mom, you don't sound right. I think you should go to the hospital."

She says, "He won't remember me."

Confused, I ask, "Who won't remember you?"

She says, "I don't know." In my mind I keep trying to figure out who "he" is but to no avail. This continues for least fifteen minutes. Finally, against her will, I decide to call an ambulance.

I ask her if she can walk. She says, "Yes." I tell her to go downstairs, unlock the side door and sit on her couch by the phone while I call for help. She agrees. When I hang up the phone, I can feel my heart pounding against my rib cage. I realize that I'm responsible for her life and that I don't have any of her friends' phone numbers.

My hands begin to shake out of control and I can barely dial 911. I get New York instead of Montana. I hang up and dial 411 for the name of an ambulance but I get into delays. Suddenly, I remember that I have the number of the hospital. I call and they say they will send an ambulance immediately. I give them instructions to come in the side door and that Mom will be waiting in her living room.

I call Mom back and tell her that an ambulance will be coming to pick her up. I explain that she probably had a stroke and that she will be taken care of at the hospital. I tell her that I'll check on her when she gets there. I'm relieved by the tone of her voice, which is suddenly calmer.

When I hang up the phone, my mind reels into a hurricane. Waves of emotions grow huge and chaotic, threatening to pull me out into a wild, dark sea of panic. I hear my breath sounding like a crazed beast, exhaling and inhaling in giant wails for life to return to normal. After I calm down, I realize that maybe her statement, "He won't remember me," means that her doctor won't remember her. I call him immediately.

2: **The Aftermath**

Mom has had a stroke. My older sister has volunteered to fly out and take care of her. She just called to say that Mom can walk fairly well but her speech is slurred. It's hard for her to retrieve words or hold a conversation for long. After the phone call, I record the dream in my journal and the thought of writing the story of her life recedes into the hinterlands.

Four weeks pass and my turn to visit Mom comes around. For the first time in all the years I have flown home to Great Falls, I take a taxi from the airport to Mom's house. It feels strange to be greeted by her at the door and I'm shocked by her appearance. She is thinner, slightly shaky, and frail—not the strong mother I visited several months ago. But thankfully, she still has that sparkle in her eyes.

After spending several hours with her, I realize that her shakiness might also be anxiety. She is continually getting up and walking around like a caged lion and is not interested in her usual afternoon nap. By the end of the day, her anxiety has gotten into me and I can't imagine how I'll get through the rest of the week. Each moment feels like an eternity and I'm grateful it's finally 8:00 p.m. and Mom is in bed.

Morning arrives after a long restless sleep. I dread the day, not knowing what to do or how to be with her. I want to go back to sleep, but instead I force myself to get up and go downstairs.

There's Mom sitting at the dining room table in the same clothes she wore yesterday. She hasn't even made her morning coffee. Giving myself a pep talk, I make some coffee and the smell fills the room with its familiar warm comfort. I lean into it and fortify myself. Usually, we read the newspaper as a way of easing into the day; but at this moment, I am the lone reader, informing her about the news in town, working hard to spark some familiarity and calm.

We have lingered over coffee for nearly an hour and I finally ask her if she wants to shower and wear a new outfit. I can hardly imagine how we will fill the day. She responds "No." Suddenly I sense her fear.

I sense her confusion, as well, in her hesitant steps as she goes from one room to another as though looking for something that has been lost.

She must feel like a stranger to herself, unsure of her world and how she will navigate through it alone. I remember her telling me years ago that her greatest fear was being disabled by a stroke. My heart breaks up with that thought, dissipating my agitation and I soften to her.

Almost immediately Mom responds, becoming more relaxed. As the day moves on she seems more like her old self and I, too, relax into me. I am aware, however, that she answers "No" to almost every question about going somewhere or doing something, wearing something new, taking a shower, turning on the television. I spontaneously point that out to her. To my surprise and clear as a bell, she says that "No" gives her a sense of control. We break into laughter.

A staff person from Eldercare comes to arrange some services for Mom before I leave for home. The three of us sit down and I quickly become annoyed at the soft tone of her voice which makes it difficult for Mom to hear. She also keeps looking at me as though Mom is not in the room and I feel uneasy as though we're hiding something from Mom. I tell her in a polite yet firm way to talk louder so that Mom can participate but she continues as though I haven't spoken. Mom is beginning to look anxious.

I give the woman one more chance to no avail and end the meeting. When the door shuts behind her I am relieved and almost exuberant that this disrespectful being has been banished from the room. Mom is happy also, as though we now have a common enemy as we join forces in determining the future quality of her care.

3: Dawn Magic

Mom is taking a nap today—something she has always enjoyed. I tuck her in to make sure she is comfortable and as I sit here with her while she falls to sleep, innocence emanates from her being. My heart fills with tenderness as I watch the blankets rise and fall, protecting the fragile form underneath. Somehow, I have a feeling that she never will recover the strength of her former self. I am deeply saddened and also in some strange way enjoy this new feeling of closeness in caring for her.

A memory comes to me. When I was eleven years old, Mom took my younger sister and me to visit her parents at their ranch outside Calgary, Canada. This was special because we were taken out of school for a week and it was also the first time I experienced Mom away from my father for any length of time. I became aware as the days passed that a happier side of her was coming out. The three of us slept together in a big feather bed and woke up every morning at 4:30 while it was still dark, eager for the day to begin. A mug of coffee with fresh cream from the milk cows, the down comforter sealing in our warmth, and conversations about our night time dreams drew us softly into each other and into each day.

Mom brought us into her childhood life wholeheartedly. She took us to the place where she grew up. I couldn't believe my eyes when I saw the small wooden skeleton of a shack that her family lived in for many years, surrounded by miles and miles of open, treeless territory. Several times she got out all of her old cowboy records and we listened to them on an old wind-up Victrola. She showed us how to milk a cow and squirt the milk into the mouth of the patient stray cat that lived in the barn.

She had much experience with this. As a young child she had many animal friends. Being the only girl with three brothers, she spent hours alone playing with feline friends that gathered around her. She would dress them up and pretend they were her children. Often she was seen walking in the fields with a trail of cats following behind. She earned the nickname, "Puss," which lasted until she left home to attend nursing school.

One morning, while it was still dark, Mom drove us to pick up a horse which our neighbor had said we could ride while we were there. I was in love with horses at the time and was not deterred when we were told that he was old and hadn't been ridden in a long time.

I was taken aback, however, when I set eyes on him. Standing in the middle of the corral was a tall, muscular pinto horse with a shaggy winter coat of large black and brown spots. His neck was huge and his wild brown eyes lit up when he saw us approach.

Bursting with excitement, I begged Mom to let me ride him back to the ranch. Without hesitation she consented. With my sister behind me on bareback, the ride was tinged with early dawn magic: The bulging muscles of the pinto rippled beneath our legs; my hands gripped the long, tangled, coarse mane and my sister's warm arms wrapped around me as we galloped along.

Anything my sister and I wanted was granted here. A camaraderie grew among the three of us that has stayed with me all of these years. It was a blessed time where my sister and I enjoyed the divine meaning of Mother, a being who opens her heart to her children, offering them slices of life that nourish and serve the spirit and the longings of the soul.

4: The Garage Door

Before returning to New York, I make sure Mom can get around, cook, and take care of her bills. The main problem is transportation. So for now, I hire a woman to shop and clean for her and I also arrange Meals on Wheels so she doesn't have to venture out.

Soon after I leave, she fires the shopping woman; but, thankfully, she is satisfied with Meals on Wheels. Despite numerous warnings from my siblings and me, she took her car out one day, and in her words, "I just stepped on the gas." Luckily no one was injured. She turned around, went home and hung up the keys.

I flew out soon after this with the sole purpose of helping her learn to drive again. In Great Falls, public transportation is almost nonexistent; Mom would have to depend on a taxi, and she's a penny pincher when it comes to herself. I know she isn't ready to submit to being dependent and that she probably will try driving again soon. After a week of practicing on country roads, she's back in the driver's seat.

Today a package from Mom arrives in the mail. She called earlier to tell me she had just finished a pastel she wants me to have. Eager to see her new painting, I rip off the wrapping and am shocked at what I see. Peering up at me is a portrait of a Native American man, his face blotched and scarred with dark colors and a faraway expression in his eyes. It gives me an eerie feeling. Usually her pastels reflect a joy and beauty in whatever she portrays.

I call to thank her and she says that she fell the other day and hurt her face which resulted in a big black and blue area around her eyes, just like those in the painting. She also tells me that she locked herself out of her house while she was out on her deck watering the flowers. Instead of calling out to her neighbors for help she climbed over the railing of the deck so that she could come in through the side door. She was halfway over the railing, which is at least six feet from the ground, when she lost her grip and fell.

She laughs and says, "Boy, did I leave a big dent!" I join in the laughter too, but an uneasy feeling grips my heart. I ask her if she really is okay. She says, "Don't worry, it was just a little accident." At the same time, she mentions that people she meets in the local stores ask her about the black and blue marks.

I suddenly feel guilty, as though I'm remiss in my responsibility to her—and the memory of a terrifying experience I had several years ago, before she had the stroke, comes to mind. I was flying back for a visit and when I arrived at the airport, I heard an announcement for me to come to the information desk. Mom was supposed to pick me up but she wasn't there. The person at the desk told me to call Mom at home.

She answered very weakly and said she had fallen backwards down the stairs and hit her head on the corner of a wall. She was bleeding and wanted me to hurry up and get there. When I hung up, I found a policeman and asked if he would give me a ride home. He agreed and when I finally got there I ran in and found Mom in bed covered in blood. I rushed her to the emergency room.

She had to have fifteen stitches and was hospitalized so that she could have blood transfusions. It took me days to clean up and I finally had to take the blood-soaked pillows to the only dumpster I could find downtown. I quickly flung them in and ran back to the car as fast as possible, feeling like a criminal leaving the scene of a crime.

After that incident, every time the phone rings, my heart jumps.

Continuing our conversation with this memory haunting my mind, I ask her if it's still easy for her to shop and get around. She says, "Yes." But she also tells me that sometimes while shopping at the mall, she forgets why she's there. I ask what she experiences when this happens. She says it feels as though something exits out of the top of her head, leaving her with a blank feeling. Feebly, knowing that she is determined to stay put in her home, I suggest that perhaps she should make a list before going shopping. She says that she will in the future.

Then she lowers her voice as though telling me a secret and asks me how to use the garage door opener. We both know this is a bizarre question since, for years, she has been using the remote on the sunshield of her car. I explain how to use it, but I know that trouble is just around the corner and she won't be safe for long living on her own.

When I mention this to her, she gets very upset and says she's perfectly fine. She is not about to have help or move into an assisted living facility. I tell her that I'm grateful she can be honest with me. I know that she confides in me because she trusts that I will respect her wishes. I want to keep that line of honest communication open and at the same time I struggle with concern for her safety.

I sense her struggle, her ambivalence about her situation also. Part of her wants me to know that she is having trouble. Another part of her insists that nothing is wrong. Today I am resigned to her insistence that nothing is wrong and I let it go. I tell her to see her doctor and pray that nothing terrible will happen.

5: The White Ducks

An awareness is growing in me that Mom is functioning in a minimal way at home and that time is moving swiftly along, demanding more attention from me. I will need help, but it's not just about getting advice from others. It's about becoming stronger internally so that I can stand up to the imminent decisions and happenings we will be facing.

I've been turning to contemplation for solace and wisdom. I find a place to sit and light some candles. I focus on my breathing and when I sink into its hypnotic rhythm, stillness comes over me with its sheltering presence. Mom's situation begins to feel less scary and I gain a sense of strength and clarity. Slowly I'm realizing that her trials are unavoidable events on the precarious path she is now on, and that I am a participant, unable to protect her from the gods of Old Age and Death.

Today, as I drop into contemplation, an image from the other day at the beach appears in the darkness of my mind: Mom has entered a transitional space, a period of time where independence struggles like a fish on a hook, hoping to set itself free from the firm hand that holds its face into eternity. Just for now, I accept that it's alright that we both want to stay here at the edge of the land of denial for a while longer. We both want to rest in this familiar place that will allow us to hold on to that last scrap of life as she now lives it. Neither of us is ready just yet to face the inevitable.

I have made a commitment to my innermost self that I will honor, to the last possible moment, how much she loves her life in her home, the home she bought and decorated from scratch several years after Dad died. She chose all of the colors, the furniture, and the carpets with an excitement that bubbled up from her spirit. It was here that she came into her own.

She studied pastels and became an accomplished artist. One of her paintings, a portrait of a Native American woman, won a grand prize ribbon at the local fair. She also had several offers on her portraits of roosters but was unable to part with them.

Her home is filled with her pastels of elk, lions, flowers, rabbits, wolves, and birds of every description, as well as portraits of Native Americans. One of my favorites is a pastel of two luminescent white ducks standing on the edge of light blue water. It is late in the day and there is a soft, misty light in the sky. They are not looking at each other, they are each tending to something in their own world, and yet the way they are standing conveys a deep feeling of rapport, of deep communion. They seem to personify contentment and grace, seeking nothing more than the present moment together. Immersed in this state of tranquility, they appear holy. Honestly, I cannot imagine Mom leaving her sanctuary behind.

6: The Accident

Mom fell over before a hand could grasp or an eye could blink. She was standing, talking with my brother and sister, firming up plans for a family reunion when she collapsed, breaking her left hip. My sister, who stood a foot away, was horrified. She felt certain she could have somehow prevented it. This happened one hour before my plane was due to arrive from New York. I had called Mom from the Minneapolis airport and she said she would pick me up. Only two and a half hours later, my sister-in-law greets me instead. She tells me that Mom has just broken her hip and is in the hospital waiting for surgery. I go completely numb.

The dry hot wind swirls around the corners of the airport, like miniature tornadoes, spiraling dust particles into the air. The hot, barren landscape mirrors a strange emptiness I suddenly feel inside. All the vacation plans evaporate and my mind goes blank. When I speak, my voice sounds disembodied like an echo rising out of an empty chasm. Somewhere inside, in the deepest chamber of my heart, though, something begins to boil. It is fury. I am *furious* that something has happened to her. I am furious that she is slowly being disabled by time and that she has to experience the brutal breaking-up of her body, one accident at a time.

At the hospital I find her in a room on a disheveled bed, waiting for the surgeon. Frail and frightened, she can barely greet me. There are tears of pain in her eyes. I stand there momentarily, totally helpless, witness to the inevitable. I lean down and kiss her soft wrinkled cheek.

7: The Corridor

I want to fix her. I want to mend the hip she just broke and take her home. I want to see those pioneer hands, once more, grab that golf club. I want to hear her speech unaffected by the last stroke. I can no longer keep at bay the knowledge that our time together is fragile.

She heeds the instructions of the nurse and grabs her walker. Eager to recover her former strength, she slowly stands. Her hands grip the pink ace bandage wrapped around the handles of the walker, and she begins her long journey down the corridor. She takes one step and drags her other leg. Shoulders raised, breath turning into little gasps, she continues on this mighty task.

Time slows down, and my heart begins to break into tears; tears of compassion for her; tears knowing that her spirit wants to keep walking down the hospital corridor, unaccustomed to this battered body. My tears are overflowing as I realize that life on this beautiful planet does eventually come to an end. The sounds of loved ones, the feel of cotton, the joy of having a healthy body, the enchantment of puffy white clouds fades and then vanishes forever.

As I drive away from the hospital, a sparrow is struck by an oncoming car. I stop and get out of my car. Lying in the middle of the road, its head wobbles to one side. I pick it up and feel its pounding heart beating out of control. Each beat presses down against the palm of my hand. Suddenly there is stillness, like the quiet that follows a storm. What is left of this tender being that only a moment ago could fly up and away with the vigor of a sparkling light?

I hold the body of the sparrow close to my heart even though I know it is dead. I feel the little legs, lifeless and brittle against my hand. When I arrive home I take it over to a silvery poplar and place it in the deep, soft grass near the trunk. Its head drops gently, nestling back into the embrace of the earth. Somewhere within, a light breaks into my dark sorrow.

8: Rehab

Mom has been in rehab for ten days. John is her speech therapist. Beth is her physical therapist. Tom is her respiratory therapist. Cindy is her occupational therapist. Ed is her group exercise therapist. Linda is her LPN, and Sue is her nurse. Debra is the coordinator of her discharge.

Charles is her shrink because they think her asthma is really a panic attack. He just finished giving her a test to evaluate her mental functioning. He pours out the contents of a Ziploc plastic bag and says, "Point to the pencil, now the keys, and now your nose." She does this perfectly. It's strange to see Mom point to her nose. It makes her look stupid. I hate this man before me and I want the test to end.

I wheel her back to her room. I want to get her out of here and take her for a drive but we have to get permission from the doctor first. Finally we're off to the car. I feel her eagerness to get in and she momentarily forgets the procedure for turning with her walker. After eighty-five years of moving in a particular way, now she must not cross her legs or point her toe inward or bend at forty-five degrees or her hip will dislocate out of the socket and she will need another surgery. Her physical therapist quizzes her on this procedure after every session, "Now tell me the three things you are not supposed to do." Breathless, Mom always remembers the first two but not the third.

Driving away from the rehab building, I look over at her and the childlike expression begins to fade as her old self returns, as though the car from her 'life before the broken hip' brings her back to herself. We talk as we did in the old days. We could be out on one of our favorite jaunts to the local cowboy coffee house for a single shot latte or mocha.

I ask her if she wants to drive by her house and she eagerly says, "Yes." Barely able to walk with a walker, home seems very far away to her. Her sanctuary of many years is slowly fading out of reality and even though I know she wants to return, I'm aware now that it will never be the same. She will probably need someone by her side, guiding her, helping her with all of the mishaps of her frail existence.

Mom has been proud of her strength and independence growing up in that one-room shack of a homestead on the plains outside Calgary, Canada. Her parents used newspapers to insulate and cover the walls and when it rained, pails collected the drops that seeped through the roof. She really did walk several miles to school each day, even in the fierce Canadian winters.

Unlike most of her friends, Mom wasn't interested in getting married. She wanted to be a nurse and have a career. At a young age, she developed a hunger for books and would ride into Calgary with a neighbor so she could go to a paperback bookstore and get lost reading until they picked her up in the evening. The harshness of her daily life was softened by the stories of great women who lived lives of luxury and adventure, and the door to new possibilities opened in her mind.

Poverty forced Mom to earn her own money. She told me that she set traps for weasels on her way to school and gathered the little victims on her way home. She got five cents a pelt. One time, she was carrying three weasels and halfway home they sprung to life in her hands. Despite their desperate clawing she hung onto them even tighter and made her way home, bloody arms and full cargo. I was hoping against hope that she would say that she let them go; but when she got home, she killed and skinned them all.

She made enough money to buy herself a horse she called Old Yellow Face. He was very old and became increasingly ornery. Reminiscing, she told me that he was not quite worth the price.

9: The Conference Call

At 11:30 a.m. Montana time, we're having a conference to determine Mom's future home after rehab. My oldest sister is currently there with her, my brother is on a phone in California, and I am on a phone in New York. All of her therapists are there to give their reports on whether she can return to her home. Mom is there also.

I visualize her surrounded by all these people, struggling to keep her composure as she listens to the verdict that will determine her future home. She isn't one to call a lot of attention to herself. I know that a big part of her is hoping they'll say that she can go home without assistance. Another part of her is afraid to go home unassisted.

She told me yesterday that during the night several nurses came into her room because they thought she had passed on. Reluctantly she said to me, "I guess I do need someone around at night." Fear of being alone at night in such a tenuous state has broken through her strong hold to independence.

Each phase of her aging has held its challenges but this one is the most difficult thus far. When the stroke first limited her mobility, she gave her fishing pole and gear to her grandson. I was upset to see the empty hooks that once held her pole up on the wall. The tan and brown checkered tackle box no longer occupies its rightful place on the floor behind her golf cart. Her old fishing hats now hang lifelessly on the wall. The golf clubs still remain in her golf cart but they no longer reflect the order and shine from use. But at least then she was still able to live at home.

Then she could still drive herself to the store, even though at times her memory would forsake her and her speech would crumble into unintelligible comments. She could still slowly but surely ascend the stairs and walk out on her deck and water the flowers that have always been such a deep source of her daily joy. She could still make her coffee in the morning and look out on her birdfeeder to greet a couple of finches that have been there as long as she. She could pick up the local newspaper outside her door and spend the morning leisurely reading about the happenings in the world.

Now she must face the fact that these moments will never be part of her creature habits in the same way. What will happen to the old plastic milk container that still holds the extra onions and potatoes? Who will feed the finches and water the flowers? Where will the Glady (Mom's nickname) who fed and watered her loved ones go? Will she revive and continue this part of her in a new life or will her spirit wither and die into a lifeless smile, a cold vacant stare?

These daily routines are the beloved glue of her life, the strong threads that weave the colorful tapestry she calls home. How will she ever be able to say good-bye to this life she so loves? How will I ever be able to help her?

As each report is given, the hope of her returning home grows dimmer. I am beginning to experience a sinking feeling. Somehow, I imagined that she could live at home with some assistance. Debra, her coordinator, and all of the others say that she needs care twenty-four/seven. This adds up to an unimaginable amount of money and even if we do hire nurses, Debra says we'll also need backup help from neighbors or friends in case an aide should get sick at the last minute. It is clear to me now that the door to home is closing.

10: **An Old Journal**

Today, I'm in a window seat on Northwest Airlines and so full of emotion that I could burst into tears and never stop crying. The tightness of the physical space is adding tremendous pressure on the sudden explosion of feelings inside. It's as though all the previous months of fear and sadness that have been kept under wraps are suddenly beginning to unravel.

Desperately, I reach for my journal and pen just as my heart cracks open. Everything pours out of me onto the pages. I write steadily and as the hours pass I begin to feel calm inside. The words I choose seem to hold me in an embrace, like the arms of a great muse awakening, reaching out to me, offering comfort. Lost in time, it feels as though someone else is writing. I finally close the journal as we make the descent to LaGuardia Airport. I know something important has happened to me: I am seized by the call to write.

The wind is howling outside my car. There's a threat of a hurricane hitting land in full force later today and I've come here to the ocean at Robert Moses State Park to see the wild waves. I can see the ocean from my car and the waves are rolling and gray, foaming at that mouth. It's too windy to take a walk but I'm content in my car, eager to write with some journals from the past two years to inspire me. The crashing waves and the sound of sand pelting my car is my only distraction.

I open a journal from the year 2000 and begin reading. Suddenly, before me is a recording of "the dream" that told me to write the story of Mom's life. I completely forgot about this dream and yet when I see it here in front of me, it's as though it happened yesterday.

I now have written over thirty pages and in this moment I feel awe, awe for the unconscious process that we all experience at one time or another that seems to move us along in our lives with a direction unbeknownst to our conscious mind. There is another feeling, too. My journals suddenly feel sacred. I sense their presence here beside me in this lonely, turbulent landscape, like a secret lover hungry to delve deeper into my being, my soul, as I accompany Mom on her journey. I will follow this siren like a sailor lost at sea. I will write "the story of Mom's life."

11: The Sanctuary

Off the beaten path, past the poison ivy and several fallen trees, is a circle of Norwegian pine. I have spent many hours here communing with the spirit of this woods I call "my cathedral." Bluebirds flit from tree to tree, leaving trails of iridescent blue light. Several red-tailed hawks screech as they circle above and today I answer them back. The smell of pine perfumes my inner being with the promise of peace. Even though this forest is only five miles from my home, I am transported to a wilderness that holds no scent of another human. Here, my wild soul loves to wander. This place is my sanctuary, a place that makes all my burdens bearable.

Today the forest brings me back to a time flying home from a golf trip in Hawaii with Mom. We had bulkhead seats so we could stretch our legs and the sun was pouring in through the windows. The hum of the engines and the smell of coffee lulled me into a sleepy state of mind. Memories of the week prior began floating back—of green fairways and humpback whales breaching, bright pink blossoms of bougainvillea and the smell of orchids. I leaned over and put my head on Mom's shoulder. It felt soft and warm. I remember the sweet smell of her skin and the familiar freckles on her arms. Even though I am no longer her child, there still remained a place for her to return.

My sister arranged for Mom to move into an assisted living facility. She said that when they went to fill out all the forms, Mom noticed a tray of home-baked cookies on a nearby table, got up without help and ate several in no time. Sweets are her favorite thing. Mom refers to this place as a hospital and I am surmising that she calls it a hospital because it implies a temporary stay. My sister says it is comfortable and the people are friendly.

I have not spoken with Mom since she moved in but that will change now that her new phone has been connected. It seems strange to suddenly dial this new number. For fifty years, 406-452-2134 has been home, Mom, my history, the lighthouse in troubled times. I feel deeply disturbed, as though the bedrock of my existence that once was like granite is starting to give way to the unforgiving determination of the ever-pounding sea of time.

Today I am worried because my sister has to return to her home in California and this will be the first night Mom has been on her own since the accident. She will not have a shoulder to rest her head on or a forest to embrace her. Where will she find shelter? Will she have a dream like the one she told me years ago where she felt her head cradled in the softness of a pink, heart-shaped pillow? I'll call her later and tomorrow and the next day and the one after so she won't feel forgotten.

12: The Box

Mom has been in her assisted living place for almost two months. I haven't seen her room or the particular building even, but my younger sister just returned from a visit and says that Mom has been moved to another room. It is very small with a bed, a television, a hospital dresser, and a bathroom. The window is painted shut.

She offered to bring Mom some of her paintings from home but she refused, saying that she doesn't want to make this home. She made it clear that this is a place of continued rehabilitation, not a final place of residence. When I asked her in a phone conversation if she is joining the other residents in activities, she responded in an irritated way, "Yea, can't you just see me getting into that little bus with all of the others!" I laughed and felt like an idiot. The truth is I cannot.

She is still trying to manage the walker and the two oxygen tanks; one is portable and the other is stationary next to her bed. At first she often got the walker tangled up in the oxygen hoses. One day my sister came into the room and Mom was having difficulty breathing. She had attached the hose to the wrong oxygen tank.

Today Mom tells me that she's resting and enjoying not being responsible for anything. I ask if she wants me to send her a hot pot for water for tea. At home, she always used to wake up from her afternoon nap and make a cup of Constant Comment tea with cream and Equal and toast with Skippy peanut butter. She assures me that she wants no part of cooking on any level.

I tell her I want to send her a package anyway, but without the hot pot. This need arose in response to the fear I experienced the other day when she told me that she spent a lot of time staring at the four walls. What scared me about this? Have I not experienced this myself, that sense of existential despair, that emptiness, that abyss? Shouldn't I protect her from this, this place where there is no "other" around, not even God? Is this when the spirit begins to wander away because there is nothing reflecting it back, nothing engaging it in life? Is this the place where madness makes its way slowly into the psyche?

I want to make sure she doesn't fall into this void and I immediately begin to think about what I can do to help her fill out her day. I also wonder for whom I am doing this.

I remember someone telling me once that isolation is the opposite of healing. Love and connection orient us in time and space. I begin to imagine ways to fill up those four walls and banish that emptiness, that madness that lurks there. A care package is the perfect remedy. I relish this renewed sense of power and begin my shopping list: Skippy peanut butter (crunchy style), homemade raspberry jam, crackers, Constant Comment tea bags (she can ask someone for hot water), catalogs, modeling clay to keep her fingers dexterous, vitamins, lavender soap, sweet-smelling shampoo and conditioner and, best of all, a tiny stuffed Scotty dog to keep her company. I want her to feel love come into her room and oh, I'll send a framed picture of all her children. She will have us to look back at her.

13: Doctor's Orders

I notice a different tone in Mom's voice lately. It's the sound of contentment. She is resting a lot and she especially enjoys her meals which are at 7:00 a.m., 11:00 a.m., and 4:00 p.m.

My younger sister, who lives in Portland, Oregon, found a perfect place for Mom nearby. It is small, beautiful, and well-managed. She imagines Mom coming over for holidays and taking her to doctor's appointments. When she asked Mom about that possibility she replied that her doctor wants her to stay where she is for another month or so until she is recovered. My sister decided to call Mom's doctor to verify and he had a totally different story. He said that she could move any time.

Mom has found a way to stay where she is. I sense that she still believes that when she gets better she will return home. I have a deep knowing inside to trust that Mom knows what's best for her. She still exudes an inner strength and a desire to be in charge of her life. I am determined to honor that and in this trust I will be able also to see beyond my own needs and fears that lurk around dependency and aging.

The other day a friend said that Mom was being difficult wanting to stay in Great Falls, rather than move closer to one of her children. But the truth is she has never really been someone who could allow others to take care of her. She is always the first one to grab the dinner check or clothes at the register. She likes giving and has never been able to be anything but mother to her children. I don't think she's being difficult. I do know, however, that she would be difficult if she were forced into a situation that she did not want.

As strange as it may sound, I learned a great lesson about appreciating the uniqueness of another from my cat Bear. I always wanted a lap cat and when I first got Bear I was determined to make him into one. Often I would pick him up and force him to sit on my lap. He would get furious and bite me and then jump off and run away. Set on having my way, this continued many times until one day instead of biting he just looked at me with this look that stopped me in my tracks. I knew that he was drawing a line, warning me that if I continued with my plan he would seal his heart off from me forever. I put him down immediately and from then on I always took my cues from him. Amazingly, he is now a lap cat five years later. Mom demands this respect.

I wonder how she will navigate through this part of her life. I know that if I impose my needs on her it could threaten the life of her spirit and our relationship. Will she make choices that will challenge my sense of right and wrong? Is it more ethical to be concerned about her safety above anything else? Or should I be more concerned about the health of her spirit? Is it possible to gratify both? Will I know when it's time to break through the denial and make decisions for her?

I do know that she lives deeply connected to her inner voice, something that became steadily stronger after Dad died. This prize was hard won and she is not about to let it go. It's easy for me to honor this because the foundation of my work as a psychotherapist is based on the belief that each individual has a deep longing to wake up to their inner voice, their pathway to wholeness and fullness of being. If believing that the doctor is ordering her to stay at this residence makes it easier for her to be there, then so be it. She has found a way to control her situation and, unlike her children, she's sleeping through the night.

14: The Adventure

Mom has been at the assisted living facility for almost a year. Her discontent is growing as the months pass. The other day when I called she said, "I am getting out of this hospital and going home tomorrow."

"But Mom," I asked, "how can you go home tomorrow? How will you manage with the walker and the oxygen tank?"

She said, "I don't want to talk about it anymore."

I find it difficult to talk with her lately. One day she feels one thing and the next day another. Sometimes I have no idea what is really going on or how to help her. When I ask her if she misses her home she says no, but then in the next breath she says she is going home. I mentioned to her that she could stay with me in New York for awhile but she says that she doesn't feel up for traveling.

My sister and I agree that certain times of the day, especially the evening, are difficult for her and for us. She will implore us to take her home. In the morning, she is perfectly content with her situation.

I keep holding on to the idea that this is an adjustment period and eventually she will grow to like it there. I am also aware that, a year later, this still hasn't happened. I feel guilty that I am failing her, especially when I imagine her sitting in her room alone, longing for home. At the same time I feel helpless because at this point, the only thing that would truly make her happy is if I gave up my life and moved back to Great Falls!

She told me the other day that one of her friends came by and asked her if she wanted to do something different for a change. Without telling anyone, Mom took off with her friend on an all-day adventure. They went to Gibson Park and spent the day feeding the Canadian geese and ducks. When she got back everyone was frantic. The nurse who was assigned to give Mom her medications came into her room and there was Mom's walker and oxygen tank, but no Mom.

This kind of spontaneity was not unusual for Mom. You could always count on her to join in an adventure. When I was first embarking on my career as a psychotherapist, I asked her if I could practice my skills on her. She was a very good sport and said yes. I had just been hired as an elementary school counselor and had no experience in counseling.

I made an appointment with her for the following week. Meanwhile, I hurriedly read some guidelines for counseling children and when the day arrived for her appointment I was feeling very competent and eager to begin. At 6:00 p.m. I was waiting for her. She drove up at 6:10 and sat in her designated chair. I, in my therapist hat, asked her why she was late.

She was a little taken aback by my seriousness and replied that she had been shopping. After a few more questions she replied that maybe therapy wasn't for her. We both started laughing and decided that probably it wasn't a good idea to try this out on family. I did learn that confrontation in the first session is not a good idea.

Soon after this Mom decided to go back to school and finish up her bachelor's degree in nursing at Bozeman. She drove off to school, terrified that she was too old. She rented a little room and graduated two years later. She told me that her professors took pity on her (which I doubt) and gave her a great deal of encouragement as well as compliments on her high marks. After graduation, she returned home and began working at a hospital where she eventually ended up teaching for quite a few years. It felt as though she had reclaimed that part of herself which she had given up during the many years of her marriage.

It is interesting that one of the wards Mom loved most was the psych ward. She began to understand herself and her marriage in a whole new way and we would often joke about relating and empathizing which came out of her first session with me. Our relationship began to grow in a new direction. She turned to me for my knowledge in psychology and we had frequent discussions about how she felt her children were affected by her marriage and the passive role she played in it. She saw herself as unable to stand up to her husband which both angered and distressed her. For many years her anger took the form of berating him.

No matter what we might be talking about, the topic would soon turn in the direction of the past and the mistakes she had made. It wasn't until a few years before her death that this stopped. I think the stroke had a lot to do with it. Either it was too difficult for her to get the words out or she no longer thought about him, but it was then that our conversations began to concern issues in the present moment and the bitterness of the past began to drift away.

15: The Other Hip

It's now only two months later and Mom just broke her other hip. I cringe to think of her body being so frail and vulnerable. I plan to fly out several days after she has been in the hospital, buying time because it's hard to get away and right now she's in good hands. I'm also adjusting to the fact that these mishaps are on the rise and that in some way I'm getting used to it.

At the hospital, I stand outside her room for a moment. I'm curious to see Mom from a stranger's point of view, to get a glimpse of how she is when I'm not around. She's not aware that I'm outside her room and when I look in I get frightened. She's staring off into space, totally lost. The left side of her face is drooping as though she had a stroke. I take a few moments to get my bearings and then walk into her room. She recognizes me at once, which is a relief, and we talk for a brief time. I tell her I plan to be in town for a while and that she'll be in rehab for several weeks.

Before flying out, I told her doctor about something Mom had shared with me over the phone just after she broke her hip this time. She confided that she was having nightmares and wasn't sure if they were dreams or reality. She told me about a "dream" in which she was walking in Gibson Park and suddenly ended up in a building very high off the ground. She was terrified of falling off a stage. She tried to call for help but suddenly the phone lines were cut and she thought she was going to fall. She said it was one of the most terrifying moments, because the bottom was endless space. I assured her that it definitely was a dream and that she actually had been in the hospital the whole time. I was concerned, however, about the dream imagery. Could the phone lines being cut symbolize that another stroke or her death is approaching?

When I informed her doctor about this I suggested that she should probably take an anti-anxiety medication. He agreed and put her on a medication. Unfortunately, it produced a terrible reaction where she couldn't even talk on the phone for several days. I was mortified and felt totally responsible. Very slowly, days later, she recovered.

Outside the snow has made a beautiful white blanket. I love to walk after a big snow because the secret life of various creatures is revealed. Deep in the woods, I find tracks of deer and a place where several bedded down for the night. Seeing the imprints of their bodies touches me deeply. I see how closely they have lain together and how the scattering of leaves left from their grazing forms trails of intimacy. Further up the hill I find the body of a raccoon almost buried in the snow. What happened?

As I wander deeper into the woods I notice a small moth walking on the snow, caught unprepared in a cold white universe. I feel for this creature struggling to stay alive and place my hand down for it to crawl up on for some refuge. The moment it contacts my finger it dies. Did the warmth of my hand allow it to die in peace or did the warmth actually shock it into death? I will never know.

As I walk on in the soft white world of the woods, an awareness of death permeates my thoughts. Death is inescapable.

16: Passages

For two weeks, while Mom is in rehab again, I'm busy visiting her and setting up another assisted living situation. This one will be smaller and more intimate than the last.

An employee at the current place told me that Mom fell and broke her hip in the elevator. Mom has different story. She says that someone accidentally bumped into her and she fell. I'm disturbed and realize that this situation is much too large and impersonal.

My siblings and I decide that she needs something more homey and friendly immediately. A staff person mentions a small, cozy, and well-managed place. They have an opening but I, up until the last moment, am not certain that she will qualify because of her diabetes and erratic blood sugars.

I am mindful of how precarious life seems at times. One fall can, in a moment, totally change the quality and direction of one's life. Last-minute decisions, chance meetings with certain people, fleeting intuitions that we act on can steer our lives in an entirely different direction. This feels like one of those moments because we're also thinking that maybe she would be better off living near one of us.

Before deciding what to do next, I call one of Mom's best friends to get some down-home advice. She invites me over for a cocktail and we speak for hours about Mom's situation. I ask her if it would be better to move Mom at this point in her recovery to a place near one of her children, or should I respect her wish to remain in Great Falls if the living situation works out. Her friend suggests that Mom will probably be happier in her familiar surroundings.

I realize that Mom's psyche is oriented to her surroundings. She has lived in Great Falls for over seventy years. The landscape calls her back to herself: the streets and stores, her friends, the open space, her doctors. With her increasing frailty and her memory failing, a new town could be very disruptive to her sanity. At least here, past memories, even though fleeting, act as minute anchors in her ever-changing world.

As I drive over to the rehab center, the moon is making its way over the horizon. The first star appears through the dark blue clear sky. I ask for guidance from above to help me continue to be open to Mom's circumstances. In this moment, heaven and earth seem to form a warm cocoon of comfort and support in this uncharted territory.

Each person's journey is so intimately different and yet similar in many ways. Very few books or programs on the aging process have offered me wisdom. But that's okay because somehow this journey with Mom is forcing me on a path that's filling a deep hunger. Writing and my ritual of contemplation are giving birth to an inner friend that is warm and expansive, comforting and wise.

Carl Jung, the famous psychoanalyst, wrote about this place in the psyche and called it the Self, which is very different than the ego. The Self resides in the deeper layers of our psyche as wisdom directly linked to a divine order. This Self has to be cultivated, through self-reflection, dream work, and being open to our intuition with a trust that there is an innate wisdom in all of us waiting to awaken. The stars, the moon, and the night sky affirm this in a resounding epiphany.

When I enter Mom's room she's watching television. She tells me to come and get into bed. Feeling a little awkward at first, I sit down next to her. It feels suddenly cozy to be next to her enjoying *Animal Planet*. Then she says she wants to go home and sadness wraps us in its arms.

I suggest that maybe going home is a wish to return to her former way of life. I begin to talk about how every stage of life has its challenges: birth, infancy, young childhood, going to school, teenage years, college, finding a career, finding a life partner, midlife, retirement, and old age. I tell her she's being challenged with losing her sense of independence and trust in her body. I let her know that I'm learning about this stage of life through her and that she is my model.

The conversation ends and we turn our attention back to the television. I can tell she feels better knowing that her struggles might have some meaning to me, but more importantly I know that the warmth and intimacy of our visit is the real salve to her longing for home. We stay like this for a while longer with the moon shining in upon us.

Driving home I feel grateful for this time, this intimacy. I get a sense of myself aging as well, and somewhere deep under the layers of denial, a vague fear has dug in. Here, in the domain where an awareness of death is a constant presence, my sense of security is as steady as the shifting sands.

17: Before Dawn

As I pull out of Mom's garage the next morning, I am met by the presence of the constellation Orion overhead. It's still dark at 5:00 a.m. and I'm headed out of town to the Pishkun where I hope to find some solace. The Pishkun is twenty miles outside Great Falls in the middle of open prairie, sage brush, and huge shale ledges where Indians used to run buffalo over the cliffs to ensure their supply of meat.

As I drive down the winding gravel road, the vastness of the land and dark sky fill me with awe. The road takes me up to the top of the cliffs where I park. A dark blue halo is forming on the horizon as the sun still hides beneath the distant mountains. As I close the car door and begin the mile walk to the edge of the bluffs, I'm aware that the protective shield of my car has disappeared and I am alone in this vast expanse of space.

Out in the middle of this land I make myself vulnerable. Although I feel fear, the cool mystery of the darkness and roughness of this place pulls me forward with wild tastes of stars and sagebrush. Slowly, as the light begins to change from darkness to dawn, the landscape softens; tall prairie grasses rise up out of darkness into silvery wisps; rocks begin to take shape on the path; now and then I hear the deep lowing of cattle below. The landscape all around me is gently waking up.

At the edge of the cliffs I can see for miles. Far off the twinkling lights of Great Falls form a necklace around the distant mountains. To the right Square Butte rises up like a giant table, offering itself to the sky. The first rays of sun break out over the horizon, coloring the layered rocks in purple, red, and orange light. The stillness of twilight cracks open as the wind comes down from the heavens and sweeps across the land.

I sit sheltered from the wind on a great stone chair, covered with light green and bright orange lichen that has formed over thousands of years. Behind me several abandoned sweat lodges appear like strange skeletons of some vanished species that once sheltered the ceremonies of the first people of this land.

Sacredness still emanates within the emptiness. I feel humble in this simple encountering. I am aware of my body and the coldness of the stone.

When I stand up and make my way along the shale edge, time seems to slow down. I notice a beetle making its journey with steadfast determination. It opens my vision to all the small communities of other life around: prairie dogs pop their heads out of their earth dwellings, barking warnings to each other of this strange visitor; the wild hare blends into the branches of a thorny bush, sitting so still that it looks like a stone; the skin of a rattler is hidden deep in the dark corner of a shale ledge; the red-tailed hawk glides without effort, its red tail catching the first rays of sun.

I am penetrated by the presence of these other communities that live on beside, underneath, and all around me and they are deeply connected to my well-being in this moment. Their existence enhances my own with mystery and the joy of living in an awareness that is so multi-faceted. As the day warms up, I make my way further along the shale cliffs. Immersed in the wildness of this place, my imagination begins to recapture the huge herds of buffalo that grazed here and the smell of campfires coming from the circle of teepees. Taking a moment to rest, my eyes sweep across the land below. Out behind a rock appears a coyote. Its long flowing gray coat is ruffled by the wind. It looks right up at me as if to say, "You are not alone,' and then as quickly and quietly disappears as though it, too, were a phantom of my imagination.

18: The Meeting

Back in town I decide to visit a second-hand store which sells Indian jewelry and clothes. Last year I bought a pair of black cowboy boots for only fifteen dollars. I want to find out if there is someone who does sweat lodges or healings. The woman at the cash register gives me the name of a man.

Later that day I call. He tells me to come to his office and when I arrive at the address, I'm surprised to find that he works in the same building my father did some thirty years ago. As I follow him into his office I'm overwhelmed by his presence. Long black braids sprinkled with silver fall down his back. One half of his face is handsome and the other half is scarred and has the look of an old bird like a hawk or eagle.

We talk for a little while and I tell him that I need a healing and that I want to pray for help with my mother. He agrees to do a healing and later we meet at his house. Many Indians live in this part of town and you can see native symbols, animal skulls, and other wild objects hanging on the sides of their houses and trailers. I realize that a whole other world exists here and the mystery of this place intrigues me.

He greets me at the front door with an austere look. I don't think he really thought I would show up because there are no signs of preparation. He tells me to wait while he goes downstairs. He emerges with an abalone shell, a package of sage he gathered on the reservation, and two huge golden eagle wings.

He lights the sage and the smoke curls upward offering a peaceful feeling. He smudges all the corners of the room, the windows, and the doorways. I feel protected, as though the sage has created an invisible chamber for the healing.

He tells me that some plants are regarded as more sacred and powerful than humans and sage is one of them. It is a medicine that guards sacred space so that evil spirits cannot enter and at this moment, I can sense the awareness of the smoke hunting around for bad energy.

He tells me to stand and begins a prayer for me and my Mom. I silently ask for help and guidance. He begins to pray in his native tongue and with several strong movements of his arms sweeps the huge wings, pungent with the smell of sage, all over my body. The breeze and sound of the wings feel as though the giant bird has flown into the room. My ears tune into the sound of his deep voice speaking a language I have never heard. Sometimes the words—her mom, Liza, grandfather, grandmother—break out of the strange sounds and I feel transported back into another time, when the land and all that lived on it was revered with the utmost sacredness. Tears begin to fall down my cheeks, and they feel good against my skin.

Later on, the sun begins its orange descent and this strange, rich world I have encountered recedes as the glass doors to the rehab open for me to enter where Mom is struggling to recover. She beams me a big smile and I begin to tell her about the healing. I also mention my encounter with the coyote and that I'm a little concerned about returning to the Pishkun.

She tells me that one time when she was walking to school, she came upon a band of coyotes. She slowly turned around and went home. She described the encounter to her mother and her mother told her to go back to school, that the coyotes wouldn't harm her. She did, bearing her brave child's soul. And I guess I, too, will go back to the Pishkun.

Just as that thought enters my mind, her golden eyes with dark brown speckles twinkle with prairie wildness. As I gaze more deeply into her, an ancient face of eternity appears and disappears, just like that coyote.

19: Temporary Solution

Everyone is telling me that I shouldn't bring Mom to her home when I visit in February. But I'm steadfast in my decision to bring her with me for the week I'm there. I want to offer her something she has desperately longed for . . . home. I want to see her face when she walks in the door.

When I arrive at the assisted living facility, she's ready. I know on some level I'm taking a big risk. What if she refuses to return? What if she breaks down in tears and I'm not able to take her back? Despite these considerations, I go ahead with my plan. I do ask her, however, to promise me that she won't give me a hard time when I bring her back. She agrees. I put all that she needs into a flannel pillowcase and, without further ado, take her home.

When we arrive I try to remember how to help her up the stairs with her walker. To my surprise she grabs the handrail and starts up the stairs, leaving me to follow with her walker. She hasn't been in her home since she broke the first hip more than a year ago.

For the first hour she goes from room to room looking at everything. She looks in the closets, in the refrigerator, out the windows, checks her birdfeeder, and finally settles on her bed while I open the closets in her bedroom. She wants to see all of her clothes and shoes. We take out an outfit and she eagerly casts off her clothes that smell of assisted living.

Later, we go to the supermarket and she relishes walking around, especially in the bakery section. Her residence has kept an eye on her diabetes and she's been deprived of her favorite thing—sweets!

That evening we talk about all the things we will do and I ask if there's anything in particular she has been longing for since leaving home. She says she is just happy to be with me at home.

When I first arrived at her place, I was taken aback at the cold feeling. There was stillness, a lack of color—no soul giving things a loving order. It was eerily empty. As we settle in, that empty feeling is slowly filling up with our conversation and laughter. We relish the idea of a whole week open to adventure and make some plans for the next few days.

Initially, I was worried about Mom getting up and down the stairs. I even entertained the thought of sleeping at the top of the stairs so she wouldn't wander down them in the middle of the night. After she had the stroke, she used to wander down the stairs, go into the refrigerator, and eventually there would be some mishap, like falling or knocking something over. One time I found her in bed eating an ice cream bar and the next morning she remembered nothing about it.

Again I ask her to promise that she attempt the stairs only if I'm nearby. She nods her head "yes" and I see a little sparkle in her eyes. After several days, I'm surprised at how well she's getting around her house without her walker. She gets support from walls and chairs at times and as each day passes she gets steadier on her feet.

Near the end of the trip, we take a picnic lunch down along the Missouri River where we can watch the flocks of Canadian geese descending on the river. She has always loved the haunting sound of their calls, going back to childhood. As we eat our sandwiches, a rich silence falls upon us. Neither of us feels a need for conversation. We're lost in the moment, as though infinity itself is making its presence known like an invisible river carrying us along on a timeless journey that will go on forever.

The next morning I pack all of Mom's things back into the flannel pillowcase and we drive back to assisted living. I'm overcome with sadness as I glance over at her and sense a childlike innocence in her obedience. At the same time I'm filled with the closeness we shared and a new feeling of tenderness fills my heart.

True to her word, after we put all of her clothes away, we kiss good-bye and she tells me to go without a tear in her eye.

20: My Garden

It is a beautiful, brisk morning. I'm standing in a sunny spot, feeling the warmth of the sun penetrate into my being. There's a feeling of life within me, reaching for that warmth as though I were a seed nestled in the dark earth waiting to awaken to a blessing. My hand feels the cool hard shape of coins in my pocket. I become aware of how the material world and all the fears it brings—of needing money, of needing various things to feel secure—clash with this serene moment.

I notice the bright green leaves of the hydrangea and the young, scarlet cardinal that has just landed on a nearby branch. My body casts a shadow on a small azalea. I think, something will have to give up its life for me today: The lettuce I eat for dinner will have to leave its soft, nourishing place in the earth; the plump olives, filling up with sun, will be crushed into oil; the fish that rejoices in the deep sea, shall be taken. How will I make my day worthy of their death?

Mom and her fierce thirst for life are worthy. I remember when, at eighty-four, she first went into rehab for the broken hip. She came down with pneumonia and was having difficulty breathing. Standing outside her door, I heard a staff person tell her that she needed an antibiotic, that she had pneumonia. He asked her if she wanted to take one—in my mind implying that if Mom wanted to die, she could choose to forgo treatment. I waited for her answer. Without hesitation she said, "I want it." I remember the way the sun filled her room and how the wrinkles on her face and her bony feet and hands suddenly appeared primal, enduring, sacred.

21: The Jewelry Box

As a child, I was always fascinated with Mom's jewelry box. It sat on top of her bureau, inside her closet, black and square with corners bitten by age. I would open it only with her permission. No matter how many times we meandered through its contents, I always begged for a story or two about her life.

The amethyst necklace from my father sleeps curled up in the corner, like a magical creature with its multitude of clear polished stones held in gold, lacey trim. A large pin of polished agate with a curled silver sword nestles nearby. Mom tells me that one day while she was walking down the streets of San Francisco, an old woman approached her and told her that this pin had a powerful charm and that she should always guard it from harm. Many years later my brother played with it and accidentally broke the sword. Mom was upset for a long time, wondering when misfortune would come hobbling around the corner.

As we open the jewelry box today, there is a different agenda. This time she wants me to take whatever I want. She no longer needs these things. Sprawled on her bed, I pick up the black and silver pencil she bought herself in nursing school. While many things have come and gone in her jewelry box, this pencil with its look of antiquity has always remained a steady occupant. I loved the idea of her starting out on her career with such self-indulgence. She says, "Take it. I want you to have it." I can barely imagine its absence from the jewelry box. With mixed emotions, I carefully tuck it into my purse.

As I sit on her deck in the quiet twilight, I watch the blue sky slowly fade into darkness. The round globe lights around the swimming pool make dancing reflections on the water. The sparrows are settling into the branches of the scrub pine. Mom is already asleep in her big waterbed. A wind picks up and the song of the copper chimes outside her kitchen window breaks out into the starry night.

22: The Little Book

October has arrived and there's a feeling of fall in the air. I'm back in Great Falls for a week and it's a relief to come for a visit instead of an emergency. Mom has just slipped into bed for her daily nap. During this time I like to meander through some of the antique stores in town. My favorite is the Bull Market on Commercial Avenue. There used to be a great restaurant for lunch on the first floor called The Bay Leaf. Mom and I would often eat there. Everything was homemade and their desserts were always a special treat.

Today on my trip I have ended up at the Bull Market. As I walk around, my mind preoccupied, I am drawn to a dusty shelf of books at the back of the store. Usually, I'm interested in old bowls or relics from the "Cowboy and Indian days." As I quickly scan the book case, a tiny green book on the very top shelf captures my attention. Barely able to reach it, I jump up to grab it. I am struck by its outward beauty. Only three inches by five inches it exudes a big presence. The title is written in gold print in old English lettering and the cover is a luminescent forest green with wavy patterns. Opening it I notice a woman's signature, G.E. Grace from Kansas City. I become intrigued with this book's journey here to Great Falls. The title also sparks curiosity: *In Tune with the Infinite* by Ralph Waldo Trine. It was written in the late nineteenth century, around the time Mom's parents were born. I look through the table of contents and am captivated by Chapter VI, Wisdom and Interior Illumination. I read, ". . . there is an inmost center in us all, where truth abides in fullness. This is the interior guide. This is the light that lighteth every man [woman] that cometh into the world. This is conscience. This is intuition. This is the voice of the higher self, the voice of the soul. . . . Thou shalt hear a voice behind thee, saying: This is the way, walk ye in it." I'm sold. I buy it for only three dollars and leave immediately for home, eager to read more.

When I return home Mom is up from her nap. As we drink our usual cup of tea, I tell her about my adventure and show her the little book. We begin to talk about spiritual beliefs, intuition, and psychics. She tells me that when she was in college, she and my Aunt Ann would go to San Francisco on a monthly basis to meet with different psychics. I am surprised since she has never spoken about this. I am aware that there are so many things that are a mystery about Mom, stories and happenings in her life, that are like those flowers that bloom in the wilderness, unseen, unknown by anyone.

For the rest of my visit I read the book slowly, savoring each word, while Mom watches TV. I carry the little book around with me everywhere as though it were a long lost friend. I enjoy touching its soft malleable cover. The lettering on the cover soothes me as though I'm witness to a sacred craft that cared about the spirit of its product. So here I am with this little book as a new companion on this journey with Mom.

It's early in the morning and Mom is still asleep. I decide to sit on the small couch in the living room for a while with my new friend. I light several candles and begin to imagine the small area where I'm sitting becoming imbued with the sacred. I ask my friend for wisdom and then sit with candlelight flickering on the walls. It is quiet, still and fresh from the long night.

I begin to focus on my breathing and as I do so my breathing begins to slow down and become deeper, reaching into the dark unknown places within. The sense of "me," which I usually call my ego, my ordinary conscious self, begins to expand and then slowly evaporates leaving me with a sense of inner spaciousness. I stay like this for a long time until I begin to notice the blue light of dawn slipping into the room.

I open the book randomly to see what message it has for me. I read, "Let there be many windows in your soul, that all the glory of the universe may beautify it. Not the narrow pane of one poor creed can catch the radiant rays that shine from countless sources . . . let the light pour through fair windows, broad as truth itself and high as heaven. . . . tune your ear to all the wordless music of the stars and to the voice of nature, and your heart shall turn to truth and goodness as the plant turns to the sun. A thousand unseen hands reach down to help you . . ."

The first ray of sunlight casts an orange glow into the room. In a state of deep gratitude, I am ready to greet this day.

23: "Chrismess!"

Mom always made Christmas a special occasion when I was a child. She decorated the house, baked cookies, and bought many presents for all of us. I think she wanted to make up for the neglect in her own childhood. She doesn't remember celebrating Christmas.

Hers was a childhood of labor. She helped her mom cook meals—and because ranch hands would gravitate to ranches where the food was good, the investment in cooking was similar to a solid stock in the market. As a treat to the ranch hands, Mom's mother would make dozens of doughnuts in the mid-morning and Mom would have to take them out into the fields and was told not to touch one. Amazingly, she told me she did not. Maybe that feeling of not being loved choked her indulgence.

There was a time when I wanted to know more about Mom's family. I asked her if she had any living relatives that knew her mother. She told me about Aunt Edie in Indiana, who was still alive. I began a correspondence with her and found out that Mom's mother used to make dolls and had given one to Aunt Edie a long time ago for Christmas. Mom got very upset that Aunt Edie got a doll from her mother and asked, "Why didn't she ever give me one?" She even called Aunt Edie to talk more about it. After that, Aunt Edie never wrote back to me.

When we all grew up and left home after my father died, Mom would spend Christmas with my older sister and her family in California. When she was unable to travel, one of us would usually come to Great Falls and spend some part of the holiday season with her. Last year, however, was her first Christmas alone. My sister planned a trip in late January and because we had to spread out our visits so that one of us would visit her every couple of months, this was how it had to be.

We thought we could make up for it by making it special via the mail. My brother and sisters, as well as myself, sent her many beautiful presents, cards, and flowers. When we called to see if she liked them, she said she didn't get anything. Upset, I called the director who kept a keen eye on everything. She informed me that Mom did, indeed, receive her presents, cards, and flowers.

At first I felt angry at Mom because I had spent so much time and money trying to make it a wonderful Christmas. Now, all of these efforts lay shattered before me like a broken vase. What I had to realize was that my wish to make her happy in her assisted living home was fruitless.

Later, after calming down, I realized it was no one's fault. Mom can only remember a few things—mainly, when one of her children is coming to visit. She remembers the flight, the date, and time. Oh, and there is one other thing she remembers. This year I decided to enclose in her Christmas package, among other presents, a box of hand-dipped chocolates. She did remember this gift and also told me she ate the whole box in two days. Thank God they were sugar-free.

24: The Ranch

I think Mom's love for sweets filled in for a lack of love in her childhood. She did, however, get much joy and love from the animals on the ranch. Her parents leased a small herd of cattle. Mom had to help milk cows before and after school.

She told me one time that she nursed an orphan calf which eventually became her friend. She called him "Orphie." When Orphie grew up, her parents wanted to sell him for beef. Mom became very upset, but later came up with a scheme. It was often a chore to get the milk cows to come in for milking, so one day when they were out in the pasture and her father was getting ready to bring them in, she called out, "Here, Orphie." Sure enough, Orphie came quickly and all the milk cows followed him right into the corral. From then on, Orphie was a celebrity.

I begged her for more stories and, indulging me, she told me how she had been in awe of her friend's beautiful ranch house and wished she could live there. She said that one time this friend invited her to a birthday party and when the day came she realized her shoes were dirty and ripped. She decided to wear her older brother's shoes because they were new even though a little too big. When she arrived the mother of her friend approached Mom and asked her if she wanted another pair of shoes to wear. Mom, who was always very prideful, said "No."

Many years later, her parents bought that ranch. They ended up very wealthy, especially after their death. The ranch house was huge and filled with priceless antiques. Mom's mother eventually became a collector of English teacups, and I have a few in my cabinet today.

The ranch also held a special appeal to my siblings and me. We loved to visit in the summer because of all the things to do and see and our grandparents always let us do whatever we wanted. They had every kind of animal and we were endlessly fascinated.

We learned how to feed the chickens and gather their eggs without getting pecked. I loved to milk the cows and then make slop of milk and grain for the pigs so that I could hear their smacking sounds of delight. The turkeys were always a little scary because they would chase us and seemed almost as tall as we were. We would run up bales of hay to get away from them.

The most thrilling animals were the huge hogs that were kept in a large pen. There were probably twenty of them and they were extremely hungry all the time. They were about three feet tall with dark bristly hairs that stood up on their backs like sharp quills. Unlike the other farm animals, they exuded a wild, aggressive spirit that sent shivers up my spine. I remember noticing that the ground in the pen was completely bare. They ate every little thing, even at times gnawing on the fence posts—ugh, just looking at them made me feel like part of their food chain. In the middle of their pen was a big flatbed truck with grain. Because the hogs would eat anything in sight, they were on a strict feeding schedule.

One day my sisters and I decided to feed them. When we got near the pen they all ran over and were too threatening to just go in; so one of my sisters distracted them while my other sister and I snuck around to the other side of the pen, climbed the fence, and ran to the flatbed. When the hogs saw us up there they stampeded over. We shoveled grain over the side and watched them go into a feeding frenzy.

While they were completely absorbed in this activity we suddenly realized the problem of how we would get out alive since they had surrounded the truck. We immediately thought to shovel more grain over on one side and when they all were lost again in a wild banquet, we leaped off the truck and ran as fast as possible to the fence, our hearts pumping adrenalin.

25: The Shopping Car

It's springtime now and Mom's ability to get around has decreased rapidly since Christmas. This time when I take her home, she can barely make it up the stairs. It has been only months since I was here last. I'm also struck by the loss of her long-term memory. Events and names from the past that she can usually recall are forgotten. She doesn't even recognize her own artwork on the wall.

To reorient her, I gather a bunch of her pastel paintings that she had long ago put in the back closet and tell her that I will help her finish them. She had forgotten all about these, and one is more beautiful than the others.

After completing the paintings we drive to a nearby store where, coincidently, there's a sale on frames. We purchase at least fifteen of them. While we're there she notices a poster of several huge white daisies and wants me to buy it and frame it for her. I'm taken aback since the poster seems so unlike her usual taste, and I wonder if she will change her mind or even forget about it later. But when we get home she puts it in front of me to frame and even remembers (later) to take it back to her residence.

It's satisfying to hang her pastels up on the walls. As each one is hung, a new light and energy flow into the room. I can also see a new light and energy come into her as well, as she looks around the room filled with her artwork. I am grateful that spark can be ignited and realize how that spark is an indicator of the quality of our time.

I'm dedicated to activities that bring her back to herself, and shopping is one I can usually count on. Today on our shopping trip, however, I have to find a wheelchair for her wherever we go. This is not an easy task, as many stores are unprepared for the elderly—except for one! Target has motorized wheelchairs. "This one," the clerk says, "goes no more than five miles an hour." That seems perfect.

I help Mom into the chair, and before I have time to gather our purses she takes off. Five miles an hour in a store seems like seventy on the highway. I run after her just as she heads for the jewelry case.

Soon, however, she gets the knack of it, and I watch in amusement as she maneuvers through racks of clothes. It's as though she has reclaimed the speed of her younger years and is enjoying the ride as much as the shopping. Every now and then clothes get stuck in the wheels and I help untangle them.

Letting her browse in peace, I search through a rack for some jeans. When I look up to check on her, there's Mom with a whole rack of clothes on wheels trailing behind her. She's unaware that a blouse sleeve is trapped in one of the wheels and the look on her face is one of pure pleasure.

26: The Divine Web

Early morning has left a soft mist over the open water. A celestial light rises from the golden path the sun paints on this salt marsh. A starling takes its bath alongside the road.

I'm looking forward to my morning run and a visit to my pine cathedral. When I arrive there, I spontaneously begin to pray to the four directions, East, South, West, and North, in a circular movement as the Native Americans did hundreds or maybe thousands of years ago. As I pray and face each direction I seem to fall into the essence of a giant invisible wheel. I experience myself in the center of this wheel: It is cool, calm, quiet, and sentient—a place that holds steady, like the wisdom of a great chieftain.

This place seems to instill harmony. I sense the presence of ancient beings who once stood in this place. Deeply moved and without conscious thought, I begin to honor the pines, I honor the birds flitting from tree to tree, the ants making their way among the leaves, the wind that rocks the mighty pine trunks back and forth, back and forth. I am mesmerized and sink deeper into time, deeper into my own presence. Here gratitude and grace seep into the empty places of my heart, connecting me to all that is around. The Native Americans call this experience "Mitakuye Oyasin," a term meaning "all my relations," and I call this moment bliss.

When I decided to go inside the tourist center at the Pishkun last year, on one of the walls in the back room I found a quote by a Native American. It's called "Walking in the Dark" and it goes like this:

My heart fell down when I began to see the dead buffalo scattered all over our beautiful land. The whole country smelled of rotting meat, not even the flowers could put down the bad smell. Our hearts were like stone. Times have changed and they have left me behind. I do not understand these times. I am walking in the dark. Anonymous

This haunting story describes what it was like for Native people to witness the destruction of their land—which was sacred to them—

and to live without access to their spiritual practices that connected them deeply to the spirit of the earth. The realm of the spirit and soul that gave meaning and light to their existence was knocked out, and darkness prevailed.

For most Native people, recognizing and honoring the spirit world forms the center of their world view, which is that everything alive has a spirit, including rocks, insects, trees, water, wind, clouds, animals, you and me to name a few, and we are all linked together by an invisible divine web. This web makes everything in the universe, visible and non-visible, an important participant in life and engenders the attitude that if one element is disturbed or honored, all other elements will be affected. This belief system encourages a deep respect for all living things and a great conscience about how one's actions affect the entire web.

I understand now that the experience I had in the pine forest was an encounter with this divine web. It feels as though it comes from another realm, bearing the sense of another world, sometimes within me, sometimes outside me, carrying me into a great wave of grace. It seems to be born out of reverence, of living deeply in the moment, and the experience of time seems to shift into timelessness. When I tap into this place, I feel as though I'm never alone.

Tonight I'm back, dropping Mom off before I return to New York. We are feeling very close and I sense her deep attachment to me. She definitely doesn't want me to leave.

She says, "When will I ever get out of here? Will you take me home?" Tears fill her eyes and I sense her deep longing to return home. Torn and feeling desperate I think to call on the experience of the divine web, hoping I can bring in some comfort and wisdom. I begin to connect with my breathing and as I do so, my beating heart begins to slow down. I take the focus off these questions for a moment and feel into the peaceful atmosphere of her room.

I tell her, "Let's just be in this moment." I turn on the bedside lamp and turn off the overhead light and the soft warm light makes her bed look inviting. Very consciously and slowly I help her change into her nightgown. I do this as though I were in the presence of royalty. Each gesture is reverent and imbued with the intention of bringing in peace and comfort. Finally peace settles into the room. My sense of time slows down as she snuggles into her bed.

I take her hand and hold it while I ask her if there's anything she enjoys. She tells me that the most important person is the director, and also the minister who comes every Wednesday. I ask her why she likes him. She says, "He is really friendly and his sermons give me a sense of belonging."

I'm struck by her insight and also by the need to belong. So often Mom and the other residents seem to pass each other like ships in the night, detached, often silent, and wanting to be somewhere else, wanting to be somewhere where they belong, wanting to be home. With the loss of comfortable speech and memory, how can one develop relationships with these strange companions? Mom doesn't even remember what she had for lunch or dinner.

Even though I hate to leave her, peace for now seems to be taking the place of fear and longing. I tell her I'll keep her in my heart and that I'll call her in the morning. We make that kind of eye contact that goes right into you and I'm ready to leave.

"Mom of the past" is quickly fading. She used to be able to deal with anything. She would take her dryer apart and fix it when it went on the fritz. She mowed the lawn, cooked the meals, trimmed the trees, cleaned the house, and washed the cars. She knew how to handle practically any situation. This woman now can barely make it from her bed to the bathroom. Every now and then, however, that old spirit is still there, like the ancient Sphinx, silent, in the background, portending a greater mystery of what lies beyond.

27: The Swan

The wind is blustery today. The sun is bright and as I drive along the causeway, whitecaps from Long Island Sound smash into the rock wall, spewing white foam into the air. There's a wild energy in this wind and spring is on its way. Even though the trees show no sign of buds yet, there' a feeling of energy beginning to rise up the strong trunks.

As I look out over the marsh on the other side of the road, I notice a white swan resting on dry grasses. Its neck is tucked deeply into its body. The wind is blowing the back feathers around in a swirling white flame. At first I thought maybe the swan was dead. But I returned later in the day and saw it gracefully floating on the dark blue waters bordering the marshland.

How strange it is to see this swan alone. They usually swim in pairs this time of year. I realize that maybe this is the swan I saw at the beach nearby, swimming by itself this past summer. As I look at this swan now, I wonder if it is feeling its nesting instinct, despite being alone. It's not flying to another place where there are many swans. Instead it remains here alone. Why?

I feel unsettled today. My sister says that Mom has to wear Depends all the time now. It's hard for me to hear that she has a rash because of this, and also that she can't make it up the steps to her home.

I feel a huge loss on the phone, too—Mom can't talk for long and is finding it increasingly difficult to express how she's feeling. Often after only a few minutes of conversation she wants to get off the phone.

Many times recently, I've regretted not moving her closer to one of us. It would have given her time to adjust, but now it almost feels too late. My sister and I wonder if the airlines even transport someone in her condition. Mom keeps telling me that she doesn't know if she'll recover. It seems as though she's still experiencing her assisted living situation as temporary, though, and that if and when she feels better she'll go home.

There's also a different tone in her voice. I can't describe it yet. It's as though there's some new feeling or presence, and I don't quite know what to make of it. It arouses a renewed feeling of protectiveness in me, and I keep thinking about how to arrange a trip out there. I feel as though I need to see her, touch her, help her, protect her. Maybe, like that swan, she's feeling abandoned, and life no longer brings her joy or pleasure.

Earlier this month she developed an infection in her hand that landed her in the hospital. Her hand blew up to three times its size and had to be drained. She was put on intravenous antibiotics. At the same time, she began to experience pain all over her body that was excruciating. We all thought that maybe she was dying.

My older sister flew out immediately and when she arrived at the hospital Mom said, "It is crucial that you are here!" Because dementia has set in even more, Mom didn't understand why she was in the hospital. She became suspicious and depressed. My sister continually explained why she was there, but she would forget the moment my sister walked out of the room.

One day while my sister was visiting her in the hospital, a friend called and said she wanted to visit. After my sister hung up she told Mom that her friend was coming over and Mom exclaimed, "Hurry, let's clean up the house, it's a mess!" They both laughed when my sister said, "Mom this is your hospital room!"

I am just beginning to imagine how terrifying and confusing it would be to have dementia. Without memory, chaos and confusion set in and there's no rhyme or reason to things. I think this makes her scared and that's what I sense in her voice lately. It's as if she has no interpreter for her experience in an alien world, no one who can help her make sense of things. Nothing holds steady, orienting like a landmark.

And yet, even if on a daily basis I or anyone else could be reminding her of what has happened, it still wouldn't fill the gap that has formed between her experience of reality and her ability to anchor that experience so that things make sense to her, and there is an ordering to her inner world. Her aloneness, confusion, and helplessness are hard for me to bear. Her condition fills me with fear, maybe an archetypal fear of insanity where one is lost to the self.

Recently, I had a shocking dream that filled me with a panic that I never knew existed. I dream that I can't find my car. Everyone I reach out to for help either doesn't hear me or can't understand what I'm saying. Fear begins to build and take hold of my being. I suddenly become so disoriented and scared that I forget how I got to work—maybe I took the train instead of my car? Then I can't remember my name or where I live and suddenly I end up in a dark side of town where everything, even the buildings, take on a strange, threatening, ghoulish energy. Even though I thankfully wake up, the feeling of the dream has stayed with me, helping me relate to some of what Mom is going through.

I hear the voice of a Buddhist teacher: "Drop the story line and breathe in fear, breathe out peace and compassion. Every fear has within it a teacher, so do not run away from it. Turn around and face it and something will come out of it."

More and more often now fear is a visitor to my heart, waking me up in the middle of the night to my pounding heart and my clenched fists. This fear is related to what Mom is going through and also an anticipation of what I may go through in my elder years. I continue to force myself to turn around and face these fears as they arrive. I will sit with this one for a while and wait for the teaching to come out of it.

In the morning, I light some candles and begin to breathe deeper and deeper until the briny seas calm down. As stillness begins to penetrate into my being, I can feel into Mom's dependency and how it is shifting and moving to a deeper level. I sense that she is going to need someone around her more and more.

I become aware of how she looked at me the last time I visited. I see her looking to me for something. Yes, it's that feeling of her innocence, helplessness, and confusion—the child within her, coming through, looking to her parent, or in this case to me, for help and answers that are beyond me—that is haunting me.

28: A Window of Opportunity

Mom has just been hospitalized again for an infection in her other hand. Her doctor thinks that maybe she was bitten. The assisted living place has a resident cat that always ends up on Mom's bed. She enjoys the cat but says it can get nasty at times. I ask her if it bit her and she vehemently says, "No!" I believe her but we're worried that maybe her immune system has weakened along with her general physical state. Her speech and memory both have worsened and it's become almost impossible to carry on a conversation.

After much discussion, we all agree that Mom should be moved near one of us. The imminence of a full-blown stroke is creeping into all of our psyches. Just as we make this decision, a placement opens up in a small cozy assisted living place near my sister in Portland. This is the same place that had an opening several years ago. We begin to mention this to Mom over the phone. My sister describes the place to her and she is warming up to the idea. After a few more discussions, she has no objection to moving.

I talk with Mom daily about this new place so it will get imprinted in her mind. I tell her I'll fly out and accompany her there. After much paperwork, everything is set.

Several days later Mom had a diabetic incident where her blood sugars got so high that she fell over and lost consciousness for a few moments. An aide came into her room and at first thought Mom had died. She told me later that when Mom came to she acted like a scared child, not knowing what had happened.

Even though Mom has been in the hospital for only two days and her sugars have come back to normal, when we speak on the phone she has completely forgotten that she's going to be moving. I'm worried since we've already made all the arrangements and maybe now we have to start all over again or forget the plan completely. She sounds different also, more confused, and her memory is worse than ever. She doesn't even remember that we talked on the phone yesterday.

In the back of my mind I wonder if she's had another small stroke. I know we have to act fast.

The huge responsibility of my role in her situation begins to break into my consciousness, sending a chill down my spine. I am being chosen as the one who will have to move her from her home, her hometown, and the myriad webs that have shaped her life for the past seventy years. I know deep in my bones that if I give Mom the impression that this move will be a good thing, she will trust me to make the move.

29: The Red Buffalo

Before embarking on this move with Mom I have a very disturbing dream. It goes as follows: I am entering a dreary brick building where Mom has been moved. I'm worried about how she will be in her new place. The room is an awful green and very dark. Mom is sitting in bed and I am at the door. She's not happy. In the next scene I'm at the beach and it's foggy. I notice something dark in the waves and, all of sudden, buffalo are being washed up on shore. There is one very large, reddish colored buffalo that is recovering, lying down on the sand. It suddenly begins to stare at me out of its right eye, and I wake up with a start.

My whole being is filled with an uneasy feeling. Mom's hair, in her younger years, had that same reddish color. A thought comes to me that she trusts me totally. I am aware of how responsible I feel moving her. I decide to work on the dream with a teacher of mine. He helps me go deeply into my experience of the dream, similar to my experience of contemplation.

After some time, I'm suddenly bombarded with every powerful emotion imaginable: fear, guilt, anger, love. I feel as though my own psyche is beating me up. The tension increases until I can barely stand to be in my own body. All I want to do is run away from my and Mom's situation. I want to run so far away that I will disappear into a small speck of dust, hurtling through the Milky Way.

Just at that moment, I hear a rushing sound. It sounds like the wind sweeping across the prairie. This evokes an eerie feeling of being in two places, in the dream and in reality, at once. Time slows down and suddenly I become the wind sweeping across the prairie. A sound emerges from the core of my being moving out like that speck of dust. I hear it, I speak it, I am it. "Whuuuuuuuuuuuuuuuuuuuuu, whuuuuuuuuuuuuuuuuu, whuuuuuuuuuuuuuuuu, whuuuuuuuuuuuuuu. It gets louder and more encompassing. I suddenly hear myself saying, "We all are going to vanish. There will be nothing left. We are all going to die and there will be no human on the prairie, no buffalo, no birds, just the grasses and the wind . . . a huge emptiness . . . like the mind of Buddha . . . or maybe like the stone at the grave."

Realizing that I will die and that Mom will die makes me somehow have more compassion for myself. The thought that death cannot be avoided fills my mind and makes its presence known quietly like a soft breath. There is a turning point here, and I'm the player who will open one door and close another. Who knows except the great mystery that resides beside, underneath, alongside my journey and within the deeper layers of my psyche, what is to be?

I do know, however, that I will move her and that her death is imminent.

30: The Move

Friday I'm leaving for Great Falls to help Mom make the big move Portland. The director there is a wonderful woman named Mary. My sister and she are colleagues and she intends to spoil Mom rotten. Mom laughs when I tell her this.

I'll bring her home when I arrive, so we can spend a few days packing and just hanging out. I want Mom to feel relaxed and enjoy this visit. Then we'll fly together to Portland, which will probably be her last home. Mary says Mom can stay there until the end. It's comforting to hear these words and I'm relieved, because I don't want Mom to end up in a nursing home.

My sister says that Mom's room is in a private part of the house, looking out on a garden and water fountain. She will be fixing up her room while I pack up the basics of Mom's clothes to get her ready to fly. I've had moments of deep sadness knowing that this may be Mom's last time in her home, her last time in Montana.

When I arrive in Great Falls, I drive immediately to get Mom and take her home to prepare. I see her through the glass windows eating lunch and am deeply disturbed. She is totally unaware of me as I approach the door. Normally she would be looking up expecting me, but she's totally engrossed in her lunch. When I come in she says, "Oh, what are you doing here?"

I take a deep breath and say that we're going to her home.

She says, "Oh!" Her face looks funny, almost childlike, and I'm certain that she's had a small stroke.

When we get to her house, she barely makes it up the stairs. It takes us literally five minutes to climb five stairs. I'm grateful that we have six days here so I can determine if Mom can in fact make the move.

A vacant lot separates Mom's home from the bright lights of a casino that has suddenly sprung up behind her. A magnificent cottonwood tree that was home to many birds once stood there. Now there are weeds and forsaken garbage from the Dairy Queen. It's not a pretty sight during the day.

Tonight, however, as I take my walk, I'm struck by the shimmering light dancing on the wispy soft hairs of the dandelions, transforming them into fairies swaying in the soft breeze. They move full of grace and beauty, lifting up my spirits, reminding me of the eternal beauty of that which comes forth from the earth, despite our reckless lack of consideration and reverence.

31: The Spirit in Nature

Mom is happy to be home. She has no desire to talk about the move to Portland. Every time I bring it up, she says let's talk about it later.

It's Saturday, and I have tickets for us to fly this coming Thursday. I figure I have several days to work on her about the move. I'm a little worried that she won't want to move, but I just let that go and keep praying that it will get easier. At some point, I'll have a heart-to-heart talk with her. Helping her make this move suddenly feels like transplanting a giant cottonwood tree.

Tonight on my walk the almost-full moon shines over head. Venus in her glory watches me from the horizon. As I make my way into the darker regions of the golf course near Mom's home, I begin to feel like a wild being, skulking around a darkened landscape. At times blue spruce and pines form a safe passage for me out of the light of the moon.

Walking on, I find a grove of pine and cottonwood trees that forms a sanctuary for me. I stand in the middle and feel their sheltering presence. They seem to care about me. Their moon shadows move as I slowly walk on the crunching pine needles in a walking meditation. I feel a deep communion with them which then spreads as a feeling of compassion for everyone in the world.

As I continue to slowly walk in the midst of the trees, I'm suddenly aware of a huge cottonwood tree. It's calling my attention. The tree is very old and has the feel of an ancient wise elder. I feel small in its presence. At the same time, in this moment, it's as though we are in relationship. I'm mesmerized and a sense of timelessness pervades my being.

I walk over and as I stand near the trunk and look up at the moon, millions of wet moonbeam sparkles appear on the tender new leaves. A state of rapture comes over me. It's as though I've passed through an invisible doorway and entered a magical world. Here all my concerns about the move and all my pain about the situation in the world begin to drift away. The doors to my heart fly wide open and

I absorb this blessing as the most delicious nectar on earth. I ponder, so simple, an experience of beauty and reverence moves me into a whole new healing frame of mind.

32: Conversations with Don

Don, my friend who gave me a healing several years ago, is coming over to catch up. We haven't spoken in a long time and I need to talk to him about moving Mom. He has been an important figure in this situation. I feel comforted in his presence and he always seems to have some wisdom to offer me. He has a way of making something complicated very simple.

We take our glasses of iced tea out on the deck and for quite a while we sit in silence, taking in the cool night breeze. I tell him that moving Mom may be much more difficult than I anticipated. This is her home. She is rooted in this land, as I said earlier, like an old cottonwood tree.

He says that her roots are very strong here. His people believe that those roots are sacred and that they anchor the spirit and soul. He says I should tell her spirit and soul to come to Portland. I feel goose bumps when he says this because somewhere within, I know it's true; her spirit, her soul are deeply embedded in this land and, frankly, I can't imagine right now her living anywhere else. He tells me that we can do a ceremony for Mom and in the meantime I can begin to visualize Mom moving, all of her intact, knowing it's the right action.

The next day Mom and I have our heart-to-heart. I tell her how her life might be different with family around; that she would be driven to the doctor by my sister instead of a taxi; she would be taken out to dinner and there would be more things for her to do. I tell her that she could easily have a major stroke and that we really don't want her to end up in a nursing home here in Great Falls, alone. If this were to happen, she most likely would end up in a place where she'd get minimal care and we wouldn't be able to talk to her on the phone.

Remembering that she was in the hospital three times this April, I gently mention that she might not be able to climb the two flights of stairs to her home much longer—she can barely lift her leg from one step to the other now. On this visit we've only ventured out several times, and even she says the stairs are getting to be too much.

I hate to be the bearer of these facts of reality as I witness her slide into that contemplative space that seems far away. After a while she agrees that the move makes sense; but later in the day, when she speaks to my sister she says she isn't sure. I tell her that if she really wants to stay so be it. I also tell her that if she hates Portland I will move her back, which I would.

Mom is tossing and turning in her bed tonight. I know she's thinking about the move. I help her get out of bed and watch television for awhile. I can always tell when she's thinking, even though she says she's not. Instead of looking up and out at the world her head is faced downward, as though she is tuning into her innermost being. Then she begins to twiddle her thumbs, a habit she developed just this year.

33: The Turning Point

Morning has arrived and Mom greets me at the top of the stairs. Her bony hands grip the handrail and her silvery hair is tousled from a tough night. I give her a big hug and plant a kiss on her wrinkled cheek. Her golden eyes with brown speckles look bright and smiling and the first thing she says is, "What kind of clothes do people wear in Portland?"

Totally surprised I say, "Mom, does this mean you want to move now?"

She says, "I've made up my mind!" I know that when she talks like this, there's no turning back. She has come to this decision on her own through much struggle in the middle of the night. I feel deeply relieved and I ask her if it's based on our conversation last night. She says, "Yep."

I tell her I think it's the best decision and that I know it wasn't easy for her. I mention what I said to Don about moving a giant cottonwood tree and she laughs, agreeing that it's true. I won't tell her just yet that Don offered do a ceremony for her. She's not someone who takes easily to that sort of thing.

With this cleared up, I go down under her house and bring up some suitcases. We have three days to pack and begin to sort through a small closet. It feels right for her to be an active part of this process. I hold up a garment and she says "yes" or "no." Every now and then I make the decision for her, but basically she chooses everything. Little by little, we eventually pack four suitcases. It's actually going very smoothly.

I've kept in mind a story she told me years ago about when her mother wanted her out of the house immediately after graduating from high school. She said that one day her little brother innocently brought her suitcase out and she burst into tears. She didn't want to leave home, but she had no choice. I would hate to repeat this terrible memory.

With her suitcases packed and put into the car, there are two last events: a healing from Don to ensure a good move, and a good-bye party at the assisted living. I explain to Mom that I want her to have the healing with Don before embarking on her journey. It feels important to me that she has his blessing to be sure that her roots, her soul and spirit accompany her. She agrees, even though there is some trepidation. The spiritual world of Native Americans is foreign to her so I explain, as well as I can, some of the ceremony. I know that if Mom definitely does not want to do something she will tell me, so I proceed with her assent, even though some apprehension still lingers.

After dinner, Don arrives and the three of us talk for a long time sipping iced tea. He asks Mom a lot of questions about herself and shares some of his personal stories. There is a warm feeling in the room and Mom seems more at ease.

Finally, Don gets up and begins to smudge the room with sage to create a healing chamber. He wants Mom and me to hold hands while he prays to his ancestors for help and blessings. We close our eyes and I tune into Mom's hands, which feel thin and cold. I feel soothed by the tone of his beautiful voice. He speaks in his native tongue and after a while, the words seem to take the shape of ancient guardians that he's calling on to help me and Mom.

Mom's hands begin to fill with warmth. I open my eyes to check on her for a moment. Her eyes are closed and she actually looks peaceful. I'm surprised by her concentration and can tell that she's starting to allow this blessing to wash over her.

Don ends the ceremony by presenting both of us with a piece of wood from the central pole in the Sun Dance ritual that he participated in last year. This is a very sacred ceremony of the Blackfoot Indians and I am deeply honored. We both tuck our pieces safely into our wallets. Then he gives each of us some tobacco. He tells us to put our prayers into it for Mom's well-being. I am instructed to take it later that evening and bury it next to a cottonwood tree.

After Don leaves and Mom is tucked into bed, I set out to find a cottonwood tree on the golf course. I find myself back at the giant tree

I visited the other evening and sit down with my back against its huge trunk. I tell the tree that Mom is moving soon and ask if it will safe-keep our prayers for her to move, spirit and soul intact. Carefully, I dig a small hole with my hands and place the tobacco safely in its cocoon. I feel comforted that this mighty tree is now a part of Mom's journey.

The next day, before I even remind Mom of the good-bye party, she asks when are we going to the party. It surprises me that she remembers, and suddenly it dawns on me how important this place has been to her. They are going to serve coffee and strawberry shortcake.

When we get there everyone is happy to see Mom and even the resident cat comes running into the room. They serve us a huge portion of cake and coffee and then give Mom a card. She spends a long time reading their messages and saying good-bye. There is a finality in the air when we leave, and it hovers around us for the rest of the day.

In the evening, Mom asks to call Dorothy, her sister-in-law. Throughout her life, Dorothy has been a steady friend and every now and then in their later years they catch up on each other's lives. It seems strange to have Mom initiate something. They talk for a long time and she tells me that Dorothy approves of the move. I think Mom needed some outside support.

It is very late and I'm up, thinking about everything. At 4:00 a.m. I get up from a restless sleep and look in Mom's room. She's sitting on the end of the bed and I wonder what's going on. For some unknown reason I decide not to bother her and go back to bed.

When I enter her room in the morning with coffee, I find clothes strewn everywhere. She's wearing a pair of shorts. I comment that I didn't think they would be appropriate for the plane ride and we break into laughter.

34: The Plane Ride

I pack a healthy lunch for our plane ride. I want to make it an adventure for Mom, knowing this is her first plane ride in five years. Her life in assisted living had narrowed down to a small safety net of nutritious meals, naps, and occasional visits to her doctor. Her big adventures were staying over at her house when one of us would visit.

Everything has gone smoothly, I think to myself as I drive us to the airport. We have plenty of time to deal with wheelchairs and boarding the plane. I park her car in long-term parking since I'll be back in three days. Every now and then, the thought occurs to me that this will probably be Mom's last day in Montana. I try to keep focusing on making this an enjoyable trip, an adventure into new territory.

I leave Mom near a big window in the airport so she can see me while I park the car. When I come back, she's re-reading the good-bye card. These "ships passing in the night" residents have touched her more than she ever let on. Hopefully she is taking in their blessings as she departs into a new world.

Getting on the plane is a huge production. They usher us behind the ticket counter for security reasons. We have to go through security and there's Mom in her wheelchair, looking like a little kid as the checker goes over her body with a big wand. I explain to her that this is the new method to detect for terrorism. They ask me to take off my jean jacket, which I place on the counter. Then they take the wand to me, too, as Mom watches intently. When they finish they tell us we can board. I pick up my jacket, laughing to myself that after all that they failed to check it.

Since we're boarding a little plane, Mom has to ride up a ramp in a small motorized wheelchair. Finally, when we're in our seats, we sit back to enjoy the flight. It is a surprisingly long journey—changing planes in Seattle, and then flying to Portland. At one point I notice Mom is shaking and I zip up her jacket and put my arm around her. I reassure her that this is going to be a good move and that if she doesn't like it there, I'll move her back home. She says, "I trust you."

After we eat our lunch I give Mom some gum, which she relishes. I haven't seen her chew gum in years. Before arriving in Portland I notice her fumbling with the tray. I ask her what she's doing. She says, "I'm getting rid of my gum!" We break into laughter as I take it from her.

We finally arrive at my sister's house and I cannot believe the hike up to her back door. I almost cry. The steps wind up the back of her house, at least fourteen in all. I'm worried Mom can't make it. The front steps are even steeper. I look over at her and say, "Do you want to give it a try?"

She nods and we begin the ascent. We stop many times and I notice perspiration beginning to form on her forehead. I think how brave and determined this woman is and amazingly, never complains. At the top she exclaims, "Here I am!"

Once inside, we're greeted by my sister's three dogs that are very curious about Mom and her walker. When she comes out of the bathroom and starts down the hall, the big poodle and little cocker spaniel run in between and under Mom's walker. There's a happy, silly mood in the air and I think we all feel a sense of relief to finally be here.

That night Mom stayed up way past her bedtime, watching a movie with us while the little cocker spaniel lay fast asleep on her lap.

35: Mary's

Today we're all going to visit Mom's new home. As we get closer to the place, anxiety rushes through my system like a poison. I suddenly realize that I have gone on blind faith with my sister's recommendation and haven't seen the place myself. Even though she and her partner have told me many wonderful stories about Mary and her place, seeing is believing. I suddenly berate myself that I never flew here to really check it out.

As we round the corner and begin the ascent up a beautiful street, I calm down a little. I'm not entirely relieved until I begin to wheel Mom down the sidewalk where roses of every color and description line the walkway. At the back of the house are several beautiful fish ponds and a friendly porch. Mary comes out immediately, and greets us with hugs and the smell of home cooking.

She takes us to Mom's room, which is freshly painted a light yellow. On her dresser are a dozen yellow roses picked from her garden. Mary even planted a special yellow rosebush outside Mom's window so she can sit in her recliner and smell the roses. My sister and her partner picked out an electronic recliner and a television. They sanded a beautiful wood side table and put pictures of family on it. Mom immediately gets into bed and takes a nap while we fill out the paperwork. That evening we eat a delicious dinner of salmon, fresh spinach, and potatoes with the residents and Mary. After dinner we all leave, including Mom.

Around 6:00 a.m., before my flight back to Great Falls, Mom, my sister, and I drink our coffee together, wrapped in throws in the cool dawn. When my sister leaves to get us more coffee, Mom turns to me and says, "This is special." She gives me a big smile that warms my heart. I feel like my mission at last is accomplished.

36: Alone in Montana

Flying back from Portland, I wonder what it will feel like to step off the plane knowing Mom no longer lives there. I feel numb, as though I left some important part of me behind. Mindlessly I leaf through the Sky Mall catalog. Each time I meander through, it's as though for the first time. The senseless items and endless gadgets make no impression on my mind. The only thing that remains in my consciousness is an herbicide that's advertised to kill plant life in ponds. They claim it won't kill fish and I wonder who on earth would use this product and what would the fish do with no plant life? The absurdity of our culture rings out like a grotesque bell from hell.

I have no luggage to pick up and head straight for Mom's car. It's noon and the sun is brighter than I ever remember, making it almost impossible to open my eyes. As I look at the distant mountains that appear light blue against the brown yellow color of the prairie, tears well up in my eyes. The once loving and captivating landscape is now barren and hollow like dry hay.

My heart is ready to burst, and when I reach the safety of her car I cry for a long time. The tears feel empty, as though there's nothing to give them meaning. The vastness of the landscape exaggerates the aloneness I sense inside. This place, which has always given me so much comfort, suddenly folds in on me like the last page of an old book and I have nothing waiting for me to dive into.

I feel the same way when I walk into her home. The peace and quiet that always rejuvenated my soul now wrap me in heaviness and I must get out of here. Even though it's hot and I'm extremely tired, I can't hang out here and immediately jump back in the car and drive to the Pishkun. Surely there I can get some comfort.

When I arrive, the man at the tourist center below the bluffs says that I have one hour to hike before they close. Normally, I drive to the top of the bluffs where I feel free to wander without restriction. Today, however, I need some human contact.

He asks if I have water for the hike. I never take water on hikes and especially today I need to feel the harshness of this place. I say that I'm fine without water. Then he warns me that there are a lot of rattlesnakes around. That's something I don't want to hear. Nevertheless, I head out, unable to truly enjoy the freedom because my eyes are constantly alert to the threat of snakes. I do manage to watch a lone antelope in the distance who takes one look at me and bounds off.

Fitting for today, even the great Pishkun can't dispel this loneliness.

37: The Big Bird

On my last evening in Montana I call Mom and my sister. I tell Mom that everything is okay at her home and that I will lock everything up. I reassure her that we are keeping it in case she wants to return.

When she realizes that I've spent several days here she says, "How come you're not here with us?" I tell her that I need some time to clean and prepare her home for the empty months ahead.

Also I need some time to get used to this huge change and rest from the strenuous move. For ten days I have poured all my energy into Mom to ensure that this move would go as smoothly as possible. I felt like her watchful mother, keeping the magical eye on her for protection. I enjoyed making her feel safe and comfortable during the transition, and now I feel a sense of accomplishment that the move was successful. She's in a secure place and actually having fun in the company of my sister, her partner, the dogs, and Mary.

Later in the evening, Don and I drive out to the Pishkun. It's cold and windy and the stars are just beginning to break through the haze of the evening sky. As we drive down the lonely highway, I notice a big bird dead on the side of the road. I stop the car and we get out to take a look. Don seems surprised that I noticed the bird and says we should pick it up and take it with us. He wraps it up in a red bandana and puts it in the trunk of the car.

When we return to Mom's house we smudge the huge bird with sage. In Don's culture, this bird has great healing medicine. He carves off one wing for me and keeps the other wing for himself. We decide that this way we can share its healing powers. I watch Don silently. His concentration brings me peace as we give back meaning to this almost lost bird of the night.

I sense an era dying and become very sad. I don't want to walk out into this night knowing that Mom is no longer living here. I know that a part of me has to die, but I feel fierce about not letting it go, not now, not tonight. The sadness that is with me suddenly vanishes as my eyes focus on the sharp talons. I want to hold on like I imagine that bird did, with those talons curled around a branch and my beak shut tight. Only my eyes shall remain open. No tears, no sadness, no grief, just an unrelenting determination to hold fast shut.

After Don leaves, I take my time cleaning up the stray feathers. I am meticulous, concentrating the light of my mind into a single ray on the carpet before me. Carefully I gather up each feather, even the almost invisible down, bringing the scattered pieces of this magnificent bird together. When my task is completed I step outside and with one big sweep, I toss the feathers into the night wind and watch as they swirl upward to the stars.

38: The Phone Call

Mom is spending her first Mother's Day in many years with family. My sister bought her a golden chain with her initial "G" in diamonds. They're having such a good time that they extended her stay. At first I thought it would be best for Mom to go straight to Mary's, but I haven't heard her sound this happy in a long time.

Apparently, when my sister first saw me taking care of Mom, she exclaimed, "I can do this!" She told me that when she saw how loving I was with Mom that it got right into her. She suddenly felt as though she had received instruction, a new way of being with Mom that allowed her to open her heart in a way that she never had. She became filled with all kinds of plans and activities that she and Mom could do and actually had a hard time dropping Mom off for her first night in her new home.

Now it's Mom's first night at Mary's. I call her to see how she's doing and am totally caught off guard. Her speech is perfect, the way it was before her major stroke. She's using complete sentences and it is almost eerie how present she sounds. She asks me again why she's there and I explain that we were afraid she would have a stroke and end up in a nursing home in Montana alone without family and unable to speak with us over the phone. This time I know she understands when she says, "Oh."

The next day I get the dreaded phone call. Mom woke up unable to move or talk. They rushed her to the hospital and started her on anti-stroke medication. The next day she was out of bed, walking down the halls with her walker, working on rehab. Unfortunately, her speech is completely gone and she can't swallow. They try to tube feed her but she pulls it out every time.

I call Mom while my sister is there so she can help me talk to her. It's chilling to hear the sound that comes out of her. It freezes my heart. Fighting back tears, I speak at length about how I love her and how brave she is. When my sister gets back on the phone she says that

Mom is smiling and pointing to the clock, which means that it's time for my sister to go home.

I, in the meantime, become consumed with guilt. I keep thinking that if only I had let her be maybe this would never have happened. I call Don and tell him about Mom. He reminds me that this was the reason I moved her in the first place, and yet I continue to be riddled with guilt.

For several days I keep thinking about flying back so I can see her face to determine if she's mad at me. I know this is totally irrational, but for the first time in many years I feel a distance begin to creep in between us. It makes me feel impotent where I once felt powerful; it wipes away all warmth, and I feel totally alone. Nothing and no one can comfort me.

The afternoon sun is casting shadows of dancing leaves in my office. I look at them blankly and go through the motions of my work. The only source of energy is the numerous phone calls to my sister, helping her decide what to do next for Mom. At least I feel somewhat important to her and I channel all my support and energy toward her. There are so many decisions: what to do next and, if she gets better, will she be able to go back to Mary's.

I'm afraid of Mom now, afraid that she'll turn on me and blame me for this horrible situation, even though deep down I know she couldn't possibly hold me responsible and besides that she can't even talk. My God, she's just trying to survive!

For the first time, I don't even think to turn within for help. I've become lost in the dark forest of ghouls and witches. The look of trust and love in her eyes, that has always shed a glow in my innermost being, has turned to stone and her words to me, "I trust you totally," have shape-shifted into a dark ghost.

39: The Stomach Peg

My sister asked Mom if she wants to try one more procedure, inserting a tube into her stomach so she can have nourishment. Hopefully, this will build up strength and maybe her swallowing reflex will come back. The doctors encourage us to try this last procedure, and Mom definitely wants it, so in two days this will happen.

My sister calls me several hours after the procedure and apparently it went fairly well. Later in the day, however, when she went back to check on her, Mom had her head in her hands crying. In all the years of Mom's travails, she has probably cried only a few times. My sister was heartsick. She put her head in Mom's lap and just let Mom cry.

The next day Mom refused all further therapies. My sister knew she had given up and called me and my older sister to come out there. She didn't think Mom could go on much longer. I drop everything and fly out immediately. I dread seeing Mom and am still afraid of what kind of look will be in her eyes. At the same time, another part of me can't believe that I'm so preoccupied with this concern.

When I finally walk into the room, Mom seems confused that all three of us are there. There's a blank look in her eyes and she hardly recognizes me. My guilt revs up to full capacity, leaving little room for anything else. Months later, after hours of research on death and dying, I learned that this expression of blankness precedes one's death.

Mom keeps putting both hands up in a gesture that seems like, "What now?" I feel bewildered and totally helpless. The guilt has disabled my connection to myself and I can't find a way to respond to her. I do know that I definitely don't want to tell her that she's dying. How could I say that to her? I can't even accept that myself. And what is she supposed to do with that knowledge?

I just know that right now that feeling of paralysis is suddenly shifting into intense hatred. I hate this hospital even though it's the most beautiful hospital I've ever seen. Every window looks out on a misty blue mountain range and the rooms are large and clean. The staff couldn't be more thoughtful and skilled. But I'm exploding inside with hatred. I hate seeing Mom confused, unable to talk or even get out of bed at this point. I hate that she can't even make a sound. I hate seeing her tongue red and covered with sores. I hate her for dying after all of the effort I put into this dream of happiness for her. I hate feeling like a robot with no words of comfort or wisdom. I hate. I hate feeling hate.

When I'm alone with Mom, after the hateful feelings subside, I am mostly silent; and when I speak it is hollow and empty once again. There's nothing in me. I'm a dried up riverbed, offering up a shadow of what once had life and renewal. I still feel angry at myself, which only makes the riverbed drier and more desolate. All day long, I vacillate between rage, emptiness, and guilt.

She recognizes the necklace I'm wearing, which I gave her a long time ago. She couldn't wear it because she was allergic to silver.

Deep in my heart I know our love is more powerful than what's going on now but I can't dip into that place; it's lost and I can't find it. I tell my sisters that I want to spend the night alone with Mom, hoping that maybe this lost place will come back.

40: Alone with Mom

After dinner I go back to the hospital, prepared for a long night. As the night moves on, softness begins to return to my heart. I have some rose oil, which Mom loves. When she gets restless in the night I take a warm wet cloth with a few drops of rose oil and stroke her face and hair with it. Her eyes are closed and there is tension in her brow. As I begin to stroke her forehead, the tension leaves and peace settles in. I do this for the longest time and I begin to feel like a big cat licking its young.

Words are spare, and I'm totally absorbed in this activity. I wash her arms, her neck, and her hands with tenderness, soothing my wounds and hers if she has any. I will never know. As dawn approaches she turns on her side to look out the window and I join her as we witness the shapes of the mountains move slowly out of the darkness into dawn.

When I get up to take a walk, a staff member approaches me and basically tells me that Mom will probably die in a day or so. Since her lungs are slowly filling up she suggests that we could ease her pain by administering a narcotic drip. I tell her I'll talk with my sisters and let her know. I thank her for her honesty and her permission to stop any further procedures. The realization that we now have to help Mom die, not live, spits me back into reality.

I drive back to my sister's house and get lost several times, wrapped up in a cocoon of feelings. After much discussion, we agree that this will be best for Mom. We return to the hospital several hours later and spend the day there.

She seems happy to have us there. We watch a tennis match on the television and some golf, which Mom loves. Then we call our brother in California so they can have one 'last conversation.' I watch as she holds the phone to listen. Her knuckles turn white from gripping the phone so hard. She smiles the whole time and then hands the phone to me. I tell him how she was gripping the phone and that she hung on his every word. At this point, Mom can't even make a sound, but her gestures and the look in her eyes say everything. Oh, how she loves her boy.

After a while, Mom wants to get up. We all struggle to help her sit on the side of the bed. When she finally feels steady, she reaches out her shaking hands, for my older sister's hand, and holds it in both of hers for several minutes. Then, very slowly, ever so slowly, she bends down and kisses her hand in the most sacred way. I have never witnessed anything like this in my life. It feels like a blessing of the highest order. We are all in awe of this gesture that seems to have come out of nowhere. It feels as though she is showing her deep love and appreciation for all of our care and even perhaps now as I write this, she was saying good-bye.

My older sister bursts into tears. My younger sister and I look at each other unable to speak. All of our hearts seem to join as one. She, our Mom, we, her children each one unique yet bound by history, fate, and in this moment, the sacred feminine. It is here that the jewel of humanity appears, giving back wisdom and strength in a moment of greatest hopelessness and pain. Here in the wellspring of love, the great goddess rises up, bringing love tears out of a place of darkness and mourning, watering the flowers of our souls, leaving me to ponder . . . even in this condition, at the edge of her known existence, she imparts a dignity and grace that will impact our lives for years to come.

It is now 5:00 in the afternoon and Mom is very tired. The nurse has come in and set up the drip. Suddenly, Mom pulls the plug out that keeps her on medication, as though to say, "Get rid of all life supports. I am ready to behold the Creator."

Five minutes later Mom's gaze turns upward toward the heavens. Her breathing is beginning to sound raspy and this may be the last conscious moment we have with her. The woman who brought me into the day light of the world, I am now following into the darkness of death.

41: The End Is Near

Tired and hungry, we drive back to my sister's for dinner. We also have something important to discuss. Both of my sisters want Mom to be baptized. I like the fact that she is pagan, a child of the earth, free from the reins of any religion.

I remember Mom saying many years ago that she was never baptized and sometimes she wondered what her fate would be when she died. She was not a religious person, but she was deeply spiritual. She carried a deep respect for all living things, and our house was often an infirmary for injured animals.

I remember one time our bathtub was home for two mallard ducks. My dad, a doctor, put a splint on the wing of one and bandaged the wounded leg on the other. They made a huge mess and a lot of noise but they certainly were enjoying their stay. After some time, Mom took them and all of us out to see if they could fly. Sure enough, they took off, circled several times over the house and then sped on their journey.

Tonight they convince me about the baptism and we set up an appointment with the chaplain at the hospital. After dinner my older sister and I plan on going back to the hospital to spend the night. Around 8:00 p.m. I begin to feel a pain in my stomach and chest. It feels like someone gripping my heart so hard that I have to lie down. My sister leaves and I struggle to recuperate. I'm so weak that I can't get up and my hearing is so acute that I can hear a conversation on the phone two rooms away. What a strange feeling.

I finally fall asleep but at midnight my sister calls and says Mom's condition has worsened and that she probably will pass within hours. My younger sister and I rush to the hospital. The night nurse informs us that Mom regained consciousness around 8:00 p.m. looking scared and disoriented. She asked Mom if she was afraid of dying and Mom nodded her head. The nurse spent some time comforting her. This was around the same time I experienced that dreadful feeling in my heart. Since then, I've learned that some people have described similar experiences happening to them when a loved one was close to passing on. Mom is now unconscious again.

I keep looking at her, almost in shock. She's sitting up in bed, her head slightly back and her mouth wide open trying to take in as much oxygen as possible. I feel the urge to shake her and wake her up but I know I can't. Her hands look strange with dark red patches on her palms and fingertips, just like the nurse said would happen when death is very near.

I wish I knew what she was experiencing, but now there is no expression on her face, no clue as to where she is. Maybe this is part of the mystery of afterlife . . . that you have to develop a new system of communication because the old one doesn't work any longer. Her eyes still look upward but they no longer are beautiful golden brown with dark brown speckles that always made her look like some magical feline. They appear almost gray, glazed over with a silvery light. I know her spirit has begun to leave.

42: The Birch Tree

It's late. It's 2:00 in the morning, and nothing seems real. My sister and I decide to find a place outside to get some air and relief from the sounds of Mom's breathing and the smell of death. We find two large rocks near the trunk of a white birch and sit down. The branches reach over us and there is comfort in this shelter. The streetlamps cast flickering shadows of light on the trunk and the small heart-shaped leaves make whispering sounds in the cool breeze. The rocks hold us in our silent retreat as we adjust to the imminent passing of Mom.

Even at eighty-six she has maintained an important position in our lives. She has been the link to my sisters and brother and everyone else I know in Montana. For me, there has always been a comfort in her wisdom. You could count on her for an honest opinion even if it didn't sit well in the moment. Like these rocks under the birch tree, her appearance, weathered by sun and wind, reflects a familiar landscape to me.

Tonight I sense her brave presence filling the night. She is sharing her last moments on earth with us, forcing us to have courage, allowing us to witness and participate in her dying. There is an intimacy that is mystical rising up out of this unknowable event and tonight I feel as though I am witness to her giving birth to her spirit. Her strained yet persistent breath is pushing and releasing it into another world that I can sense but cannot see. I also feel unreal and slightly detached, unable to fully comprehend that Mom is actually dying.

It is hard to believe that just two days ago, my sister was calling every place in Portland to see if they would take Mom in her condition. I was very upset to find out that she wouldn't be able to return to Mary's. Finally, my sister actually found a place that had accommodations for her. She said they even had a beautiful dining room where patients with stomach pegs could eat with each other. We've become accustomed to the bumpy road that now is about to end.

43: The Baptism

Around 2:30 a.m. the chaplain comes into the room. She explains the ceremony to us and to Mom as though she can hear. I'm very touched by that. In her quiet, regal presence she places her hand lightly on Mom's forehead and says, "I am anointing you with herbs from the sacred land of Jerusalem and the calming herb of lavender. Glady, I baptize you in the name of the Father, the Son, and the Holy Spirit. May our Lord embrace you with his promise of eternal life and salvation this day. May you be blessed with his peace and know that you are loved by a God who will love you always, a God that does not abandon. And let us pray as our Lord has taught us to pray:

> Our Father who art in heaven,
> Hallowed be thy name.
> Thy kingdom come, thy will be done
> On earth as it is in heaven.
> Give us this day our daily bread
> And forgive us our trespasses
> As we forgive those who trespass against us.
> And lead us not into temptation,
> But deliver us from evil.
> For thine is the kingdom
> The power and the glory
> Forever and ever. Amen.

"In this baptism you are claimed as priestess, prophet, and queen. May you be blessed for as you witness your faith in this baptism, we as community promise to support you in this journey. Go in peace for it is a wondrous adventure. Amen."

She places a white cloth with a red cross on Mom's chest. A sense of peace begins to fill the room, making the lights look softer. The fragrance of the herbs softens the smell of death. The night nurse comes in with warm blankets, pillows, and comfortable chairs for all of us. We surround Mom's bed in a huddled softness, each touching her, each in our own reverie. This is how we spend the night.

Many images begin to appear in my mind as I sit here crunched up in my chair. After a while, a vision appears . . . I see Mom entering her home. She is not the same age she is now, but younger, in her sixties. She looks around at everything. Checking the closets, the appliances, and of course her bird feeders which she always did. She looks out the window at the grounds, noticing the pool in the distance and the scrub pines nearby. And then she sits down in her favorite chair of soft pinkish lavender fabric with a suitcase at her side. She sits there for the longest time waiting.

Finally, a soft, almost iridescent blue light from the dawning sky begins to make its way into the room. The pillow I'm resting my head on and the white blankets turn blue just like the misty mountains that have been witness to us all along and slowly that vision vanishes with the light of day.

At 5:00 a.m. I decide to visit the chapel. I noticed it earlier and was in awe of the beautiful quilt on the back wall near the podium. As I enter the room, pieces of red, gold, and orange cloth patches from the quilt rise up into giant flames and in the background are pieces of blue, silver, and pastel lavender that hint of another world, another state of being, cool, calm, quiet, over there.

Stained glass windows line the walls near the ceiling and a circular light bordered in silver forms a giant halo in the room. It is still dark but a light shines on the fiery quilt. I stand in the center of the room and before I realize it, I begin to pray to God. These are the words that pour out of my soul: "Dear God, show Mom the light when she is ready. When she comes to you take her in your arms and hold her. I now give her care over to you. Please take really good care of her." Then I pray in the Native American way: "Creator, and all of the four directions, all beings in the higher realm, please show Mom the light when she is ready. I now give her care over to you. Please take good care of her and hold her in your arms. Make her feel safe and blessed."

I want Mom to have the care she never had as a child, to feel welcomed and loved.

44: The Final Hours

When I return to the room it is about 6:30 a.m. My sisters go to the cafeteria to get something to eat and I stay with Mom. When they leave I sing some of her favorite songs. I start with "Born Free" which she always used to sing, off key of course. Then I sing "Hey Jude" and "I'm tired and I want to go home." When I finish I sit down in an 'unreal' state and wait for them to return. Mom's breathing is labored and I notice the rhythm of her breath slowing down. I still cannot believe that she is dying.

I'm absorbed in this state of mind which feels like an eternity when they return, startling me back to reality. For a while we take our eyes off Mom and focus our attention on food. We chat about various things like birds waking up in the morning. We begin to talk about Mom's brothers and how one of them had done some research into the family tree and discovered they had American Indian blood in the family line.

Just at that moment I notice the quiet and turn around. Suddenly I am aware that Mom is passing on. We all jump up and go over to her as she takes two last breaths. My younger sister, an R.N., reaches for the suctioning hose and suctions Mom's throat for the last time. The nurse comes in immediately and lays Mom back on the bed and then leaves us alone.

We all take turns laying our heads on Mom's chest to feel the warmth of her body for one last time. As moments pass, Mom's skin turns a translucent silvery white and all of her wrinkles disappear. She looks noble with her smooth face and high cheekbones, like an Egyptian queen.

I'm not sure why I keep saying that to myself, but it's the truth. Was she a noble queen in a past life in some far-off region of the world? When I express this out loud, even my sisters agree. We spend several hours with her saying our personal good-byes and then slowly begin to throw away things she no longer needs—the white gloves she wore to keep her from pulling the feeding tube out, the half-used

89

packages of bandages, her hospital toothbrush. Several hours later the nurse comes in and tells us it's time to leave.

Before leaving, I ask my sisters if they would like a lock of Mom's hair. They do, but this is difficult for me since Mom always took great pride in her hair. I decide to ask her permission and then cut off a lock for all of us. Even though this feels taboo, I am determined to keep some part of her with me forever, as though in some strange way this is an act defying death.

We arrange for Mom to be cremated, and then we leave the hospital. My older sister and I plan to return for the service later that day so we can learn more about the Day of the Pentecost. Mom died on this day and we know generally that it is the day to turn fear into courage but we want to know more. Later we find out that this is the day that Christ's disciples knew they were being hunted down and were full of fear. At that moment a light came down from the heavens and spoke to each of them in their native language.

I understand this to mean that if you have a spiritual connection you can turn your greatest fear into courage. I know Mom was afraid of dying, but from the expression on her face when she passed on, I know that she had more than courage, she had a noble ending. She has found peace I tell myself.

Maybe it's because she felt her loved ones around. Maybe she felt that light of the Creator guide her to the open arms of heaven. I will never know, at least that's how I feel today. Temporarily, though, I do feel as though my world has expanded, knowing Mom is on the other side.

When my sister starts up the car the Celine Dion is singing "A New Day." Finally my tears break through the hard shell that has been around me and we both cry for a long time. It is definitely a new day, a new era.

In the evening we decide to get the Will out and discover, penned in her hand, "Please do not be sad for I have been blessed with a good life. I will watch over all of you when I am gone."

45: Back Home

It's strange to have no funeral, but that was Mom's request. I'm back at work as though I have flown out of one world into another. There, in that other world of Oregon, the blue misty mountains, and smell of pine, Mom still lingers.

My sister informed me that Mom had been left in the hospital morgue over the weekend. She was mortified. The crematorium couldn't pick her up because the death certificate wasn't ready. She felt horrified that we had left Mom that way, but I told her Mom was probably laughing at the mistake. She had that kind of humor. Also I knew from the expression on her face when she died that she had definitely departed. I can still hear the door close to her room when we left, and feel the chilly emptiness that followed us down the hall and into the elevator.

Today I'm calling all of Mom's friends to let them know she has passed on. After a few calls of sharing stories about Mom I feel better. I feel close to her again. The director of the assisted living place was very surprised and upset to hear the news. I let her know how Mom kept their card close to her heart during the flight to Oregon. I call her doctor. On her last visit with him he made her laugh when he said he had been her doctor as long as he had been married to his wife. I have no one else to call.

The weeks have flown by and now a month later, I realize that this is the longest I have ever gone without talking to Mom. I am suddenly missing her. The thought to call her has been entering my mind often. I want to know how she is doing and what it's like wherever she might be.

I am aware how I felt more secure somehow knowing she was in the world. It's not that I need a mother, but rather that she represents a generation that will never return to this planet, like an endangered species vanishing.

She was a pioneer. She was born in a wild land that had not yet been tainted by humans. The spirit and soul of the land shone through her being. Her hands looked rugged, like well-used tools. I remember her telling me how her father bought an old car and they packed everything they owned into it and moved from Wyoming to Calgary. They lived in close relationship to the land, depending on it for their food and money. They were far from any store and Mom described in detail how her mother canned everything in sight until their whole basement was loaded from floor to ceiling. She knew how to can everything, even meat.

One time during a visit to the ranch, her mother made a picnic lunch for me and my sister. We went outside with our brown paper lunch bag and sat under a tree. It was a hot day and very windy and the grass was brown, dry, and scratchy. I pulled our sandwiches out of the bag and noticed something red in a plastic container at the bottom. We couldn't wait for the surprise and I immediately opened the lid to find two shiny scarlet candied apples sitting regally in clear pink nectar. The taste immediately filled my child's heart with joy. For the first time food was not just food. I knew Grandma loved me.

From that moment on, I understood that deep in the natural world is a spiritual essence, just like that within the candied apples. Somehow, these people knew how to reach into that place. And maybe too, the spirit in the land was very strong because there were no chemicals or poisons diminishing its sparkle—only sun, water, stars, and wind.

46: The Empty Void

It has been five months since Mom's passing. I've had no dreams of her or any sign that she's around. I have hardly cried, or shared my grief with anyone. I feel as though there's a huge frozen lake within and no signs of a thaw. I feel alone, even with my partner, as though I'm surrounded by an invisible wall. Is this grief?

The loss of her is huge. My visits to Montana the past few years became a pilgrimage to my spirit home, that link to my source— Mom, home, the West, that place within that is as spacious as the skies, the clouds, the rolling plains, and distant mountains. Despite the worries about Mom's well-being, I always looked forward to the distant approach to Great Falls on Northwest Airlines. My lungs and heart would open as I viewed Belt Mountain, the square patterns of wheat fields, the white-capped mountains, and last but not least the long winding rope of the Missouri River. The familiar patterns of the landscape are forever etched in my psyche, shaping my desires and experience of things.

I finally adjusted to Mom being unable to pick me up. It was a landmark on her journey when she could no longer do this and Diamond Cab became her replacement. Usually within ten minutes of my call, I would see the old beat-up cab making its way toward the airport. Driving down Gore Hill, the location of the airport, I enjoyed the thought of taking Mom home. I would plan all of her favorite meals for the week and shop the minute I got to her house so that I wouldn't have to leave her alone for long periods of time. For one week we both could return to the way it used to be and Mom would always come back to herself.

Our days had a familiar routine. One of our favorite activities was gin rummy. Around 5:30 p.m., I would make us a cocktail, usually bourbon and ditch (water), and we would play many games while dinner was cooking. We were staunch competitors and the winner would treat for dinner later in the week. She was very sharp when it came to cards and I would usually lose. The last game we played, however, she lost and it was her turn to treat for dinner.

We went out to our favorite Italian place, Borries, and after our meal she asked for the check. Unfortunately, we had forgotten her purse. I said I would pay and that she could pay me later, knowing full well she would forget.

I also did this on shopping trips. I would let her charge up a bunch of clothes because she loved shopping so much. But many times when we got home she wouldn't remember what she had purchased. And she certainly didn't need many of the clothes or shoes she charged. So I would take most of them back later and she would never miss them. This was something I discovered shopping with her in these later years. I would find the new garments in her closet with the tags still on them months and sometimes years later.

47: The Little Angel

Yesterday, one of Mom's best friends called and asked for my address. She said that she had something Mom gave her many years ago and that she wants me to have it. Days later a package arrives in the mail. I handle it carefully for a long time, relishing the anticipation of wondering what could be inside. In this moment it feels as though Mom has come back to life. I want this moment to go on forever.

Finally, I open the package. Inside is an angel made of clay by a prominent Montana artist. In the note, she said, "You deserve to have this angel watch over you." How strange to read these words, the same words Mom had written to all of us in her Will. Suddenly a memory of a conversation Mom and I had some years ago surfaces in my mind. She told me that I was born under a lucky star. It gave me much comfort at the time to imagine a star in the heavens actually caring about me. That same feeling is here with me now.

For the first part of my life, my relationship with Mom was very distant, almost estranged. I rarely shared anything about my life with her or my father. However, after my father died, she and I and a group of her friends became very close. Most of them had lost their husbands and were ready to dive into a more adventurous side of life, which was right up my alley. We spent quite a few years traveling to various places where we could play golf, and in the winter we would take cross-country ski trips into remote wilderness areas in Montana. This was a time when Mom became my friend and I enjoyed the way she let her spirit loose

On one of our first adventures we took a cross-country ski trip into Yellowstone National Park. One night we went out to dinner and after a few drinks we were laughing and being loud like teenagers. At the end of dinner, one of Mom's friends decided we should take the butter left on the table so that we wouldn't have to buy any the next day. Quickly, before the waiter came over, she put the butter in a small napkin and stuffed it into a purse sitting on the table. Later, when we were leaving, another friend who was laughing and being silly accidentally leaned on the purse when she got up and the butter squished onto everything inside. This memory and many more always brought laughter to our get-togethers. The phrase "good fresh butter" became our code word, and we gave ourselves a name: "the gang."

48: Visitor from the Dream World

Last night I awoke from a dream. For nearly eight months since her death, I have had no dreams about Mom. Last night, however, she came to me as real as ever, looking exactly as she did when I last saw her:

We are at the airport and I'm helping her with her plane ticket to go home. The ticket agent won't let Mom board because she has an e-ticket instead of a regular ticket. Frustrated and short on time, I ask to speak to her supervisor. She leaves and is gone so long that I begin to look around for someone else to help us. I notice an Asian ticket agent and ask her if she can help. She slips me a pass and we go through the gate. Before us are wide white stairs that are outside. There is a white atmosphere to everything and only one wall on the right-hand side of the stairs. We begin the climb slowly. Mom seems frail and yet seems to hold steady. Halfway up the stairs, she goes over to the wall where there is a slight discoloration in the stone and begins to move her hands over the spot in strange gestures. I'm disturbed by the hand gestures because they appear so alien. After a few minutes I tell her we have to hurry or she'll miss her flight. We finally make it to the top of the stairs. Mom turns around to look back. We are met by the beginning of a sunrise over the landscape of Great Falls and the mountains in the background. It is breathtaking. Suddenly Mom begins to make slow bows in prayer. She has both hands on her heart and her eyes are closed. I am swept up in this moment with her and join her in prayer. I feel reverence in every part of my being as we both deepen into prayer.

The dream feels holy, a passage into timelessness. I'm filled with reverence as I wake up. The experience is so real that I'm slightly disoriented. Did we really meet somewhere? It feels as though we did and it's clear that she can still come into my life and affect me. I wonder if she has transformed in some way, wherever she may be. Since I've never had this kind of experience before with her, I begin to wonder if it was a visitation.

Later in the week, curious about this experience, I revisit that

...e sunrise with her. I light some candles and sink into a ...emplation. The experience of bowing to the sunrise with her ...ack with great clarity, as though it were happening now. I can ...r tranquil face and those rugged hands on her heart. I watch she bows slowly with sacred intention and I too can feel that ...ovement within my being. She emanates gratitude and grace that ...eaches out beyond her, into the whole landscape, and it also moves right into me. I am mesmerized by her hand on her heart.

As I continue to bow, in my mind's eye, I begin to feel a strange sensation in my heart. Suddenly, I feel a huge eye begin to open in the center of my heart. It feels as though it is my eye and yet it feels bigger than me. The strangeness of this eye and the location of this eye in my heart suddenly transport me into a sense of timelessness that feels eternal, as though I existed before I was ever born. I feel intrinsically connected to Mom, the sun, the landscape of my birthplace, and the innermost realm of my being, my soul. I'm called back to that sense of Self, that inner sanctuary, I have been alienated from since her death. This is the Self that guided me into all the different ways I joined her in the challenges she had to face, and which I did too.

Sometimes I was her daughter, sometimes her mother, her friend, her soul sister, sometimes her enemy as the bearer of bad news, at times that hand of fate. I could walk beside her, often stumbling and falling here and there but nevertheless, continuing on, knowing that if I could be as present as possible and open to the unfolding of outcomes I couldn't predict, the journey would unfold into wholeness, enriching both of us. Surprising to me once again, this journey I shared with Mom continues to connect me to my spirit and soul.

I hope she continues to be a teacher from another realm, accompanying me on this wild journey into the interior of my being. My vision has expanded from the narrow range of my eyes, to an inner source of wisdom that can transport me to the transcendent. As I look out the window in my room, I am mystified and curious about who in me is experiencing the soft white flakes of snow falling through the bare branches of the sweet gum tree.

49: Afraid to Tell

It has been almost a year since Mom's death and a thought keeps circling around me like a hungry dog. I wonder how things might have been different if I had told her that she was dying. This thought disturbs me like that choice-point at the crossroads where the beckoning light of the road not traveled stirs the soul. I know my fear got the best of me. I remember the conversation with my sisters about whether we should tell Mom that she was dying. I was vehement about not saying anything. I couldn't bear to see her react to this news. Now I consider that this was my fear, not hers. I am terrified of death and dying.

I decide to go back in my mind's eye to the afternoon before her death. I light some candles and begin to bring back the memory of being with her in the hospital. I can still see her sitting in bed, looking expressionless and childlike except for an occasional time when she would raise her hands in a gesture of what I imagine to be, "What do we do now?"

I decide that I will tell her. This, by the way, is not coming from a place of regret or remorse. I have accepted what happened. I just want to explore this place within me that I avoided. I know, however, that by avoiding this place in me, Mom's experience was also affected, for better or for worse.

So, now in my mind I am back at the hospital. She is looking at me with a childlike helpless look and then raises her hands in that gesture of, "What do we do now?" I go over to the side of her bed and I take her hand and hold it for awhile. Then I look at her and in this brief moment it feels as though I'm waiting for a bolt of lightning to strike me right to the ground. I say, "Mom, you are dying, do you know that?"

She looks fearful and starts to cry but nods her head yes. I look into her eyes and watch as she looks headlong into the face of death. It is awesome yet private, sacred, and terrifying. I am joining her here on the bridge where death is on one side and life is on the other. As I lift the veil off the face of death to her, I also encounter death and silence falls over me. In this strangely mortal-immortal place, stillness makes its presence known like cool darkness and I am lost and at the same time caught in an eternal cramp.

There are no words to release me, there are no thoughts that make me feel hopeful or safe. There is just me, Mom, and Death.

50: The Historical Link

Several years ago I volunteered for a local wildlife refuge to rescue injured animals. When I signed up, I really didn't fully understand what this would entail. But later it dawned on me. I called up in a panic and said that I couldn't volunteer: I realized that I was afraid of confronting a dying animal.

Pondering this now, I remember a time when I was seven years old. I was playing on a swing with my neighbor friend. We took turns hanging from the top bar and then let each other hang from our legs. When it was his turn to hold me, he lost his grip and fell on top of me, fracturing my back. I was taken to the hospital by Mom and was wrapped up in a body cast. On the way home, lying in the back seat of the car, I said to Mom, "I don't think I'm okay." She replied that I would be fine.

But deep in my being I was having a panic attack, feeling totally helpless, encased in a hard shell, knowing that I would be imprisoned in this way maybe forever. I developed a panic disorder called claustrophobia which, thankfully, I have now overcome. The panic I felt as a child was an overwhelming fear of what I now realize was my own death. It seems as though the panic protected me from falling into a dark unknown abyss that would have ripped my sense of being into a million pieces.

It is a chilly spring day and I'm spending the night in Montauk, New York, where the dark green sea and gray sky and the rugged sand dunes caress the muse within. From the deck I see white-capped waves rolling into shore. Occasional seagulls take flight and glide on the invisible jet stream of the wind. The sand dunes lie before me in colors and textures of winter. Dark brown stalks and silvery dry sea grass cover the dunes. There are patches of light green lichen and bristly brown stalks of wild roses.

As I take in this landscape my gaze comes to rest on the carcass of a deer not far away. I see the curl of the white rib bones and imagine how this mysterious structure protects all the vulnerable inner organs. Its head is tilted back towards the ribs, raised upwards to the sky. I am struck by a deep beauty in this posture. I know that in time it will disappear into the landscape. I feel a need to go over to it and look more closely.

As I take in its being more fully, I wonder whether it was a peaceful or painful death. I begin to imagine that moment just before it crossed over. Did it feel the canopy of stars overhead and the warmth of the earth from which it incarnated? Here, in my imaginings, death seems almost gentle, like an embrace that dissolves all misery and pain.

Mom and I rarely spoke about death. I remember, however, many years ago that I wanted to suggest an object that we could communicate through after she passed on. For some reason, we never had that conversation.

51: The Psychic

Several years ago, before Mom passed on, Don invited me to his family's land. Each year they have a huge spiritual gathering there, in which contact with their ancestors who have departed is an important part of the ceremonies. Native people gather from all over northern Montana and Canada to participate.

The "ghost trees" marked my entry into this land. Faded white pieces of cloth are wrapped around hundreds of ancient birch tree trunks from previous sacred ceremonies. On this hot afternoon a breeze whips through and around the trees, stirring these diaphanous white pieces of cloth into a mesmerizing dance of ghosts. I've never seen anything like this before and my footing in reality slips for a moment. Where am I?

As I drive on, I glance westward to behold the giant gateway of mountains that opens skyward into the entrance of Glacier National Park. In awe, I am witness to Heaven and Earth rejoicing in their relationship. This land emanates such beauty that a power gets right into you. I have passed through this reservation many times on the way to Whitefish where my family spent summer vacations. It is very desolate looking, with few trees and mostly dry prairie land. The town seems poverty stricken and has a broken feeling to it; but behind the scenes, back in the interior, there is this breathtaking land and sacred ceremony going on.

The most powerful ceremony I experienced at the gathering was the sweat lodge. The sweat lodge, in my understanding, is the Native way of creating a portal into the womb of the Great Mother for rebirth and communing with those who have crossed over. Here, through prayer and purification, connection to the spirit world of their ancestors is possible. It is built in a sacred way with each branch serving a particular purpose. The structure is covered with tarps and cloths of various natures to ensure that it will be completely dark inside. Pungent sage, their "guardian of sacred ceremony" plant, is spread throughout the floor and intertwined in the branches that form the roof. On the ground, in the center of the enclosed space, is a hole where hot rocks, called the grandfathers, are placed after they have been purified in a sacred fire for several hours. After we all enter the lodge, and it is totally dark, water is slowly poured on these rocks in intervals of time until we are all covered in steam and sweat.

The leader of the sweat lodge begins to pray to the Creator for blessings for all of us to purify ourselves and renew our connection to our spirit and soul and reconnect with the ancestors. I feel primal, yet holy, linked to the ancestors of homo sapiens. The boundary between the land of the spirit and physical reality vanishes, and though I personally have no contact with an ancestor, I feel in awe of the power of this ceremony. All around me I hear the whispering prayerful voices of my Native companions and I am drawn deeply into the mystery of this transitional realm where life and death, past and future are one.

Don tells me that his people have no word for good-bye. People cross over to the "Happy Hunting Ground" and continue to be a part of the lives of the living. Not only can the living benefit from help from those who have departed the earth plane, but those who have crossed over can benefit from the living.

Don told me that one time a friend of his was killed in a terrible automobile accident. He appeared to Don in a dream extremely deformed. Don performed many ceremonies throughout the following year to heal this friend and eventually he appeared to Don in a dream, no longer deformed. This brings a whole new way of thinking about life into me.

Recently, I keep wondering if Mom's spirit is back in her house. I sense her there sometimes. Living so far away, it's not hard for me to imagine that she's there doing all of the things she usually did. I've decided to visit there soon and am wondering what it will be like. No one has been there since last year at this time, when I closed it up and locked it away, wanting to keep everything as we left it when I flew out last year to move her to Portland.

We plan to have a ceremony in July in which we will release

her ashes to the wind in the Wolf Creek Canyon in the same place we released Dad's ashes some thirty-four years ago. She wanted her ashes to be cast in the same place, even though she still harbored resentments. Sometimes she changed this location depending upon her frame of mind. She told me of a dream several years ago where he greeted her at the pearly gates of heaven and she walked right past him. At that time she wanted her ashes elsewhere.

Before I leave, I decide to see a psychic. A good friend of mine has the name of one who will come to your house and read for a group of friends. There are eight of us and I am second to last to be read. I'm feeling anxious, because she has been amazingly accurate so far. Finally it's my turn, and I ask her about Mom.

She says, "She is still alive right?"

"No", I respond, "She died a year ago."

She says that Mom has not crossed over completely and that her spirit is still in her house. I immediately get goose bumps, affirming my decision that it's time for a visit. I am curious as to what I will experience when I spend some time there. She says that Mom wants me to have the picture of her as a little girl. She also says there's something with flowers on it that she wants me to have. I have no idea what that may be.

52: The Return

The plane touches down with ease while my mind races, aware that I'm back in Great Falls, one year to the day that Mom passed on. I decide to have a taxi pick me up instead of a friend because I want to feel unencumbered by conversation.

Walking up the wooden steps to the side door, I stare at it with apprehension. I have no idea what to expect when I pass through the door. Will her ghost greet me in some way? As I turn the key, I almost feel like an intruder entering her sanctuary. I look around much the way she did when I took her here to visit. I look in the cupboards, the closets, the garage, the refrigerator, half expecting some sign of her.

Silence follows me into every corner. Several times I call out, "Mom, are you home?" Then, as always, I check to see if the car will start. As usual, the battery is dead and there's a flat tire. I call AAA and then go food shopping to make myself feel better.

I feel as though I'm in a dream, disconnected from myself and everything around me. When I return from shopping, I look around for the picture of her as a child. It's in front of some books on the bookshelf. She told me that it was the only picture of her as a child. She's about four years old and is sitting, wearing a little white dress, with her two brothers, one on each side. She has a worried expression on her face.

Next to the picture is a journal she kept when she traveled for the first time in Europe. She had always wanted me to read it but I never found the time to actually sit down and go through it. I pick it up and begin to read a few pages, hoping to enliven her presence.

The details of her writing take me into England, Ireland and Wales, France, Italy, Switzerland, and Australia. She describes in detail most of her meals, their nights out in pubs, and quotes from many locals. She vividly portrays her awe of the paintings in the Louvre and the walls of the Sistine Chapel. I lose track of time for a while and when I put it down, I notice the flowers on its cover. It dawns on me that this is what the psychic was referring to.

Later that evening, loneliness begins to settle in all around me. I decide to go downstairs and open the closet where she stored many of her clothes and shoes. I lean in and grab a whole armful as though I have my arms around her, and the lingering scent of her earthly being washes over me. I cry for a long time.

This visit will be the last of its kind because in July all of us will gather here and begin dividing things up. I also am beginning to realize that maybe her spirit has finally left forever and that everything I've believed about the spirit living on is not true. This moment feels like a crisis of faith.

The next morning I drive to the outskirts of town where we roamed with our horses many years ago. The wind is making large swirling patterns in the winter wheat and tall grasses. Spring circles everywhere—in the air, in the soft mint-green shoots of sage, in the songs of the meadowlarks perched on the fence posts. It has been overcast and cold since my arrival. Emptiness prevails, affirming Mom's departure. I am aware that a big chapter in my life has ended and the next has not yet begun. I am in between, suspended in time.

Tomorrow is Saturday, the Day of the Pentecost, and I want to do a ceremony just for myself.

53: Flowers and Candy

It is sunny and windy this morning. I have decided to buy some gladiolas, since Mom's name was Glady, and some saltwater taffy which she loved, and drive out to the Pishkun for my ceremony. This is her gravestone, so to speak, until July.

As I walk down the gravel road to the edge of the shale cliffs, I remember several years ago when I drove her out here to see the Harmonic Convergence. The sun and full moon were both still visible, and other planets formed the configuration of the Star of David in the heavens, portending a time of great healing on planet Earth. She sat next to me in the car with childlike wonder in her eyes as I explained the meaning of the event. It occurs to me now that she just might have thought I was crazy. But, actually, she always showed a great interest in my esoteric studies. It was beautiful and awe-inspiring to watch the full moon begin its cool blue ascent over the eastern mountains, while the sun made its fiery descent into the dark blue silhouette of Square Butte.

Reaching the edge of the cliffs, I find a small ledge to shelter me from the wind. Here I sit for a long time, deciding what I want to say and what I want to do. Thoughts begin to come.

I'm aware that as I go through this letting-go process with her, I'm also having a new experience within myself. I truly am no longer anyone's child. I simply feel alone, alone in that there is no longer anyone I can turn to in the same way I did Mom. Her generation has departed into the great mystery and I am next.

Even though her wisdom stills lives within me offering comfort, there is a stark awareness that I am the Master of my life and that it is up to me to decide how I want the next part of my life to look. In some strange way I feel empowered, despite the huge emptiness that recognizes itself in the wide open prairie below me. As I continue to sit for awhile, listening to the wind sing its song through the shale rocks and sage, I begin to feel deep within the link to the spirit of the land that Mom has bequeathed to me. I understand in this moment that this is how Mom will continue to live on in my soul.

Slowly I arrange the colorful bouquet of red, yellow, purple, orange, and white gladiolas. I find a small ledge that looks like an altar and place the flowers so they won't be blown away by the wind. I put several candies next to them and tell Mom that I am honoring her today, the Day of the Pentecost. I tell her I hope she's in a good place and that I will continue to work on my relationship with her.

I take one of her golf balls and throw it over the cliff into thick brush where I'm sure it will never be discovered by any human. For some reason, I need to secure a place that perhaps will outlive me where I can symbolically mark the experience of our eternal connection. I think golf balls have a pretty long life, and this place is truly out of bounds.

When I return home to New York I set out for my usual run. I'm filled with thoughts about work when suddenly the smell of the ranch in Canada overcomes me. It is so strange to suddenly recognize the presence of this smell.

I suddenly ask, "Mom, are you around?" I became aware of the shimmering yellow, orange, and red of the many bunches of lilies. Lilies were one of her favorite flowers. If you were visiting her in the late spring she would always point out their return at the base of her deck. The words, "I will always watch over you," come to mind. Maybe her spirit is around but not where or when I expect it.

54: **The Ceremony**

We are all gathered here in Great Falls, to set Mom's ashes free. My sister has kept them in Oregon for over a year and has now brought them back where she belongs. They are contained in a beautiful, deep blue urn with rainbow trout swimming around on its sides. Mom loved to fish and spent many days on the Missouri River trout fishing.

Several years ago she told me a story about a time that she and a friend were fishing, gliding down the Missouri on a rubber float, when all of a sudden she hooked the underside of the float. Water started to seep in and in no time the raft began to sink. They lost all their belongings but were able to swim to shore, not an easy feat because the currents run deep and are imperceptibly strong.

It's a typical Montana summer day. The sun is strong, casting a white glow on everything, and the wind is rustling the leaves on the sumacs that border the deck outside her home. We decide that each of us will take a part in the preparations. My older sister just purchased two CDs containing Mom's favorite songs, "Hey Jude" by the Beatles and "Take Me Home" by John Denver. My younger sister is packing a picnic lunch, candles, and sage. My brother and I are at the Farmer's Market and decide to buy a beautiful bouquet of sunflowers and cattails.

As we walk through the door to the garage ready to depart with Mom's ashes, we suddenly have an inspiration. We decide to carry the urn around the house, passing it to one another, as though allowing time for Mom to say good-bye to her home. This is emotionally very difficult because it feels as though she really is here saying good-bye. As the garage door closes with the sound of finality, we head out onto the interstate to the Wolf Creek Canyon. Except for occasional small talk, we are all quiet, each in our own reverie.

As we get closer to the canyon, the landscape begins to change. The browns and yellows and vast vistas of the prairie are met by the giant and ancient rock formations of the canyon. Here, the Missouri River suddenly makes it appearance, winding in a blue green ribbon along the canyon walls. This is where many fishermen experience heaven. Every now and then a float passes by, carrying several fishermen totally absorbed by and quiet in their activity.

A silver bridge crosses the river here and we park on the side of the road. Below, an abandoned railroad track makes its way along the river and tunnels through one of the giant boulders. Our destination is near the tunnel and down to the banks of the river.

This area is familiar to all of us. As children, we used to come here to fish and often walked through the tunnel which was filled with bats and who knows what else. Our adrenalin would rise as we reached the middle of the tunnel, hoping that no train would take us by surprise. When we set Dad's ashes free many years ago, we had to walk through this tunnel so we could climb to the top of the mountain. Today, however, we aren't so brave. As we veer off the tracks just before the tunnel and climb down to the riverbank, we come upon a spot where there seems to be a ready-made gravestone, a large triangular rock. We all agree this is the place.

55: **Free at Last**

We take our time setting up for the ceremony. We put the urn near the rock and place the flowers right alongside. My older sister and brother put pictures of their children, who were unable to attend, on the branches of a bush behind the rock.

At this moment coincidences begin to happen. A deer emerges from some brush on the other side of the river. A mother duck and her four babies swim happily along. I notice a giant pitch pine just above us which seems to have sprung up out of nowhere. Suddenly, we all look up just as the sun peeks through several branches, creating a silver halo that spreads throughout the whole interior of the tree, exuding an angelic presence.

We decide to write personal penciled messages to Mom on the stone, visible to us but no one else. Then we all hold hands and my brother says a prayer for Mom's journey. I can feel all the years of our lives coming together as we bond in this sacred circle. And then slowly, we pass the urn, each of us in turn releasing ashes back into the land. Some of them fly upward; some fall into the river in long streams of white currents; and some land on the rock, dusting it lightly in a soft blanket of white. When the last of the ashes are gone we look out over the landscape in silence. We start to gather things up.

Just as we begin to play her songs, a golden eagle soars overhead and disappears behind the mountain, portending a blessing from the Great Spirit, the Native American Creator. The eagle is considered the most powerful bird of many Indian communities because its flight takes it highest in the heavens and therefore is most able to bring our messages and prayers to the Divine Creator.

Maybe my prayer for Mom to be embraced by the open arms of the Creator is, in fact, happening right now as John Denver's song "Take Me Home Country Roads" joins with the wind and the currents of the great blue and green Missouri River. She has finally returned to the arms of the Great Mother she loved so dearly. A lone puffy white cloud glides slowly away from us in the bright blue sky.

My feet feel the soft embrace of the earth as I whisper silently within, "Glady is home."

Part Two

The Storytellers

Storytelling is one of the most ancient forms of passing on wisdom. This wisdom comes from experience written from the heart to help others awaken, while leaving room for personal exploration.

Section 1

The Last Stage of Life: The Night Sea Journey and the Beacons of Light

1: Background

Shortly after I finished my memoir, I decided to develop a self-help section for this book. I posted a request on several Web sites for stories from caregivers and elders that fall into the following categories:

stories that impart wisdom and healing

stories that contain difficult and unsolvable problems, and

stories that contain mystical, afterlife, psychic, and prophetic dream experiences.

I was astounded at the tremendous response. Telling one's story about going through this stage of life with one's elder(s) seems to be an important need.

As the stories came in, I was deeply moved by their variety and rich emotional quality. I was also inspired by the storytellers' honesty and depth of feeling. These "beacons of light" stories, as I like to think of them, offer guidance, yet are easy to adapt for the unique circumstances and challenges that confront each caregiver and elder. They cover a wide range of experiences—hopefully one here will speak to your heart.

An important piece of wisdom I gained from reading these stories and going through what I did with Mom is that there is no set formula or way of doing this stage of life "right." Rather, this journey calls the caregiver to reach inward and learn how to live closely to the wisdom of his or her own heart. The awareness of the fragileness of life and the unpredictable, emotionally challenging nature of this journey enters the caregiver's consciousness, demanding greater strength and adaptability, as well as a more encompassing consciousness.

This is a time of possibility, offering much to learn about the transforming power that death and dying present to us with respect to the preciousness of life, the call to be true to one's heart, the complexity of relationships, opportunities to reconcile and forgive, and the chance to embrace a higher consciousness. If we can be conscious of Death—known through the ages as the great Awakener—a bigger, more high-minded, and mysterious part of our nature can shine through our personality. This high-minded part of us is attuned to the preciousness of life and can continue to infuse our ordinary sense of reality with gratitude long past the day our elder departs from this earth.

Like the winds that shape and shift the canyon walls in a continuing dance of transformation, this stage of life can forever change the landscape of our interior being. Those who have never prayed may find themselves praying; those who have never appreciated life may find renewed reverence; those who have been blinded by family secrets and rigid patterns may find a path to their authentic Self. And our elder is whom we have to thank for leading us into this world.

Anyone who has withstood the challenges of earlier stages and has entered into this last stage of life has earned the title of elder. For this reason, I use the word elder instead of parent.

2: *Waking up to Dependency: The Caregiver's Call to Courage*

"The last stage of life" begins the moment an elder becomes dependent on someone else for safety and emotional and/or mental support to maintain daily functioning. Entry into this stage of life is sometimes fast, as when a fall results in a need to go into an assisted living situation via doctor's orders.

For others, many increasingly emotionally difficult situations for the elder and the caregiver eventually lead to assisted living. Generally speaking, no one who has been independent wants to face the eventual reality of this stage of life. Because of this fact, both elder and caregiver usually stay in denial until the anxiety of knowing that the elder is definitely going to end up seriously hurting themselves or others can no longer be denied.

Most elders who arrive at assisted living facilities are there due to some kind of accident, rather than through choice, says a director of an assisted living facility in N.Y. This is significant and something to ponder.

Facing dependency is usually experienced as something negative and self-diminishing, and often a huge amount of resistance, denial, and fear surrounds it. Thoughts about dependency bring with them many difficult emotions, both for the caregiver and for the elder. Often elders see their dependency as a burden to others, especially the caregiver. Sometimes difficult experiences of dependency in childhood are re-awakened, adding fear and negative expectations for the elder. There are also those elders that have great expectations of the caregiver that are impossible to fulfill.

The caregiver also often faces choices that require great courage, because the consequences are usually self-defining and far reaching. For the caregiver whose elder has found a situation he or she is looking forward to it, this stage is much easier. Others, however, can be shaken to the core. These caregivers usually stay in denial longer because the task they face can be extremely emotional—uprooting the elder from their spouse or from their beloved home of many years, perhaps having to face a living situation that is less than ideal for both elder and caregiver. It is not surprising that these caregivers might feel like villains causing ruin and unhappiness to the very person they love or want to rescue.

Maybe the caregiver is reluctant to take on another burden and has to be honest and say no to taking care of their elder. Perhaps the elder is mentally ill or has been abusive (or still is) and must be placed in a mental hospital or nursing home. This is the time, just before assisted living, where both elder and caregiver can collude to stay in denial as long as possible. For the caregiver, this is often a time filled with anxiety surrounding one's elder's safety as well as the choice waiting in the wings: Where do I stand? How will I take part in this undertaking?

There are millions of stories of close calls: fires in the kitchen, falls and injuries, bounced checks, car accidents, phone calls for help. Usually there's a slow build-up of accidents, often for several years. Caregivers are prone to feel guilt during this stage—wondering if they are giving their elder the best care they can, and being forced to come to terms with how much they are willing to sacrifice. Grief, anger, terror, anxiety, and a huge sense of loss are often experienced by both the parent and caregiver each time something happens—a stroke; a fall, a heart attack.

Most of us are not prepared for this. How can we be? Often we hope or pray that our elder will return to better health, and many times they do for brief periods. Then there are reassurances from the elder that everything is, indeed, okay: "It was just a little incident."

Because denial is an unconscious defense mechanism that protects us from fear, we often have to be shaken awake. These occurrences and close calls are part of this stage of life and serve the purpose of waking us up to the imminence of our elder's dependency. At the same time they force us to become stronger and more equipped to face the eventual dying and death of our elder, and maybe even our own death. Waking up to dependency, the first beacon of light, is the caregiver's "call to courage," to thine known self be true.

"September Weekend"
Waking up to an elder's dependency

In this story, Enid Ikeda powerfully describes her experience of confronting her mother with the need to go into assisted living.

Afterward, except for brief accounts, I rarely talked of the trip and what it had meant to me. It seemed too close to the bone to express adequately. Even in my thoughts, I tended to skim the surface of the memory to avoid the ache that was a part of it. But now, years later, I needed at least to attempt it, partly as a tribute to my mother and partly to come to terms with it myself.

I left after school on a Friday in September, driving north to the Hi-Line and then east toward North Dakota. A friend had volunteered to ride along and certainly my husband would have, if I had requested it. But I felt a strong need to have the time to myself; I was turned inward and would have been alone in any case.

The call had come from my brother the week before. He farmed near the small town where our mother had lived alone since our father's death three years before. Mom was a small woman, mentally alert, unafraid and strong in spirit. But physically she was failing to the point that recently she had fallen at night and had been unable to muster the strength to get up. My brother and his family had checked on her daily for years, but this was no longer enough. For her safety, and especially with winter approaching, it was time for her to give up independent living. It was agreed that it would be better if a sibling further away would suggest the idea to her, and that person was me.

The journey to North Dakota had always been made with

anticipation and a quickening of the spirit as the miles rolled by. The sense of "home" was well-established to be in Great Falls, but there was another level at which "going home" would always mean the place I came from . . . the place of my parents. But this time, as I set out, what felt like a small stone developed in my upper chest, a lump that wouldn't go away. I faced the journey with an unaccustomed and palpable apprehension.

I thought of the small trailer home where Mom lived and its place in her life. My parents had spent years on a series of rented farms and then at last had established a place of their own, with an older house moved from another location. At the age of eighty-five, they had purchased the trailer and moved it to a lot in the middle of Fordville, population 385—a major change for two people who had spent all of their lives in the country.

I remembered vividly the first time my husband and I visited them. Mom took us on a tour and was every bit a queen showing off her palace. We viewed all the storage space and closets, the bathroom, the kitchen appliances and counter tops, the carpets, the table and chairs, all NEW for the first time in her life. Then there was the tiny sewing machine, and a dresser and bed, and other keepsakes. Seeing it through Mom's eyes, it really did look wonderful.

The trailer was both Mom's home base and her window to the world around her. She was endlessly interested in the views from her windows: people on their way to the store or post office, people going to the laundromat across the street, neighbors in the trailer park, and cars driving by. It was a parade of humanity she never tired of observing. And because she was a cheerful and positive person with a sense of humor, many of the parade's participants stopped in for a visit.

From these visits, and from the local paper, she composed a mental record of all of the births, deaths, marriages, triumphs and failures, and church and social activities of the community's inhabitants. Everything from momentous events to the trivia of a small community was part of Mom's amazing memory system. But she avoided what is commonly thought of as gossip; she would quietly change the subject or the emphasis if any "dirt" were being dished.

And the stone in my chest was partly from the thought of suggesting to Mom that she leave this small paradise that had been hers for seven years.

I arrived in Malta shortly before dusk and checked into a motel. I ordered a meal at a restaurant, but the stone made swallowing difficult so I returned to my room for a fitful sleep. Early Saturday morning I was again traveling east and the feeling apprehension grew stronger.

I thought of my trip home that past July. One day, my sister-in-law and I had taken Mom to a pick-your-own strawberry field. The expedition was a special treat and the berries were big and plentiful. Mom approached it as an unexpected adventure.

After we had picked for a while, we were walking toward the car with our buckets of fruit when Mom suddenly collapsed into the soft dirt. Immediately she said, as she was being helped to her feet, "I thought that was kind of fun!" The message, flying in the face of the fact, being, "Don't see this as any kind of weakness now!" I remembered the incredible lightness of her body as I lifted her up, a fragile frame with a wisp of covering. I was aware for the first time of a fading away of my mother's physical form.

I continued east on Highway 2 and thought of how to approach Mom about the move. I tried to imagine possible reactions but none seemed real. The only reality was my own part and the effect it would have on Mom's life.

And I thought about Mom's approach to child-rearing. Mom had the remarkable ability to provide unconditional love and safety without demanding in return the right to control. There were certain basic standards of honesty and kindness and responsible behavior, but for the most part even these were taught by example and not imposed. So I made my own decisions about friends and education and jobs with support, not intrusion, from home. And now I was about to tell this most non-interfering person how and where she should spend her days.

That, too, accounted in part for the stone.

I drove into Fordville in the late afternoon and wondered if Mom thought it strange that I had come alone or if she had any sense of premonition at my arrival. We chatted a bit and had a light supper. And later, just before bedtime, I knew I must bring up the subject that had brought me here. The thought of spending another night knowing what must be said was intolerable.

"Mom, it's probably time to think about going into a home. Glenn said there's an opening in the one in Larimore now."

A period of silence, then: "Oh, yes . . . I suppose so." Another pause, then: "Will I be able to take some of my own things?"

We talked briefly of what personal possessions could be taken to the home and then Mom went to bed. In my imaginings, it had never gone just like that. Maybe Mom had been preparing herself for this eventuality, but even so the sweetness of the response and my own sense of relief left me feeling weak.

And yet, it shouldn't really have been unexpected. It was an ingrained part of Mom's nature to put the most positive light on any occurrence; hence the automatic response of what she could bring to the home, not of what she would be leaving behind. And at another level, it seemed that Mom was aware of what the message may have cost the messenger and was trying to make a difficult situation as easy as possible. That, too, would have been Mom's nature.

Now I was left with a tangle of feelings, following the original relief. Mom had made it easy for me but I couldn't do the same for myself. The very effortlessness of the encounter caused me to feel that I had taken advantage of her compliant nature. And for me, that guilt created a space between us where none had been before. On the positive side, there was an intense respect for this valiant woman and her attitude toward the trials of life. Mom had always had the ability to make the best of any situation, without self-pity, but this was surely an ultimate test of that characteristic.

There was a bittersweet quality to the next thirty-six hours that defied sorting out. In the Norwegian way, no more was discussed about the move though the fact of it hung heavy in the air.

I slept with Mom both nights. Monday morning I awoke early because I would be driving to Great Falls in one day. I heard stirrings in the bedroom as I prepared coffee for the trip, but for the first time Mom did not get up to see me off. We said our good-byes from the bedroom door.

It was a blessing in one sense, because I hadn't known how to face the prospect of leaving Mom at the door of her trailer. But I always wondered about the strangeness of it. Was Mom, too, unable to make it a normal good-bye? Was there resentment? Or was it a final gift from someone who sensed the difficulty I would have in leaving.

As I left town, the stone began to dissolve into a seemingly endless well of tears. They flowed off and on for hundreds of miles. And as the stone dissolved, there was left in its place an emptiness, so that by the time I reached Great Falls I felt listless and drained. I stored my memories of the weekend in a far corner of my mind, from where fragments would surface when I least expected it.

But there was one scene from the second night in the trailer that touched me with such intensity that I rarely allowed it into my consciousness. I had awakened sometime during the night knowing that I had moved out from under the blankets. And then I was aware of Mom drawing the covers over me again. It was an act of such tenderness and gentle caring, especially coming at this time, that the poignancy of it overwhelmed me. The feeling I experienced was that of one of my earliest recollections, of being allowed to snuggle between my parents in bed, safe and secure and warm. Now in this unexpected time and place and circumstance, I was for one more time the daughter being cared for by her loving Mother.

"Yesterday's Road"
Waking up to choosing one's own life

*Waking up to the dependency and the tremendous
responsibility of a mentally ill elder can force one to
make a choice as to whose life you are going to save.
Here is Marsha Benoff's story.*

I was five or six when it began.

"Take care of the baby," Momma would say. "I'll be right away back."

After the first time, I knew she might disappear for several days and for the nights between as well.

I never told how I would pull my folding chair to the side of Gary's crib and reach my arm through the slats to feel the heat of his body, and how that warmth would make just enough of a safety zone to encircle us both.

Little did I know then, how much more vulnerable Gary was than I.

I used to think back then, that Momma carried with us all those huge unopened cartons from the Bronx, from one apartment to the next, to fill the empty spaces my father and brother had left behind.

But I wonder now if it wasn't the reverse—that she had packed away all the emptiness, had hidden from sight what she feared most.

And I suppose now, sitting by myself in this empty house, the monsters I imagined were creatures I created to give form to the feeling of alone.

I wish I could remember how much I understood; if when I sat on my folding chair with the ripped leather seat—did I know I was alone even when Momma was at home?

Love is more elusive than fear; love is a sparkle that may twinkle at you, tantalize you from safety as it hides behind a tree in a forest of dark.

"Come and get me," it teases. "I'm here, and here, and perhaps here."

I hang up the phone in frustration.

"She can't be released just yet, they may not release her, and who did you say you are? The doctors have to sign off on her, the head of the department . . ."

I hardly understand why I've made this choice. At twelve I left home and however unhappy I was in all those furnished rooms, I was never sorry.

But here I am, struggling with a mental health institution for her release.

Why?

Is the feeling in my heart love for the woman who must have given me that when I was still in her arms, before I was old enough to walk and to talk?

Was that enough or is the call of genetic cells responsible?

Why am I fighting to enter the lions' den, why have I changed my life to do this?

"You have three days in which to come for your mother."

I recognize the official tone that has denied my pleas in the past weeks.

"But I need time, I haven't finished preparing for her, I haven't even advertised for help. And also, there's been an unexpected emergency . . ."

"She will be released in three days. If you plan to have her live with you, you had better come for her."

He's very tall, very dark-skinned and burly; his teeth gleam white in a friendly smile. He's wearing green and I suppose he's an orderly.

"You taking her home?"

"Yes, finally," I answer.

"You gonna have your hands full with that one." His smile is gone, replaced with a look akin to compassion.

How can that be I wonder, how could he have had his hands full? I look from the body that towers over mine to Momma, who has become smaller than ever, stooped with her eighty plus years of age, and from who knows what else.

Might she become violent, I want to ask? Will there be physical struggles, will the stitches from my recent surgery open and bleed?

"Don't forget to stop at the desk and get her medication. She has a month's supply of Haldol to start her off, and they'll give you script for more."

Haldol, my mother is on Haldol—that's what they give to crazy people!

Momma has only been in my car one other time. I had driven to Brooklyn and brought her back to see my shop, hoping for once she'd be impressed, that she would be proud of me. But she hadn't noticed my paintings on the walls, the satin of the wood floors, or the dozens of blooming plants in the windows.

Her only comment was, "For what did you need to get a dog?"

This time, I tell myself I have no expectations.

"When will we be there, I need to go in toilet," Momma asks.

"It's a long ride I know, but can you wait about twenty minutes?"

She agrees. She peers at traffic signs and reads the names aloud, showing me she's still in control, and that I'm not tricking her, not taking her to a place she isn't aware of.

"They have there such wonderful washing machines; I never saw such a thing. They would take away my dresskala and right away, in five minutes, they would bring it back clean."

"Maybe it wasn't the same dress."

"It was the same one."

"Okay, I guess they do have very fast machines, wow."

"The whole ceiling was falling by them; big pieces fell from the top."

"That's terrible." I say, but wonder if that can be true? Maybe they suddenly had to empty a ward and decided to send her home.

"We're almost home; are you okay for a few more minutes?"

"I went already." She says. "Don't worry, it's nothing."

Always my eyes would be drawn to old, abandoned apartment houses. Two, three, even five-story apartment houses, often with one or more walls fallen away, the dismal interior with once-bright paint exposed.

How was it I would sense loneliness occupying the deserted walls within?

Finally, I understand.

A tree, an orange, or the ocean, all are complete in and of themselves. But a building has no need to exist without dwellers; unlike a tree or even a bug, a vacant home is useless.

Momma is home, the mission of this house is accomplished.

I'm not eager to join her first thing in the morning, but I don't know how she did during the night. I don't know if she sleeps later than she would when I knew her habits so well.

I don't know if she is awake at all.

I walk down the steps quietly, but she is awake and she greets me pleasantly.

Haldol is wonderful, I think.

"Who was that young man?" She questions with a smile.

"What young man?"

"The wonderful young man who was making music and all the children were dancing around with him." Her hands make a circle in the air.

"I don't know, Ma." I tell her. "I was sleeping, I didn't hear him."

I turn away before she can see my tears, this is not the first time I have hidden tears from her, but it is one of the times I have cried for her.

I must have been ten when she told me she had walked away from the village in Poland without a look back.

Even at that age and with my anger for her in full swing, I cried for the pain of a fifteen-year-old who would walk away from her past.

I cried at the report of the court-ordered psychiatrist during the procedure to appoint me her conservator. He had introduced himself as wanting to help her, and my mother's recorded response was, "Where were you, I waited so long for you."

Did she understand or did she think he was her father, or one of her beloved brothers, or my father or my brother?

And now her fantasy of the wonderful young man, what dream was fulfilled in the night?

These tears ache, they rip from my soul for the child and woman who might have been, for the pain she lived with, pain that inhabited her body like a cancer.

"Those dirty bastards." Momma takes a sip from her mug and I realize I've never seen her drink from a cup before, only from the rim of the saucepan.

"I was waiting for the bus; I was going to see Fiddler on the Roof, all of a sudden for no reason they grabbed me."

She hasn't asked any questions, as if this were the most normal thing in the world; that she and I would be in the same place at the same time, that we would somehow manage to live together.

Didn't she understand that while I would enjoy the first few minutes on those occasions when I would visit her, that she would, against my most improbable hopes, resort to the old tears and curses and the misery that emerged immediately after her surprise to see me wore off?

Did she not see my willingness to love turn again to the old frustration and anger?

Was she so involved in her own wretchedness that she was unable to see what she inflicted and how that would hurt us both?

But I know the answers, after all I would watch as she drove my brother, her adored child, from her, without understanding she was doing so.

She doesn't know I plan to hire a caregiver and that I intend to keep watch from afar. How can she trust herself to be happy in this new home and with a daughter she has barely known as an adult?

"And they wouldn't let me out, how do you like that?" But she isn't looking at me, or perhaps isn't asking me the question. And I do as I would back then; I make my face blank and think as I will.

"We have your mother, we have Mrs. Greenberg here."

"I'm sorry, you have the wrong number; my mother's name isn't Greenberg."

"Sylvia? Isn't it Sylvia Greenberg? Are you Marsha?

"Oh? My mother is quite short and has white hair. She speaks with a heavy European accent. She has no teeth and would be wearing at least three dresses?"

"Yes, that's her."

"Okay, she's my mother but she isn't Mrs. Greenberg," I'd answered.

"Well, we were wondering if you would consider having us keep her for a few days, for observation, you know."

I'd wanted to say why, I already know she's crazy?

But I didn't.

"Why, what's she done?"

"Well, she calls an ambulance every morning. She says she has headaches, but we can't find anything."

That's because she's smarter than you, I'd wanted to say.

She gets to ride in an ambulance, she gets a lot of attention, a free breakfast and maybe lunch, and you probably give her carfare to get home! And you think she's crazy?

"That might be a good idea," I'd agreed.

"Has she been in need of psychiatric treatment in the past?"

Are you kidding I'd wondered, would you ask if you knew we lived in poverty while she had about forty thousand dollars in a small jar inside a larger jar with chicken schmaltz poured over the two? Would you ask if you knew she left me alone with an infant for days at a time when I was five and six? What question would you ask if you knew she would steal toilet paper from public places and hang her used squares on a string to dry for reuse?

"No, never, but she's needed it," I'd answered, stifling the giggles that would bring tears of blood had I let them loose.

"Will you agree then?"

"Yes, it's probably quite timely. I'm in the process of becoming her conservator, and of looking for a house for both of us so I can keep an eye on her.

At least if you keep her, she'll be safe for a few days."

"A lot of the people there were really meshugah." Momma says.

"It's a shanda/a shame."

She nods and looks sad for them.

"Don't forget your pill." My words are deliberately casual as I hand her one, but I watch as she puts it deep into her mouth and takes another swallow of coffee.

She never used to be able to do that, she would poke pills for her imaginary illnesses deep into a banana so that she wouldn't know they were there and she would be able to swallow without retching.

It had been a relief at first that they had kept her; I had hoped she would be held for a week at least. That for one week I'd be saved the long drive from Suffolk County all the way to Brooklyn.

But going back hadn't been necessary until that last time when I passed the word to the other tenants, and opened the door for them to take away what they would.

Everything was gone in a flash, the things I'd wanted already gone long before.

For me, Momma's apartment had been empty before her former neighbors wheeled out the bedroom set I remember from the Bronx when I was three.

Empty of the only things I had wanted: the gold-colored metal box filled with papers, childhood photographs of us three children, the report cards she had saved for all these years along with photos of relatives I'd never met.

Marriage and divorce papers, everything.

Momma had finally thrown away her past.

"She had the fire department come." Mrs. Wilson had explained. "She was burning papers in the kitchen sink! After that she was scared to burn, they yelled at her! Instead, she would spend hours in the incinerator room burning boxes of things."

Momma had left her apartment empty of everything but furniture and roaches.

"Where is all her cut glass, her crystal, her jewelry?" I had asked when I spoke with Mrs. Wilson that first time.

"She sold it, she gave it away; she traded most everything for food. She would ring your bell and demand you give her food, and if you didn't she would talk you down to a dog!"

"But she has money!" I'd almost demanded of the social worker Mrs. Wilson had told me about.

"She claims she does have money, but she isn't able to get herself to the bank to withdraw her funds. The building manager and I drove her to the bank one day, but she refused to get out of the car, she was afraid we would steal from her. She was thrown out of the local food markets for stealing you know."

But I hadn't known. Why did it fall to Mrs. Wilson to contact me after so much suffering had already occurred?

Mrs. Wilson with a grown daughter and two grandchildren returned home for her help, a woman kind enough to accept the added burden of my mother, and she was not alone. Momma had demanded and received help from many of the hard-working, struggling families in the building for so many months.

And why had I not forced myself to visit Momma more often, and had I, would I have known what I could not see?

Momma had refused to take the food I'd brought that first time. I'd had to concoct a scheme with Mrs. Wilson to have her come down and fill her shopping cart with the foodstuffs Momma always liked to eat.

"I don't know who left the food, I think the Salvation Army," Mrs. Wilson would say. Momma wouldn't think they wanted to poison her.

"But she would stand in the elevator and hand out the food to the other tenants," the social worker told me.

I'd paid Momma's debt of two years unpaid rent to the manager of the project, and thanked Mrs. Wilson for everything.

I'll never go back.

There are no tears, no cursing my father, and no questions.

Perhaps she is so relieved to be free, to be released from the hospital that she is content.

But more likely, it's the Haldol.

That being so, how do I explain myself, how to excuse myself for not having stepped in sooner? What in my family was so organically wrong we each responded by complete withdrawal?

My father, who rather than to seek help for the mother of his three children, instead left us all with the woman he had diagnosed in secret and had been warned was unfit.

Both my brother and sister were barely adults when they too, abandoned our mother, fled from her insanity as if they would escape its effects.

My excuses are multiple, all flawed.

It is a line not crossed to have a parent committed, and she would have never gone voluntarily or forgiven.

Perhaps had one more family member walked that line with me . . . ?

But why on my own did I not have the will, the drive to attempt to have her diagnosed and helped?

Because her greatest fear was of being entrapped. She often quoted a movie before my time, *Gaslight*, of how the husband manipulated the wife into a sanitarium to rid himself of her.

The truth is, it was easier to ignore her, to run away as my siblings had, to justify myself with a few visits now and then, more than they ever did.

To remind myself after each visit of how it was impossible to deal with her madness.

And so this woman who had found the courage to cross an ocean alone at fifteen, and to come to a new world where she knew not a word of the spoken language, a woman who found work, and a husband, and who wrote poetry to be published with regularity, was allowed to fester in her own psychosis.

And what now?

"Diane, it's me, my mother fell out of bed and I don't know what to do."

"Is she hurt?"

"I don't think so, but I can't get her to her feet." I try, but I can't keep the tremble from my voice.

"I'll be right over."

"Lucky she didn't get hurt," Diane says.

"She's so little, she didn't have far to fall," I answer, but I'm not laughing on the inside. More than anything, I'm amazed at Momma's cheerful attitude.

I try and connect the mother I've known, the hypochondriac who never wore nylon stockings or panties because the seams hurt too much, with the woman who has no complaints after falling from her bed.

Again, I remind myself she might have led a different life had she been using Haldol all these wasted years.

I thank Diane over and over. What would I have done without her?

This time, I can't even make the attempt to hide the humiliation in my voice or the begging.

"Diane, she did it again."

"I can't help you; you better tie her into the bed or something."

"I can't do that to her."

"I can't help you; you know I'm on sick leave because I hurt my back. This is the third time and I can't keep helping you lift her.

Call the fire department."

"The fire department?"

"Yeah, that's who you call."

My hands are shaking, I am so afraid I'm ice cold on the inside, and my words sound like ice cubes to my ears.

I didn't know when you call for help, they automatically send an ambulance and that they must then take you to the emergency room.

"Are you on any medication?" the admitting nurse wants to know.

"I have a bad heart," Momma says.

She means broken heart I want to say, but I remain quiet.

"Ever have any broken bones?"

"She broke her hip a few years ago," I say.

"I never had a broken bone in my life!" Momma snaps. "Never!"

My eyes meet those of the nurse and I see the question in hers. Does she doubt me or Momma I wonder, but I don't argue.

I don't answer any more of the list of questions. Instead I replay my conversations with the hospital, and eventually with the convalescent home.

"She just won't cooperate; she won't do the physical therapy," they'd complained. "She says it hurts too much."

I'd wondered if she would ever walk again.

"And anyway, how does she know anything about me—you think you know who she is?" Momma looks shrewdly at the nurse.

"You think she's my daughter? She's not even my daughter; she's the daughter of the whore my husband ran away with."

I feel my face grow hot and my body shrink small, the same way I would feel when I was five, and six, and ten and Momma would start to scream at someone in her bad English, the way I felt when she made me lie in court and say the landlord had chased her and beaten her with a chair.

They leave Momma on a gurney and we wait.

She's pleasant to me now, either accepting me as the daughter of the whore or as her own.

"I'm cold," she complains, and I pull a lightweight blanket from an empty gurney.

I unfold it and as I cover her short hospital-gowned body I see she is indeed, as she would always say, hairless.

I always wondered at her pride in this, but assumed she meant her legs and underarms.

"Still cold." She complains quietly as if to herself, and I leave her side to search out another blanket.

The nurse has come back while I was gone and apparently gave Momma information agreeing with my own.

"How do you like that, I had a broken hip!" Momma's telling herself this, and I find it ironic she believes the stranger in a white uniform.

"Excuse me; could you get my mother something to eat? We've been here for hours and she hasn't even had breakfast."

"Actually, she's fine and we're getting ready to discharge her. Give me a few minutes and you can take her home."

Suddenly, truth hits me, and it's a hard blow.

Take her home to what?

Will she continue to fall from bed more or less often? Perhaps more often now that she has the knack of it.

Will this be a repeat of her daily visits to the emergency room?

Is she better off at home where she is as alone as she has always been, or someplace more social, where there will be crafts and nurses and doctors for her to play her coy games with?

I didn't think this out, I didn't have enough experience or support or money. I never saw beyond the step before me.

I have filled the emptiness in my home but at the expense of Momma's best interests.

"We need you to sign her out now." The nurse hands me a pad with a pen tied to the plastic backing.

"I can't take her home, I'm sorry."

"What?"

"I won't take her home, there's no point to it." My eyes sting with tears and my upper lip and hands tremble, but my voice is firm.

"We can't keep her here."

"And I can't keep her at home—how many times can she fall out of bed before she gets hurt? How many times will she end up in the emergency room confused and hungry and cold?"

"But . . ."

I hear her words of protest but my eyes say good-bye to Momma. I cannot say the words to her, or even approach her. I cannot.

I turn; I walk down the long smooth corridor toward the sign that spells Exit, my face feels swollen and my upper lip throbs.

I find my car and slide into the driver's seat where I sit shedding what feels like endless tears.

How could I have been so stupidly unprepared?

"Help!"
Hostile dependency

Sometimes the caregiver tries to do everything possible to make facing dependency easier, but is met with hostility. Resentments and anger about becoming dependent can be directed toward the caregiver, consciously or unconsciously, making her or him the object of despised dependency. This storyteller wants to remain anonymous.

One Sunday afternoon years ago I received a call from my almost hysterical mother. "Find a place for us to move to! I am a prisoner in this apartment! I have nowhere to get even a breath of fresh air and there's no one to talk to!"

My normally stoic seventy-eight-year-old mother had finally flipped and I was shocked into action.

My parents had been living in a Brooklyn apartment for about twenty-five years. They were forced to move there when the neighborhood they lived in became too dangerous. Both were crippled by arthritis and were dependent upon their walkers.

Dad was totally happy to be left to his television programs and hated almost any form of sociability. Mother, entirely opposite, longed to be with people. Her Brooklyn neighbors helped only a little to meet her needs, so it fell upon me to be her stability, company, sounding-board, and partner in hour-long discussions on all topics. My personality, much more like my father's, experienced this as an enormous burden.

At 8:00 every morning (Mother was a 6:00 a.m. riser), I knew that she was impatiently waiting for my call. Often she would be angry with someone and wanted to vent. Other times that someone was me, but I would never be told what my offense had been.

My husband and I lived then as now in a house on Long Island where we had raised two daughters who had already flown the nest. We managed to find a beautiful light-filled, terraced apartment for my parents, located less than ten minutes from our house. My parents employed a woman who spent five days a week taking care of them, doing the shopping, cooking, cleaning, and errands. A great set-up on all counts! They were miserable! They felt displaced and restless.

About four years after the move, my father had a stroke and died. Mother was left with her helper for five days a week but was alone nights and weekends, albeit with constant visits from her family. She continued to set a place at the table for my father when she ate alone.

By this time, I was taking care of one of my daughter's three young sons. He was about eighteen months and had both a younger and older brother who were cared for at home while my daughter worked. At about 8:30 one morning I received a frantic call from my mother, "I am paralyzed, I am all alone here. I can't get out of bed even to go to the bathroom. Help me!"

As quickly as I could, I returned my grandson to his house and rushed to my mother's. I pleaded with her to come to live with us and she reluctantly agreed. For the moment, we had to get her dressed and collect things she absolutely had to bring with her. These included her mink hat and her ancient potato baker. The baker had been used every day since I was a young child. It was the size of a stove burner and was topped by a rusted metal dome. I suppose to her it was a symbol of home and normalcy.

We left the apartment with mother seated in her wheelchair, sobbing and wailing and the potato baker covering her lap. Unmindful of the spectacle she was creating, Mother was lost in noisy despair going down the elevator, through the lobby, to the car, and finally to my house where she stayed the night. The next morning she insisted upon taking herself, her hat, and her potato baker back home.

The comic aspects of this story seem less humorous and more tragic to me as my husband and I grow older. We are close to the time when one of us will be left to cope alone or be forced to give up our own autonomy and that most precious place of all—our "home"—that haven of ultimate security, normalcy and belonging.

"Let Me Die at Home"
Interference from a spouse

Ruby Anastasia Sturcey's story describes a long painful process throughout which her efforts to face and deal effectively with her mother's dependency and approaching death are continually frustrated by her father, who is in a state of denial.

Sometime in March of 2006, our family "9/11" hit.

I heard the phone ringing, again and again, and finally answered it, probably around 3:00 or 4:00 in the morning. It was my sister Diane calling; Mom had fallen during the night and it appeared that she had broken her hip. She needed me to come down immediately to help.

After the phone call, I didn't rush into action as ordered, but took a short while to try to take in the enormity of what I had just been told. Grandma Jester (my mother's mother) had died from complications of a broken hip—also in March, a number of years before—at an age almost identical to Mom. I got it that it was the beginning of the end. I got it that things would never be the same, and I needed to take a few minutes to allow that knowledge to sink in.

It was the phone call that we all dreaded. Both parents were so elderly and frail. We all lived knowing that it was a matter of time before the towers crumbled in our family. In a strange sense, as difficult and complicated as our family was, my parents were still the corner stone of it all.

My mother had a prolonged, painful, difficult rehab following the fracture to her hip. I didn't think she would be able to return to her own home again, but I underestimated her strength of will. My father allowed some modifications to be made in their home—like grip bars to be placed both outside of the house and in the bathroom—and assured the social worker he would allow aides in to help with my mother's care. My mother was able to walk short distances, and she continued to do her best with physical therapy. My father allowed one person that they knew to come in and bathe my mother on Sundays, but then he cancelled any further assistance once my mother had returned home.

Once home, my mother had several more falls, each one leading to further decline. She was no longer able to participate in even small tasks such as washing dishes or assisting with meal preparation. My mother was very proud of the fact that she had been an officer in the first wave of women Marines in World War II, and her strength and tenacious spirit were a force to be reckoned with. It was that powerful independent streak that kept her going, despite the increasing and mounting losses.

As the months went by, I had the growing sense that my mother, as I knew her, had died when she broke her hip. She never recovered, which caused her to be completely dependent on my father. She became profoundly depressed, and after trying antidepressants, refused to take them, feeling that they were of no help to her. When social workers tried to draw her out, she denied having any issue or problem.

Although my father was extremely diligent, patient, and tender in his care of her, he also exercised complete, tyrannical control and would not allow anyone to visit her other than my two sisters or myself. Neighbors, friends, and her younger sister with whom she was extremely close were turned away or made so miserable that they would choose not to visit. He would not allow a ramp to be built, so my mother was confined indoors, except for the thrice-weekly trips to the local dialysis unit. He also often interrupted her phone calls, arguing with her to the point that she frequently limited the time she spoke to her friends and family.

Everyone in the family attempted to encourage my father to change, to no avail. I called in two different social workers to report the situation. My mother would then deny there was any problem, as she felt that to say anything would "rock the boat." She had been married to my father for sixty-five years, and this was the nature of their marriage. After many hours of discussion, we agreed in the end that to remove my mother from the situation would cause her more pain than attempting to comfort her while she stayed in it—her love-hate relationship with my father had been going on since the early days of their romance.

This period of time was terribly painful for all of us. At best, we could only do things to try to make a terribly difficult situation a little easier—call frequently and visit whenever possible. My sister went over almost daily to bring food and help with mother's care.

Before this time, I had always called Mom several times a week just to chat about whatever was going on in my life but now the calls were now grueling. She would talk of being a prisoner, of wanting to die, of her unrelenting misery, and there was nothing that I could do to help her. The underlying mood for me during this time, besides grief and anguish, was anger. I was on some childish level, angry that I had "lost my mother." I no longer shared any of the problems of my life. A wall hung between us. I was angry that she would not try, and had never tried to change any of the circumstances of her life. I was angry with myself for not being able to help her, angry at God for her suffering, and angry at my father for being so cruel at times. The anger ran like a submerged stream, not out in the open, but most often manifested in short frustrated phone calls. When she would complain of being a prisoner and wanting to die, I would assert that other people in her circumstances made other choices. It was difficult to watch her refuse every offer of help, whether it be Tylenol to relieve pain or truthful conversation with her doctor or social worker.

She loved to oil paint, but would no longer paint because she might get the floor dirty. She was no longer able to read because of her declining eyesight and her inability to hold up a book, but refused to listen to books on tape. She enjoyed watching TV but the television frequently went out of service, and they wouldn't spend the few dollars it would take to get it fixed, or allow their daughters to have it fixed for them.

She sank further into her misery and I went from not knowing how I would ever be able to cope with the death of my mother, to secretly wanting her to die so that her suffering would end.

So many sad images come to mind: Mom slumped in her chair in the rehab/nursing home, looking so utterly, unspeakably miserable; at the exercise machines in rehab, so tired, but not giving up; Mom so sunk into herself that I don't recognize her. The little old lady with the black crocheted hat pulled down over her head and the mauve coat that was now so big for her, was unrecognizable to me—I was shocked when I realized that this stranger was my mother.

Although she would frequently say that she wanted to try to go up and down the steps by herself, we were all painfully aware that to do so would be impossible. Mom would say at times that she felt like she could just get up and walk around, yet the awareness that her legs would no longer sustain her weight was a source of enormous anguish for her. To make matters worse, my father would yell at her at times, "Move your legs Lois!" as if by yelling, he could force or bully her into returning to the woman that she had been not that long ago.

My mother could still slowly transfer herself, with help, from the bed to the wheelchair, and back again, which allowed my father to continue to care for her at home. During this time my mother began to say that she wanted to end dialysis and die. At first, we would all try to cheer her up. However, as the months continued and she became increasingly debilitated and depressed, my sisters and I began to talk openly with her about the possibility of stopping dialysis and what that would mean.

She began talking to other people about the possibility of going off dialysis, with full understanding that if she did, she would certainly die within a matter of days or weeks. My mother never suffered from dementia and was fully alert and able to make clear decisions about her care right until the last few days. The medical staff at her dialysis center warned her that it was "a horrible way to die." When she tried to talk to her closest friends, husband, and sister about possibly going off dialysis, she was told things like "Don't talk like that," "Don't be depressed," and "What you do to yourself, you do to me."

My mother had had a DNR and Advanced Directives in place for years, and had made it clear to all of the family that she wanted no "extraordinary measures" to be kept alive. She did not want any further heart surgeries but when asked by her nephrologist, she did want treatment for pneumonia. It was clear to me she was still invested in living, and not ready to make any final decision about dialysis. She did, however, have a right to clear, honest information and support to help her make an informed decision but she was denied this.

My sisters and I talked openly with her about her options, and I read her the chapter from Handbook for Mortals—Guidance for People Facing Serious Illness, by Joanne Lynn, M.D. and Joan Harrold, M.D., about discontinuing dialysis. I asked her if it bothered her that her daughters would talk openly with her about this, wondering if she would perhaps interpret that as, in some way, a lack of love for her. She replied that it was a comfort to her and that it helped her to not feel so alone with her feelings.

We assured her that we would support her in whatever decision she made. My father refused to discuss with anyone that Mom was getting weaker or thinking about discontinuing dialysis. I would sit with her during her dialysis treatment and knew many of the nurses and technicians that were caring for her. Although many had been very kind to my mother over the years, creating a sort of "community of friends" for her, there was absolutely no honest discussion or support for stopping dialysis. I began to get a strange, unsettling feeling, almost a paranoia that the medical staff believed we were somehow not invested in taking care of Mom.

My parents had been regularly encouraged to think about some type of "assisted living" situation by me and my sisters and myself over the years, but they refused. Various family members offered to have Mom come to live with them, but not only did she not want to be a burden to anyone, she did not want to leave her home and husband. People would say "Why don't you . . ." this or that, not realizing or believing that we had tried long and hard, but had been completely powerless to effect any change with my father. He was "Mr. Charm" when in the presence of others, and no one suspected or believed us about the emotional abuse that he inflicted upon my mother.

Mom expressed strong feelings about not wanting to die alone or with strangers, in an ambulance or emergency room. She wanted to be home, in her own bed, with her family around her. She repeatedly said over the years that the only way she wanted to leave her home was to be "carried out in a box." As a Hospice nurse myself, I knew that the only way we could ensure my mother having the kind of death she wanted would be if she made the terribly difficult decision to terminate dialysis, if and when she was truly ready. I regularly attend deaths where individuals are kept comfortable, their symptoms well-managed with medications specific to their need, with their families receiving the emotional, spiritual, and medical support that they need from a team of people dedicated to their care. I knew that this could be available to us as well, but only if we, as a family, faced my mother's slow but steady decline and made clear but difficult decisions. I also knew that at that time, as long as my mother continued with dialysis, she could not be a candidate for Hospice care, as it was seen as a life-sustaining treatment. My sisters and I recognized that she was failing. My father refused to discuss it with anyone, and repeated attempts to talk to him about it drew only complete and complete opposition and total dismissal.

Anger and overwhelming loss were two of the main emotional themes permeating this period of our lives, but the power of deep love was the fuel that kept all of us going. My father, at age eighty-eight, dressed and washed her, changed her diapers, and did the cooking, cleaning, and shopping. My parents fought about everything and nothing, yet the profound love and attachment that they had for each other and their family somehow shone through all of it.

Another emotion that ran high was a strange, unsettling sense of confusion. None of us knew how long this basically untenable situation would or could possibly continue. Although my mother's physical body was breaking down, she was completely intact mentally, and acutely aware of everything that she was losing. For so many formerly independent and strong-willed individuals, the loss of their abilities is profoundly painful, their pain is often inconsolable, and their depression out of the reach of any medication. Her nephrologist continued to assure us that she was in fact quite "stable" and that her lab work was satisfactory. It was difficult for me to get a real sense of what was happening.

The American Society of Nephrology and Renal Physicians Association has established guidelines to facilitate physicians in aiding patients in making the decision to end dialysis. It is clearly recognized as being a complicated, emotionally wrought decision; and it is also recognized that families and patients need a great deal of support around this issue. Many patients at some point choose to discontinue dialysis, and the guidelines clearly lay out what steps need to be followed to allow a patient clear information and support around this decision. Yet despite the kind and thorough care that her doctor had afforded her over the years, he was completely unable to support her in facing the possibility of ending dialysis.

What further complicated my mother's decision was her strong Catholic faith. She was told by others that going off dialysis was a mortal sin, akin to suicide. So her great desire to do God's will, combined with her Marine willpower, devotion to my father, and, perhaps, fear of the consequences, kept my mother going to dialysis week after week, three times a week, for hours at a time.

My mother appeared to be slowly dying, yet, was she? Perhaps it was my experience of how incredibly frail people can become and still continue to live on and on that left me feeling completely unsure of how things were truly unfolding. Was she eligible for Hospice, with their general criteria of six months or less to live?

Each of us, in our own way, continued to do what we could to support my parents. My sister who lived locally visited frequently, brought food, cleaned, and helped to bathe my mother. When Mom had dressings that needed to be changed, she helped with that, doing whatever she could do to make their lives a little easier. Each act was met with my father's anger: "What the hell did you do that for? We don't need that shit!" My sister's ability to keep showing up, no matter what, taught me about the power of love to continue to sustain one in the face of such opposition.

Regardless of how I traveled there, each trip to see my parents took from five to eight hours each way. I struggled to balance visiting and caring for my parents while supporting my family as a single parent, taking care of our home, a demanding job, dealing with my own health problems, and graduate school. Each visit left me with a mix of feeling emotionally drained, knowing that every moment with my parents had a profound sense of poignancy and meaningfulness. Those moments of rubbing lotion into my mother's wrinkled and delicate skin, of helping to bathe her, dressing her, maneuvering her wheelchair through a too-small house, hugging her increasingly tiny frame, kissing her on the forehead, laying in the bed next to her as she said her daily Rosary, are deeply etched in my being.

My oldest sister lived quite a bit farther away. She had a very difficult time dealing with my father's tirades. Her visits were infrequent, and she struggled with her own sense of guilt for not being able to emotionally stand up to the abuse flung her way, yet she in the end was able to give my mother the imagery and prayers that helped guide her out of this life.

How do you take in the sense of how fleeting life is? One can 'know' it, know that all of our days are numbered, yet somehow there seems to be an unconscious sense that we will live forever. I would often chant to myself through the many difficult moments, "This too shall pass," yet somewhere in my heart, unconsciously, not believing it.

So we went on like this, month after month, showing up, calling, each of us doing our part and being blasted by my father for what we did as we watched Mom slowly decline ever more deeply into depression and anguish. At times, my input was successful, other times it failed miserably.

My mother tried to let us know in small ways that she had "no appetite," that she was failing. My father continued to try to entice her with an endless array of soups or meals that he had learned to cook to please her. I could see she was declining, losing weight and getting weaker, but I could see/couldn't see . . . know/not know. Her nephrologists continued to state that she was stable. She on the other hand, would at times ask us if we could "let her go." My sisters and I continued to tell her that we would support her in whatever decision she made.

THE FINAL TWO WEEKS:

I received a phone call from my sister that our father had been in a car accident that day and, thankfully, no one had been hurt. He had accidentally stepped on the accelerator and his car crashed through the plate glass doors of a laundromat, shattering glass everywhere. A few days later someone smashed into the car he was riding in while stopped at a red light. He was taken by ambulance to a local hospital and released with neck and back sprains.

Although my father was relatively unscathed, my mother had a sudden, precipitous decline. I received another call from my sister, saying, "You don't need to come, I just want to let you know that Mom seems to be weaker." One of the things about my mother was that despite her increasing frailty, her voice always stayed strong, so you could never tell from a phone call how weak or ill she was. A "gut feeling" said that I needed to be there.

What I discovered upon arrival took time to sink in. They were not "fine." Everything had changed precipitously. My mother was no longer able to transfer from armchair to wheelchair. It was clear my father could no longer care for her.

They previously had a little routine worked out that in a strange crazy kind of way, worked and my mother had actually received far better care than she would have if she was at any long-term care facility. That had now changed.

I gave my mother a half cup of tea, as I had often done over the years. She was too weak to hold it and spilled the tea, burning her leg quite badly. No one had told me that she had fallen over in the commode the day before, unable to support her own weight. My mother also told me that Dad had been threatening her. When I asked her what she meant, she said that he had been threatening to push her in her chair when she didn't move fast enough.

We were all reeling, struggling to take in that everything had now fundamentally changed, yet with no "Plan B" in place. For my family, there had never been a "Plan B." We just went along, knowing full well the precarious nature of things would eventually fall apart, but not able to predict how, or in what manner, largely due to my father's refusal to discuss any other options. That was the best we could do. So, here it was, New Year's Eve, my mother in a sudden, precipitous decline and my father unable to care for her, and his mounting threats left my mother very unsafe. My sister agreed to take a leave of absence from her job, and planned to move in with them.

Later that evening, my sister and I went to find a local Hospice facility some friends had recommended. I thought my sister had called them and that they were expecting us. It was not until we arrived at their doorstep that I realized she had not called and that we were just "showing up" unannounced.

If I had any doubt before, I learned then that there are angels that masquerade as humans, or who perhaps have such compassionate hearts that they find space to allow two complete, desperate strangers in their lowest moments some respite, some hope that a terrible situation might, against all odds, have a good outcome. We sat for at least an hour, and although it was not what I would have wanted for my mother, the thought that we had an alternative available was enormously comforting. It would take some doing to get her admitted, and then Hospice would manage her care.

My mother's breathing became increasingly labored and I alternately knew that she was dying, and at the same time, did not know that she was dying. I tried contacting her nephrologist, but he was out of town for several days. By now, my sister had been able to make an impression on my father, and he at last was agreeable to getting Hospice on board.

The doctor providing back-up did not know my mother and refused to sign for her to be admitted. I implored him to help us and after much persuasion, he finally agreed to write an order for a small amount of morphine concentrate to be administered at a very low dose. Although we ultimately ended up not using the morphine more than one time over the next few days, it gave us great relief to know that we had it in place should my mother need it.

As a Hospice nurse, I frequently come up against a great fear about using morphine, not only from individuals with no training in the health care field, but from trained professionals, people involved in patient care at end of life. It is as if morphine carries some sort of "mythological" weight of its own. For many people, it signals "the end." There is often fear that it will push someone "over the edge," hasten their death. Yet, in the small dose that we begin with, it is less than the equivalent of one Percocet, a medication that does not carry such a burden of misinformation with it and is routinely ordered for pain relief for a variety of ailments and injuries. It is of great value in alleviating the distress of end-of-life pain and difficulty breathing.

Because the path of decline for individuals at the end of life is often so unpredictable, the agonized stress and inability to really read how close she was to dying left me feeling unable to clearly read the signposts along the way. My mother was still, on some occasions, eating a small meal, perking up a bit here and there, although overall her progression was downward. I felt overwhelmed, unable to make a clear judgment. I continued to try to get her admitted to Hospice to no avail. Although my mother appeared to be clearly dying, because she was not able to disconnect from dialysis, she could not be admitted to Hospice. We were in an untenable catch-22 situation, with no relief in sight.

On Wednesday, my mother's nephrologist agreed to have my mother go into Hospice under the diagnosis of "failure to thrive." One of my hopes for my family was that by being connected to Hospice services, we might be able to have my mother receive spiritual support around the deep, fundamental life-and-death issues she was grappling with, as well as reassurance from doctors that she could in fact be kept comfortable. She was finally officially admitted to Hospice.

Hospice was able to send an admitting nurse to see my mother. Mom had perked up that day and I tried to tell the nurse that mother was having an unusually good day, but I don't think she really "heard" me. It is not unusual for a dying person to suddenly perk up at the end, and enjoy a few days of renewed energy, some improved eating, and then have a rapid decline. It is hard to recognize a beloved family member's final meal. It is only in retrospect that we usually 'get it'.

My mother was enjoying the sudden attention and family members coming to see her. My father fought bitterly against each person. In the past, we let my father push us away, but at this point, it was about Mom and what she wanted. My sister and father were forceful in trying to get her to eat and drink, as family members often are when they can't take in or accept that someone is dying, not understanding that forcing her to eat makes a dying person feel worse. Her body was no longer able to take in nourishment.

When Saturday morning rolled around, it was time to get her up for yet another dialysis treatment. It was difficult to rouse her, but she finally woke up enough to say that she did want to go to dialysis. We dressed her and the ambulette service picked her up. She was incredibly weak, and barely conscious. The dialysis technicians did not know whether she could tolerate a treatment, or if they would have to send her to the emergency room. The decision was made to put her on the machines, as her blood pressure at that point was still within normal limits. Unbelievably, she was able to assist in transferring to the dialysis chair.

For me personally, that morning was the absolute low point. My mother had made it known that she wanted to die at home surrounded by her family, not with strangers in an ER, and yet, she would not, could not take the steps to ensure her own wishes. Her commitment to do 'God's will' overrode every other instinct. The distinct possibility that she would be taken off in an ambulance while she died, or that she would die while hooked to the dialysis machine, was such a bitter a scenario for us as her family yet we were powerless to change it.

Beyond the sense of powerlessness and outrage was an underlying, hidden 'guilt' that perhaps, in some way, I was responsible. If only I forced her to eat, encouraged her more, cheered her on when she said that she wanted to die. Instead I accepted her refusals to eat, knowing that to force her only made her feel worse.

I heard her desire to die and told her it was okay to choose to go off dialysis. I tried to treat her pain the best I knew how to do; yet, in some secret, shadowy way was I guilty? The conflicting tide of feelings was overwhelming and in spite of thinking that I could never go through the anguish of another dialysis treatment with her, I knew, if circumstances unfolded that another treatment was in the cards, I would show up for her no matter what.

When we returned home, my mother was brought immediately to bed. My father was inconsolable. He was taking it in little by little, the "Fort Knox" around his heart slowly shifting, that my mother was now slowly actively dying. They had been together for so long. He had told his friends the first time he laid eyes on her that he was going to marry her! In spite of his anger and frustration, she was the reason for his entire existence, for getting up each morning, to keep going no matter what.

My oldest sister found a loaded gun next to my father's bed. As a retired cop, he had an active license to carry a gun, and we knew there was probably one still in the house hidden somewhere. We were shocked to discover it was next to his bed. The fear that he would commit suicide following my mother's death was a distinct possibility, as he fit the criteria for one of the highest risk factors for successful suicide there is. Yet we knew if we removed the gun, he would only get another one, and worse, it might destabilize him. We begged Hospice to send a social worker to talk to him, but none was forthcoming. We searched the house for bullets and another gun, and removed the bullets from his gun. It occurred to me that my father might have been feeling pushed out. He sat in the living room most of the time, his head, as usual, buried in a newspaper. I asked him if he wanted to sit with Mom and he leapt to his feet and said, "Sure!!!" After that, we all respected Dad's need to be alone with her.

My mother slept for the remainder of the day, and then on into the night. I slept in the bed next to her. At times she would wake and say she was in pain, that she couldn't get comfortable, and I under-medicated her, afraid of overdosing her. I had been accused by her nurses at the dialysis unit of "overdosing her", which was their rationale for my mother's decline. Finally by the morning I called Hospice and got new orders for medicating her. They told me I was totally under-medicating her, which was clear since she was now having unrelieved pain. The Hospice nurse told my father that my mother would not be going to any more dialysis treatments.

Mom was awake enough at times to enjoy more visitors that came to see her for what we all knew was one last visit. I had a chance to have a good talk with her. I asked her if she thought this was a good time to have "Last Rites" and she agreed. I called Monsignor Casey, and he came that morning. Ma was semi-conscious, but did one last Confession while she was alone with him. After her Confession, my aunt, sister, and I joined them. We all prayed together, and it was beautiful and profoundly meaningful for all of us. As the elderly Monsignor started to leave, he told my father that he was a good man. My father choked up and said something to disprove that. For an instant I could sense into his heart, and feel how deeply troubled he was.

After Monsignor Casey left, my mother drifted in and out of confusion. She was lucid at times, and exhibited a dry sarcastic wit that seemed so out of character and was strangely very funny. My two teenagers arrived from Syracuse, wanting a last chance to say good-bye to their grandmother. I had promised my mother that no matter what, I would see to it that she had a Catholic Mass after her death and I intended to keep that promise, despite any opposition from my father.

As my mother began to slip into unconsciousness, she stated: "I have to go upstairs to find Grandpa." Monday evening, my uncle, brother-in-law, and nephew came. They all apparently consumed quite a bit of alcohol that night. My oldest sister was due to arrive around noon on Tuesday. We all knew my mother was slipping towards death, but all believed she was waiting for my sister to arrive.

By the middle of Monday night, my mother stated again that she couldn't get comfortable. I medicated her per the orders given to me by Hospice. She had now slipped into a coma-like state, mouth open, with deep snoring respirations, common in a dying person.

I felt frantic and distraught. I tried to call Hospice, and was unable to reach anyone. I had long since stopped being a "Hospice nurse who was also a daughter," and was just a daughter, desperate to find help for my mother. I called my supervisor and while I was on the phone with her, found my father sprawled out on the basement steps. I screamed and hung up the phone, not knowing if he had had a heart attack, stroke, had fallen, was alive or dead. I screamed for my sister. We had no idea what was wrong with him. He was conscious but appeared to be drunk, and he insisted that the carpets were making him slip. It turned out that he had been "chugging" cough syrup laced with Vicodin, long expired, that my mother had been prescribed years ago for broken ribs. My father had refused treatment for a deep cough which I had feared was turning into pneumonia, and he was now overdosed on Vicodin to the point where he could not walk. With my mother dying upstairs, my father was now literally stuck in the basement. At the same time my uncle was confined to the attic bedroom, apparently having a severe reaction to the alcohol he had consumed "with the guys" the night before. My aunt closed the door, making a decision to take care of her beloved sister rather than her husband. There was a strange irony to the situation that my sister and I found funny—that "black humor" keeping us going in a desperate and unreal situation.

We were all there who would be there. All good-byes had been said that were going to be said; it was time. It was the finale to a symphony, each one of us playing a part and my oldest sister the conductor for the finale. She had arrived several hours before my mother's death, just when we most needed her. She used beautiful imagery to help guide my mother to see the light on the other side. My mother never regained consciousness. We sat with her, talking quietly, alternately praying, playing the soft music that so comforted her at times.

At 3:15 p.m. my son suddenly announced that he needed to go to the subway and return home to Syracuse. I understood his sudden urgency to leave. So shortly before 3:30, I kissed my mother's forehead and told her I had to take my son to the subway. I knew (and didn't know) that she would be gone, dead, when I returned. In retrospect, it seems unbelievable that I could leave yet I was torn by my concern for my son. As I prepared to bring my son to the subway, I heard my aunt and sister calling for me, my mother had just died, at 3:32 p.m.

My mother looked peaceful, radiant at last. My mother's younger sister, her three daughters, two granddaughters, and I all tenderly washed her body with warm water and soft washcloths. We rubbed rich lotion into her dry, wrinkled skin, dressed her in a beautiful outfit, put makeup and perfume on her, brushed her hair. Together, the women of the family laid her out in beauty and dignity, in her own bed, in her own home. We had fulfilled her desire to die at home surrounded by family, in her own bed.

My father, who was still safely ensconced in the basement, eventually made it up the stairs and spent time alone with my mother's body, who was by now, looking at peace and beautiful in her bed. For him to have been spared the last hours of her life was in some way a final gift of mercy and compassion for all of us. It would have killed him to watch her in those last hours, and we were grateful for the odd reprieve that we had been given.

When we were finally ready to have her body removed from the house, the funeral people were called. I told them that the three daughters would stay in the room as my mother's body was being taken out. Although this moment is often too painful for many people to witness, for us, her daughters, it was a final act of caring, of Honoring our mother. We stood as her Honor Guard, in silence, as they took her on that final journey out of her home. I went to the street as her body was put into the hearse, and watched in silence and alone, as she was driven away in the night.

The next day I kept repeating to myself, My mother is dead, my mother is gone—as if by saying it enough, it would at last become real. I kept getting an urge to poke my forefinger into the air. The oddness of this movement surprised and confused me. I let myself feel into it. It seemed so bizarre yet what it held for me was the sense of the invisibility of this loss. Where once was a small, broken body, my mother whom I kissed, held, hugged, cared for, now there was nothing. The sense of absence, of vacant space, was what remained.

I believe at some point, I will "get to the other side" of my grieving, that I will be able to celebrate my mother's life and her death, and be grateful that she is out of her suffering. But for now, I reach into some deep place within myself, in this silent, quiet time of winter, where we are buried by snow and cold, and feel my mourning. I light candles for my mother, and feel my love for her, and at times, my anger. I wear the butterfly pin that I took off one of her suits. The other day a patient of mine, who is facing death, said to me, "You really understand, don't you? You've been through it, I can tell."

We walk through the fire together, witnessing each other's journeys and comfort each other as best we can. I guess that's as good as it gets.

Section 2

Waking up to Mortality: The Caregiver's Call to Face Death

Facing the reality of death is a terrifying experience for most of us. It pushes us way down into the center of our pulsing hearts, forcing us to re-define what's important not only in our relationship with our elder, but within our own hearts. Just as Death begins to break down our elders' identities, the caregiver's sense of self and stability also can come into question.

We watch helplessly as our elders are stripped to the core. All the things and people that were important to them begin to drift away as we journey together deeper into Death's realm. We witness wide-eyed the broken bones, the loss of memory, the empty spaces that were once filled with life and energy. We stare in horror at the cracked teeth, the thinning hair, the shaky walk . . . and deep inside, fears of our own demise begin to stir.

Death pushes us down and we fall face-first into that brown aging spot on our hand or that new wrinkle on our face, that nagging pain that could be a malignant tumor. The haggard face looking back at us in the well-lit mirror at some point finally, hopefully, breaks into a smile, surrendering to the inevitable yet grateful for being alive in the present moment.

The role reversal in care that is slowly taking place also joins in creating a vulnerability and openness that can soften the ground of old rigid ways of relating. Those issues that we felt were most important can drop by the wayside and other needs can emerge. New insights and family secrets can unfold, bringing clarity and healing.

This is the time when we caregivers can awaken to a new consciousness, a new identity that's more expansive and humble. The alchemists called this process the death of the old king (the ruling order of our psyche) so that the new prince (new consciousness) can be born. Whether healing occurs in relationship or not, there is fertile opportunity for one of the greatest blessings of all, and that is for the preciousness of life to begin to seep into our bones, our hearts, our souls.

"Invisible Loyalties"
A time for healing family secrets

Emmelien Brouwers' story is a powerful portrayal of an elder, who at the end of her life, has a major revelation.

My mother—her name was Magdalena, but everyone called her Lena for short—named me Mila after Aunt Emilia, the wife of Johannes, the uncle who molested her when she was two. Still, she remained fond of him. My mother told me about its first occurrence rather casually one day when we were talking on the phone. I was working on a project involving our family history when she said:

"Oh yes, there was an incident with Uncle Johannes. I was sitting on the table in front of him, my bare buttocks in his hands."

"You remember that? What happened?"

"Oh it was nothing, I was only two."

She was frustrated with "the fuss people make about these things" and I too dumbfounded to know what else to ask.

She had talked about Uncle Johannes before, a handful of times perhaps. Each time she had mentioned his name a peculiar smile had appeared on her face and her eyes, set in the distance, had taken on a wayward air. She said they'd had fun together, she playing the piano while he, sitting next to her on the piano stool, made up stories. Yet she clearly had been upset recalling how his daughters had needed to lock their bedroom doors. Then again she had not seemed half as bothered when she recounted how he had grabbed her budding breasts from behind while washing dishes or when she had found his hand rimming her skirt.

My sister Margot later told me he had been convicted for his crimes (she had heard it from Aunt Constance, my mother's sister). My mother had omitted this fact, as though she thought it unjustified. On the other hand she had told me—rather emphatically in fact—that she and she alone had refused to attend his funeral. How she then named me after his condoning wife remains a mystery to me, especially since she continued to reflect on the wonderful person Aunt Emilia had been, and then added, as if these thoughts were connected, what a good mother I would make.

My father left us when my mother was pregnant with my brother Brent. Being a proud woman (she hated to be pitied, or worse, "hold out her hand") she kept the hardship of raising her five children alone, to herself. I experienced the space that was my mother as overflowing, if not with actual presence of mind then at least with color and noise. By profession my mother was a clothes designer; she specialized in people with deformities. She was gifted, made their clothes fit flawlessly, to the point where all hunches, twists, and contortions became invisible, if not actually intriguing. Her skill was a matter of professionalism; she expected no less from anyone and was critical of things improperly done.

The evocative world of sounds took place above my head on her work table. There was the swoosh of pencil over large sheets of tracing paper drawn with her swift and steady hand; the rapid ticking sound as she traced the lines, perforating the paper with her etching wheel, and the unadorned sound of scissors cutting paper along the patterned lines. When she was working with wool the sound was like the slow, lazy slide of a cat rolling over; cotton made a clean thud like animal feet stepping into the stable. Crepe de Chine had the crisp rustling sound of water running downstream or our hamsters treading their wheel and the chiffons and silks were quiet like our goldfish or the sound of a comb sliding through hair. Basting the parts was like a prolonged train ride, needle and thread going through endless seams, big stitch small stitch, big loop small loop. When I was a little older she would let me pull the two sides apart and later still, cut the threads between the mirroring pieces. Then she would tack them into their first fitting, followed by more fittings, until each client came to accept and even love the truth of their body inside the garment. Or that's the way I remember it.

When I was six my parents' divorce become final and my mother converted to the Mormon Church. Her presence at home around that time grew thin to the point of surreal—reaching for her my fingers combed air. She embraced her new Heavenly Father enthusiastically; following the way of Jesus Christ of the Latter-day Saints gave her a new purpose in life. She functioned as if by remote, walking jauntily with the self-assured allure of a puppy on a leash, as though God himself was walking her.

Still her attention to us on the earthly plane, if tenuous, remained straightforward. For the most part we wore clean clothes, or learned to rotate them industriously. She was creative with our meals, too. Conscious of color and proportions she accentuated the sparse. We enacted fairytales. Old bread was cut in strips and fried. These were soldiers standing tall in a green field of spinach, protecting the gold of a quarter hardboiled egg placed in the middle surrounded by mountains of potato. Vegetables would make their way over the hills of mashed potatoes to the pond of meat juice carefully ladled into the top. If we had sausage we played the big bad wolf looking for the seven little goats hidden somewhere in a forest hodgepodge.

All the same, there were times when nothing short of a miracle could save us; although she managed to turn even these into opportunities to strengthen her faith. Taunting us with her holy smile she'd say: "When a need draws near its cusp, salvation is sure to follow." And it would, just not always opportunely. If we dared to comment she would add with that same taunting smile: "God answers all our prayers, sometimes in the way we want and sometimes the way he wants it." And that was the end of that. She had surrendered her burden and was grateful.

My mother expressed her gratitude in sincere and abundant

prayer before and after each meal, and in the morning and at night on her knees in front of her bed, hands folded, head bowed, sometimes for what seemed like hours. The Our Father who art in heaven was of the past. Prayer became earnest, especially before going to sleep. We would kneel in front of our bed, she, Brent, and I and she would start:

"Thank you God, Father in heaven . . ." followed by all the wonderful and fortunate things we had had or done that day. She was ingenious. At the end she left a space for us to add our own desire or the desire she thought we had.

"If you pray hard enough, and if you really, really want it: Papa will come back." "Papa," however, was an elusive figure to my brother Brent and me. Her need for him was overwhelming, and my failure to "bring him back" filled me with shame. Much later I thought: If he left her, he must have had a reason.

Even so, what I remember most about her prayers is my surprise at the things she came up with:

"Thank you God for our goldfish Martine, her color looks so pretty today." Or,

"Thank you God for taking us to the park today. It was so sunny and green. The breeze was just right."

I grew attached to these surprises. It was as if each morning she dipped her brush in a different color and painted our landscape for the day, carefully placing us inside it. In the evening she'd collect them and tag them to the wall. These moments strung the week together, along with the egg on Sunday, the fish on Friday, and the juice from the meat we had on Sunday which she knew how to make last through the rest of the week.

Notwithstanding my mother's devotion (sometimes mounting debts and the needs and demands of her five growing children broke her composure) she could indulge in ungodly contempt and fling her curses, along with shoes and whatever else was handy, in all directions, although mostly towards my oldest sister Anne.

"A real Tollens!" She would spit out with venomous hatred, much larger and deeper than Anne could have possibly brought about. Tollens was my father's mother's maiden name; my mother blamed her for his leaving. The reason for this, she said, was that Grandma Tollens had found him a younger and more affluent woman, one better fitting in the family constellation, whom he subsequently had not been able to resist.

"You make my blood curdle . . ." she would say and

"You are a nail at my coffin . . ." or

"You draw the blood from under my nails. Wait till I am dead, see how you'll appreciate me then!"

I remember cowering out of sight: imagining, feeling relieved and guilty it wasn't me, thinking that had it been me I would not survive it, would not have wanted to live with that voice in my head.

My mother died last May; had she not died, today would have been her eighty-fifth birthday. Our relationship has changed since then. She has been urging me on in a most gentle and supportive way. Every once in a while I realize she is touching me. I feel her hand running through my hair, a cool calm touch by a cool soft hand. I remember my mother's hands as hot and busy, had hated her urgent, needy touch. I had not noticed how beautiful my mother's hands were until I saw and felt them when she was laid out on the bier: slender, aristocratic, capable hands. Strange how these hands seemed more hers in death than in life, except perhaps when she had played the piano. When my mother played the piano it was as if the sky opened up and God had been summoned. She would become ethereal, one with her music, her compacted body centered, a planet unto herself.

We were in France when she died. We were just about to sit down for dinner, my sisters Anne, her family, Margot, and I. Everyone was busying about. I was closest to the phone when it rang.

"Mila dear . . ."

It was Aunt Constance's voice, white spaces filled with shock and tears.

"Lena . . . I think she's dead."

I was not upset, surprised perhaps that it had come indeed as soon as it had, but not upset. Calmly I contemplated the impact of her death. I felt sad for my aunt, alone in the house with my dead mother. And I felt relief for my mother, glad she had not been alone in the end.

"Child . . . she just stepped out onto the balcony. I was right behind her. She gave a scream and fell back into my arms. I don't know where the strength came from but I caught her. She just let out a little sigh. That was it."

We had just spent a week together, the last in May, the last of her life. How well it seemed she had planned it. My mother had stayed at Anne's in spite of the animosity between them. The tension converged on the topic of my father: My mother forgave him, my sister could not. While my mother did not comprehend why Anne hated him so intensely, Anne, obstinate and exasperated, was contemptuous of her undying love.

The first inkling of my mother's impending death came to me when she pushed me. It was halfway through an afternoon. She had just woken from her nap. We were standing outside Anne's house when my mother suddenly realized she had missed out on an instant of surprise—a welcome visitor's first swirl around the bend, or a trip to the store. I had put my arm around her in a gesture of sympathy, but she would not have it. She jerked loose and flung her elbow nearly hitting my face. Then she pushed me, aggressively, her expression wrought with disdain. Perhaps she felt I had made light of the slight she had experienced, because she knew her time was running out and she needed every last bit of what was left. Either way it hit me like a smooth cold rock.

It was however not just this push which foreshadowed my mother's imminent passing. Anne had called the night doctor twice that week, and he'd recommended a stress test. When her heart rate and blood pressure were "off the chart," the doctor hushed; he suggested we spare her the results. All the same, we knew.

"Mom why do you insist on going back to Holland? Why don't you stay here with us?"

"I still have a lot to arrange," she'd answered with irritation.

"The music for one, I have to make a list." And she was right. She had wanted the Mormon Tabernacle and we never played it.

The next day Anne and I drove our mother and aunt to the airport. We had enough time to drink some orange juice, then waited for the flight attendants who accompanied them in wheelchairs through customs and on to the gate. We waved a last good-bye through the glass doors of the elevator.

Later that same evening, after we had received the news of our mother's death, we booked a flight for the three of us the following morning. All I remember of that flight is the curious sensation that we were flying backwards; either that, or the north and south had reversed poles overnight. That, and the size of the plane: small and not one empty seat. I was glad to have a place at the window. We did not talk about our mother's death. Anne was reading and Margot was calm just then.

Weeks later Margot told me, "I almost went mad when you gave us the news that Mama had died." It was true, she had not known what to do with her hands. She had shaken them and she had lifted her feet and made odd little steps in the air as if the ground underneath her was falling. I felt my heart pulled out of my chest racing towards her, but strange enough it froze mid-air. She did not want it, or she did not want it from me. Perhaps she sensed the discrepancy of our feelings, or thought I would not understand the remorse she was feeling for not having been by her side and needed to punish herself.

"I'm OK," I called out after I hung up the phone. I don't remember to whom, if anyone was listening. I did not want any sticky, needy arms clogging up my clarity. You all go ahead, I remember thinking. Perhaps it was reactive or reciprocally rejecting. Or perhaps it is just that the loss of a mother is ultimately such an intimate and private affair.

When I saw my mother's body again at the viewing, two days later at the funeral home, discreetly placed in an alcove off to the side of the reception room buzzing with visitors, she was all dressed up in Mormon whites just the way she had wanted. My mother had spoken directly from her belly and her enigmatic smile, like a soft blanket, lay draped over it still. I could feel her presence clearly, her unfettered spirit jumping up and down.

"Halloo, hallo hallo, I am here, hallo!"

All her life she had been keen to convince us of the existence of an afterlife. As a little girl she had seen two angels, one at each of the far corners of her bed. And now in her finest hour she was demonstrating, for all who cared to see, how her spirit danced along a golden tightrope leading towards a brightly glowing hoop, and like that jaunty puppy jumped right through it straight into God's arms. Her brave passion and lust for life, her denial, all of it was there, more beautiful than sad. Focused on what was important to her, she had blazed her path into the next world the way she had gone through life; no matter the situation, she had smiled her mysterious smile. It would drive me mad then but now?

Well, she is dead. Let her be, I told myself. She just wasn't attached to life the way most people are. Her attention had been on the hereafter. It had been obvious to her: Life was a burden and a lesson. She was worn out by the burden, but she had loved the lessons passionately.

"No, no make-up please," we requested.

"She is beautiful just as she is."

My mother had been proud and physically beautiful, I thought. Her energy radiated and her voice remained young until the very end. People mistook hers for a teenager's. She herself seemed unsure, until she'd look in the mirror. Then she'd say:

"Ouououghh, that old face!"

It would not have been so bad, had she not said it with such hatred, that same hatefulness which lashed and cut. I felt ashamed to be a witness and bad if I didn't think of myself as ugly, as though I should.

Talking with disgust about her aging face was not the only time my mother used that expression. She used it when I'd ask her whether or not she ever contemplated remarrying.

"I just cannot imagine having to get used to another man," she'd say, followed by that suspicious, guttural: "Ouououghh."

Actually, my mother was extremely active and social and besides her personal reasons, she in fact valued living alone. With one exception that was. Some fifteen years ago she fell in love with Michel. She was about seventy, he twenty years younger and very adventurous. Just like my father, Michel would call on her unexpectedly; invite her for an evening stroll or ice cream at the pier. They had lunch in the Rose Garden, went for walks along the beach and made all kinds of interesting day trips. My mother called me often during those months. She wanted to talk about her excitement and bewildering sensations, whether she could allow herself to have them. It was at that time she expressed her concern about having sex.

"Michel has asked me to come on a trip with him, through Germany, in his converted bus."

"That sounds like it could be fun Mom. Are you going?" I asked with some trepidation, fighting off images of him being a creep.

"I don't know. I haven't answered him yet. I wonder how we are going to sleep. It is a bus. How big can it be? He says it has a bed in it, but how . . . with him? Does he think I will sleep with him in the same bed? Do you think he wants to have sex with me?"

"I don't know Mom. Do you want to?"

My mother's conflict apparently was not about having sex with Michel. No. What bothered my mother was her concern about NOT being a good Mormon. As a Mormon she was not allowed to have sex before marriage, mind you, even at seventy! Their relationship lasted some five blissful months, and she was genuinely sad when it ended. She had treasured the affair. It had been worth the turmoil she went through. She had kept a journal during those months. Margot

169

found them. Page after page, she had supplicated God for strength and meaning.

Michel had met Marge, a young woman with two small children at a Mormon singles event. Michel liked children and they were married in less than a month. When my mother met Marge again some six months later she and Michel were divorced and he had moved to Australia.

My mother had known about the court case in which Michel had needed to testify during their dating months. The trial had involved the sexual abuse of his daughter by a previous marriage. Michel had told her that he was a witness in the case. Marge informed her that he had been the accused.

My mother became increasingly intrigued by stories of child sexual abuse and would recount them in oddly excited ways. Even so, it shook her when I later pointed out that the only other man she had fallen in love with had been just like Uncle Johannes and my father—not to forget him. How had she picked him out of the crowd?

Not long after the trial in which Michel was convicted (I did not understand how he had been able to move to Australia) there was a flood of child sexual abuse accusations sweeping through Europe. My poor mother could not get away from the topic. Belgium, Portugal, Holland, and France were all involved. The media was in its thrall. We continued to talk about it for months and if I wasn't home I would find a message.

"Mila, its Mom. I just wanted to hear your voice."

My mother had always been excitable, making it difficult to confide in her. Often she'd be laughing, sometimes even before I began. Now and again the two of us would be laughing, for no particular reason, hysterically. Or if we were not laughing, the space got filled with silent understanding, although I never felt the intimacy.

One such time, while on a trip through Switzerland, we stopped for lunch. The restaurant was located on the upside of a hairpin curve. It had been winter and the sky, a cornucopia of blues, was performing a slow dance above the large, frozen lake that lay in front of it. It was a spacious room with crystal chandeliers, lots of them with pink and yellow glows. My mother's face radiated, her eyes sparkled like the sun on ice. There was something in the way she looked at me, the way her eyes slowly poured into mine, quietly intruding, eating out my soul. I let her.

My mother had always wanted to write. I encouraged her. Perhaps it is why I am writing now, because things remained to be said. And now she is encouraging me, encouraging me with a tranquil hand, nudging me on, better than I nudged her. I have always felt too forceful, my gestures too large.

One evening, somewhere inside, I found the courage to tell my mother about my father and me. We were in the back garden of Mustache, a Middle Eastern restaurant in Brooklyn. I sat across from her. She listened quietly. As I observed her slow descent into the marsh of information, like a submarine or a whale, and watched the impact on her aging face, I saw her briefly saner than before or since. Calmly, she replied:

"I am not surprised."

It was no longer early, still warm and already dark. There were a couple of people scattered around the other end. A sultry breeze brushed our skin as if it were a membrane stretched around us like a tent. The smell of sweat, charcoal and zatar mixed with the glow from the kitchen and the glimmer of fireflies expanded the moment, invisibly the way loyalty does.

"Mila, you have to learn to forgive yourself."

She said it matter-of-factly, except her eyes were piercing me, more angry than sad. There was too much going on in her head, like when a pinball machine goes on tilt, all bells ringing just before it shuts down. A moment later she asked rhetorically:

"You know what I just remembered?"

"What, Mom?"

"When Margot was five years old she told me what Papa had done to her. She was crying. It was early in the morning. She had crawled into our bed. I had gotten up to start preparing for the day." She paused, then said:

"I did not know how to believe her. I didn't know what to do, never did anything, never spoke about it . . . with anyone."

My mother looked removed, not sad. I could not place her, and I did not want to touch her, not then. Touching her felt wrong somehow. So we stayed silent, looking no place in particular. A while later still, she said reflectively:

"Do you remember that silver thread I always felt between Papa and me?

I nodded.

"It broke, just now. I felt it snap."

"Taking Mom to Therapy"
Great patience

This story takes us into the world of Parkinson's and shows how the caregiver reaches inward, developing unimaginable patience. This storyteller wishes to remain anonymous.

I arrive at my parents' house half an hour before Mom has to be at her music therapy class. This would be plenty of time for a healthy person to make it—the class is less than ten minutes away by car. But my Mom is not a healthy person. Rheumatoid arthritis and Parkinson's have seen to that.

"Oh good," she says when I walk in without knocking or ringing the bell. "I don't have my shoes on yet."

She holds them in her hands, but that's all she can do with them. Her socks are on the table. Slowly she shuffles to the old green dining-room chair in the corner by the cupboard while I get a cushion for the chair from one of the others and hold her hand to steady her.

She sinks down, carefully at first, and then lands with a thump as the strength in her legs gives out. She holds up a foot and I pull the slipper off, wondering how many times I've helped someone change footwear. Almost always, though, the feet were very young and chubby. Hers are skeletal and deformed from years of rheumatoid arthritis. Her big toe bends at almost ninety degrees across the top of her foot, cramping her other toes into awkward positions.

I gather her white sock, "bobby sox" we used to call them, and slide it on over her foot, relieved not to be looking at her toes any longer. The skin on her shin is dry and flaking, leaving dandruff of sorts everywhere near.

I loosen the laces of her black leather shoe, a much more elegant choice than the athletic shoes she wore exclusively for many years. I fit it carefully over her toes—it only works from one side, not the other, and she winces when I get it a bit wrong. When I tie it, I'm careful not to pull the laces too tight. Everything about Mom speaks fragility, and I know her bones are so thin it would take little force to do real damage.

"Is that okay?" I ask.

"Um-hum," she agrees. She lowers the foot to the ground and slowly lifts the other.

We repeat the process with her right foot, which is equally misshapen. I am a little ashamed at how hard it is for me to look at her feet, when she has lived in them this way for years, decades by now. It's the same revulsion I have when trimming her fingernails, which are yellowed, thick, and dirty, curving so tightly that to trim them without hurting her is a trick.

I can't let myself dwell on how damaged her body is, not while I'm with her. Worse, I can't think of how she used to be, when she was my age and hiked up Longs Peak almost every year, and square-danced for hours every Friday and Saturday evening in the summer. It makes me weep, and she doesn't want sympathy so much as compassion—a caretaker to treat her gently and tend her needs with a smile. Ever the dutiful daughter, I put my feelings in a tight dark place in my heart and try to give her what she desires.

Then begins the five-minute walk out of the house and to the car, parked only fifteen or twenty feet away in the driveway. I walk backwards, holding both of her thin and chilly hands. She shuffles, moving each foot only an inch or less at a time, until I remind her to take big steps. "Yes, Miss Ruth," she says with a smile and a bit of a laugh, for this is what her therapist tells her to do. But it helps, and she lengthens her stride to cover five inches at a step.

Her hands seek walls, door frames, anything to hold on to, not always trusting having both hands in mine. I, after all, am human, and could fall, or fail. We navigate the two front steps, which have a landing between them but not much in the way of handholds, and then it's the open, curving sidewalk to the driveway.

I sway my hips a bit, humming, "Shall we dance?" She smiles, with the twinkle in her eyes that shows she really enjoys this game, and moves her hands up and down a bit. I remind her again, "Big steps."

At my minivan, she climbs slowly into the back seat with a big boost from me. She's only about ninety-five pounds, so I'm able to do this—though only by not thinking about how my great-grandmother and my grandmother used to look just like this, entering or exiting cars at this exact point on the driveway. I can't let myself notice the slight smell of urine and chocolate Ensure that cling to her. I can only be dutiful, cheerful, and efficient as I buckle her in and go back inside the house to fetch the handicap sticker to hang from my rearview mirror.

It's not until much later, when I'm alone, that I let myself weep. Then I pull out those sights and smells and memories and let them flow out of me on tears and words. When I think of her, and of the women of her line, I want only to be strong and healthy in my old age. I don't want to hold in emotions and let them eat away at my body, and I don't want my daughters to have to stifle their disgust at what my body has become.

Yet I spend what would be my workout time driving two and half hours to take Mom to her exercise class. If I look too closely at the spiral I'm in, I am lost. And then I'm no good to anyone. Shall we dance?

"Finding Love"
Finding love for a parent who has been abusive

Taking care of an elder can awaken childhood trauma. This is Colleen Donahue's story.

As I lay in bed I find myself unable to fall into slumber. Experience has taught me not to struggle, not to fret about it, not to concern myself with any amount of lost sleep I may be forced to endure—and certainly not to concern myself with how tired I may or may not be in the morning—all because I found my brain working overtime.

My grandfather clock is chiming the Westminster melody in its usual five-minutes-too-fast manner: one, two, three, four, five, six, seven, eight, nine, ten, and finally eleven which concludes the cacophony of sound with not much ceremony and pomp. And still my mind wanders with many thoughts of the day into what seems like a small eternity, if a small eternity could really be possible. Then, out of the blue, comes my cuckoo clock's ever-five-minutes-behind-the-hour report. I didn't count those off but took it on good faith that it, like the grandfather clock's gongs, would also amount to eleven.

What a curious conglomerate of sounds at uneven hours. These ever late or ever too early happenings that are accepted, if not expected, these sought after and taken for granted and often not acknowledged things in my life that ebb and flow seemingly beyond all—I find myself thinking on these things and so much more.

I look back from the person I am today, with the eyes and knowledge I have now, and how I have come to an understanding of the mysteries of my struggles those years before. Hindsight . . . the proverbial light bulb. Of course! I understand what all of the struggle was about. Or do I?

I look back on the inner struggle, the one inside myself, the one that was hidden from my view at the time but is revealed now. For this woman who was but a year or so from her passing, this woman so ill at the end of her life, so frail, so helpless, this woman who gave birth to me was the same woman who, in my childhood, had beaten and abused me so much so that the tool of my survival was to flee my body, a flight into other realms beyond my own memories and beyond my own realization.

I found myself caring for my abuser, struggling to find love and not knowing why. The soul searching, the struggling, the fear of something unseen and unknown to me and the forlorn little girl inside the soundproof black room banging on a locked door.

Push the emotion aside.

Do the task.

Work the problem.

Separate one's self.

Be efficient.

Take control.

Secure power.

Secure power.

Secure power over the mundane tasks. Secure power from a distance, do not go to Florida, stay aloof, stay effective, keep in control.

I was driven to be the worker bee, the selfless guardian caring for the parent from another state—yes, another state, a state of mind, a state of awareness, a state of solitude and control, a physical state of New York caring remotely to the state of Florida. It seemed so easy, or so I thought.

The more of my mother I lost the more I found myself missing her. I looked for love and didn't understand it. What was love in regards to my mother? I clearly understood that I loved my father.

I had chased him all my life, sought his approval, looked up to him, emulated him, and his passing shook my world. I missed him terribly. I was convinced I loved him at the time but now, my mother, my mother, where was that love like I had for dad? Where was that love for her?

Why could I not love her? Why was there so much turmoil inside of me? Why did I have to rely on my sheer will to do what I had to do for her? Why did I resent it so much in the beginning? Why was I so empty inside? It's easy to look back and see it now . . . to understand it now. So much work have I done inside myself. I've been torn inside out and reassembled. I have reached into the deep well of myself to find my own reflection in the mirror . . . to know that it is truly me looking back.

I never resented caring for my mother. I was duty bound. I had made a promise to my father to take care of my mother. But it was more than that: She was my mother and I was her daughter and who else would it fall to? My honor demanded it. But where was the love? I was looking in all the wrong places but didn't know that. I had no idea where to look.

I was trapped.

I was miserable.

I shared it with no one.

I suffered alone.

I suffered inside.

And then I learned to live with it.

Things were getting too hairy to worry over finding love. The pressures of the guardianship were becoming extreme. The woman I had known as my mother no longer existed, for in the course of a year that woman had slipped through my fingers effortlessly, lost in an oxygen-deprived, emphysema-driven dementia and there was no going back, only going down.

All I can remember upon arriving in Florida for the final month was standing in the guest bedroom with my sister, leaning on the dresser, looking down with my hands firmly planted on it and saying, "I can't go through this again." But I know now that the love I had had for my father was not there for my mother and my unwillingness to go "into it" was missing a big ingredient. And it became all about finding love.

I found love slowly . . . with time . . . with physical contact . . . with emotional contact. It's hard not to love someone who put you on Mother Earth, who's clearly suffering and your warm hand touches hers and she clutches it desperately. Or was that compassion? But can you have compassion without love? A lifetime of blackness, a lifetime of memories placed in faraway transfiles, memories so far removed I knew not of their existence. Not only that, I knew not of their ramifications on my life.

Through all of that I did find love. I found myself caring for my mother in her final days . . . this woman who was so afraid of me as a child . . . this woman who beat me in turn . . . this woman who would hit first then yell. This woman whom my sister once mentioned had made me her "whipping girl."

I have more memories of blocking blows as a child than I do happy times for I had lost it all. To this day, I have snapshots and photos of things in my memories, of events, punishments, beatings, yelling, screaming, defiance, whimpering. Small movie reels of things unspeakable to the faint of heart. Memories . . . fragmented and broken. Shame. Shame transferred into anger, transferred into fear. This was my love.

And in the care of my mother I struggled and I found a new love . . .

My mother suffered from an advancing case of emphysema as well as the grief brought on by the loss of her husband, my father, with whom she was ever so connected and dependent. She had put up a good front and really tried to be a single woman in her little Florida retirement community. For the first year after his passing she learned to balance a checkbook, use public and senior transportation to go shopping, maintain her home, hire service providers for its care and maintenance, and learn to live without her husband as best she could.

Her daughters, my younger sister and myself, lived in Santa Fe, New Mexico, and North Babylon, New York, respectively. We were both single women at the time and had lives very involved in our communities.

It was a great shock when I was called at my office by the district attorney of Hernando County Florida to come down and take care of my mother or the State of Florida would. Like most parents of that generation, mine strove to hide the truth of their lives from us. What this translates to at the end of their lives is awakening to the reality that they were putting up a facade of "I'm all right" each time I or my sister called or visited them.

And so I traveled to Florida and did exactly what the DA told me to do. I had to have my mother declared legally incompetent to care for herself. I had to become her court-appointed legal guardian to manage her estate and her care. It was decided that as the elder sister and one who was in business, I was the logical choice. So I entered into a journey that would take me from the role of my mother's daughter to a role reversal where I became the mother caring for the child.

I pause in this writing to reflect on how paramount the previous sentence is to me and how pivotal it was in my life to witness the complete physical and mental decline of the woman who had given birth to me. This is the total human equation in which this role reversal played an essential part in my ability to maintain high quality of care for my mother as well as remove myself from the equation to give her a reciprocal façade of normalcy, love, and humanity—to keep her at ease and safe in her mind as well as in her own home and not in a nursing home.

I had to learn to find the love for my mother within myself, to express it in ways that enabled me to sacrifice parts of myself to care for her. I would hope to think that women giving birth to children make a very similar internal sacrifice and bring that love to the surface to nurture and raise their children. I would hope, not having had children myself, that I had a small taste of that in the care of my Mom in her final year.

The task at hand for the daughter and now guardian in New York was how to care and maintain the parent in Florida in the home she cherished and adored. My mother had the good fortune that her late husband had provided for her in his passing and her estate was fluid enough to provide quality in-house care by utilizing her savings, investments, and annuity. Such a task was easy in the beginning as it was like business: finding twenty-four-hour live-in caretakers; an attorney on retainer to help manage the guardianship; changing all the addresses of all incoming bills and notices to my address in New York so I could maintain the house, my mother's medical care, the live-in health aides, even an allowance for food shopping which the health aides provided in the form of receipts.

I would not hesitate to say that the State of Florida was the best place for my mother to be, as Florida takes elder care very seriously. They have a lot of options for the elderly in the form of services such as what we found ourselves in need of when my mother could no longer care for herself. I cannot say if it would have been easier or more difficult in another state, but for some reason the link between New York and Florida is strong and the business portion of the guardianship was not such a great challenge to manage once I understood it.

Every day my sister and I called our mother. She was in such a way that she did not recall each conversation and often I found myself having the same conversation with her each call. Prior to each conversation, the health aide would answer the phone. I would receive a report on my Mom's condition—what she ate for meals, who else had called or visited, her general emotional attitude. With that in mind I then spoke with my Mom and often tried to ask her things like a daughter in the beginning: questions about cooking, about laundry, and so on.

My Mom was a lifelong homemaker and a very good one. She was a seamstress/tailor and I would ask sewing questions. At times she would come out of her oxygen-deprived emphysema haze and begin to sound like her old self. At one point she made a Halloween costume for a health aide's daughter. My mother had not sewn for years and here she was sewing for a child she did not know. It was a wonderful feeling to see and hear of this and to know my Mom was still in there and not lost to us.

The challenges of a guardianship force one to learn patience in dealing with "the system" as courts do not simply say, "You are the guardian now, take care of things." It's just the opposite. They freeze all bank accounts, lock out all the financial accounts, take control of the person's estate, and then, in conjunction with the bank, form a guardianship account in which allotted sums can be transferred only by court order into the guardian checking account from which all the affairs of the estate are managed. I was allowed $10,000 increments and was held fully accountable for every penny.

For a one-year period my mother lived in her own home with me as the guardian and shifts of live-in health aides. Slowly, her mental abilities, her memory, her expectations, and the size of her world diminished. She was under Hospice watch for the final six months for the second time in her life. The first had been just before the guardianship began, when she was hospitalized and placed in a rehab center. She went down to eighty-five pounds there, and we knew that a nursing home would kill her. Upon return to her own home and the guardianship she went back up to a hundred pounds and we knew she would have to remain at home if there was to be any hope for quality of life. My Mom was a small woman, 5'1", and was always very slender.

It was in the final six months that my mother became my daughter, growing younger each day. Each phone call grew more and more difficult. I was stretched to the limit, and when I thought I could go no further, I found I had new limits, each and every time. Falling to my knees in tears after hanging up the phone became a habit all too often, but I had to keep up my strength because my mother needed that and I knew our conversations made her feel good.

Who knew I could love so much so as to give that pound of flesh so freely to another and keep on giving it no matter what? In those moments, I felt so alive—as things could not be more real, and everything that was done for my Mom was done without hesitation in love and dedication, without any hindrance of doubt and uncertainty. Things were beginning to become very black and white, so much so that all priorities in my life began to reassess and shift.

And then my Mom fell. She tripped on her oxygen tubing and lost control of her walker before the health aide could get to her.

She broke her hip.

Who would have thought that my Mom with her emphysema so advanced would not only survive but receive a hip replacement and come home! We couldn't believe it. But that was short-lived, for with the emphysema, and despite the limited physical therapy and visiting nurses, my Mom was in no condition to learn to walk again. She no longer had the strength.

It was then I got the call from Hospice to "Come to Florida."

I called my sister in Santa Fe and told her to book a flight there immediately. The plan was that I would drive from New York so we would have transportation in Florida. We coordinated her flight and my drive time so I could drive from Long Island to the airport in Tampa. Somehow, I arrived just as my sister's plane was landing at 11:00 p.m.

And so began the final month of my mother's life.

It was November 1999 and the holiday season was underway. We arrived at midnight and the health aide greeted us. We collapsed exhausted into slumber and the next day we began to express our love.

Hospice was overwhelmed with the holiday season. We didn't know just how many people die around the holidays, but we learned very quickly. We were unable to secure Hospice watch nurses.

How do I tell a story without all the extreme human emotions? Of the moment I mentioned earlier when I leaned on the dresser and sighed, "I can't go through this again," my sister had said, "I can't either" or something to that effect. We had already done this two years earlier for our father and now we were here again, but this time without a family to help.

I don't think anyone ever really knows the location of the well from which that second, third, and fourth layer of inner strength, compassion, fortitude, and love is accessed. But my sister and I—along with a health aide who gave up her job because she cared deeply for my mother—found all we needed to give care and love to my mother each day, each hour, each minute as she grew closer and closer to the boundary that separates our world from the next.

My cousin flew in with my aunt and later we were joined by my mother's two remaining siblings. A final good-bye to her brother and sister. For a brief time, my mother was able to sit in a wheelchair while the life and conversations ebbed and flowed around her. I could see a peace in her. One circle had completed itself and after that came the restlessness and resistance to the inevitable. She struggled against one of the Hospice nurses and became untouchable, inconsolable. Then began the "conversations."

No one seemed attuned to the presence of what could be termed spirit. I alone seemed to feel the crowd forming around her bedside— probably because my heart was open and my mind was devoid of any resistance and suspicion that it could not possibly be. But as I felt this crowd—a very male presence in her bedroom—my mother, who had been having a conversation with Mary, a spirit who was seated at her bedside, began to ask what all the men in suits were there for. The Hospice nurse looked at me. I could clearly see she experienced this sort of thing a lot but tried not to reveal any inkling of it. It was me, her eyes betrayed her, and I knew better despite the fact she refused to speak of it later on.

And finally, one night when my mother finally had a peaceful sleep, we three—my sister, the health aide, and myself—left a baby monitor in her bedroom and we took a break in the kitchen. We sat drinking tea and I could hear several voices whispering in conversation so as not to wake my mother. Only I heard it as I watched the two pairs of eyes at the table with me. Neither of them heard it and I left it, knowing those whispering voices were watching over my mother in a rare few hours of restful sleep.

So much happened, minute by minute, hour by hour, day by day, so much that it would fill a book. But in such a situation, those of us who must will find the ways we each need to help each other and care for that loved one in their final days, final minutes. On that final night, when the Hospice nurse told us it would not be long, we gathered around my mother's hospital bed. My sister held her hand and I stood at her side gently stroking her forehead, her eyes staring up at us, and I smiled back at her with my eyes and wordlessly they told her I loved her as I felt her body stop breathing very gently . . .

And her soul was set free as it touched each of us before it went out of the room.

"Liar!"
Unfinished business unresolved

Sometimes, no matter how hard we might try to resolve old wounds, nothing changes. This next story, by Roberta Rachel Omin, is a heartbreaker.

I felt nothing, was cold until I felt the hot surge of fury and outrage. I held myself back from calling out "Liar! Liar!" in this large room of the Ethical Culture Society where people paying their last respects gathered as a man performing the memorial service said, "He loved children."

It had been twelve and a half years since I had seen my father—since he disowned me after I married Paul in a ceremony at the Institute without the presence of my parents. I was only twenty then. I had tried to see my father, but the two times I gathered my courage to go to his office added to the trauma. The moment he saw me enter his office at 2 East 23rd Street, he jumped up, strode past me to the door, pointed furiously to the elevator and shouted, "Get out of here." I meekly left. His chilling rage still petrified me.

Three years later, I met him in a neurologist's office. My sister Jackie was thirteen and I was twenty-three then. Mom had called earlier in the day to ask if Jackie had had a fall or had hit her head—anything that would have caused her to have a fit—when she had visited me the weekend before. I was stunned and burst into tears. I couldn't tolerate anything bad happening to my baby sister. When I recovered and learned Mom had taken her to a chiropractor in New Jersey, I said I wanted to take her to my doctor.

Jackie met me at the Port Authority in New York City. I took her to my internist, who then made an appointment for a neurologist that evening. My father appeared there, as Mom must have told him what I was doing. When he came into the waiting room he kissed and spoke with Jackie and did not answer me when I said hello.

We all went into the doctor's office. Jackie was given an EEG and had to hyperventilate into a bag. Then the doctor made the pronouncement, "Your daughter has grand mal and petit mal epilepsy." He then wrote out her prescriptions and handed them to my father.

When we left the office, Jackie went with him. Never once during this whole traumatic unfolding did he utter a word to me. Mom did not fill the prescriptions and continued to believe that Jackie would not have any more seizures with the chiropractic and nutritional care she was receiving. It worked for eleven months; then Jackie began to have grand mal seizures. After each seizure my mother would call and give me the full details. Eventually she had to acknowledge Jackie, indeed, needed medication.

After that encounter in the doctor's office I did not see my father again, although I was always looking for him wherever I went—in the restaurant across the street from his 34th Street apartment, in the shops, in trucks that looked like the last one I had known him to have, in the streets and even at future office visits with other neurologists. He never appeared.

When I was thirty, I gave birth to my first child, Joshua. I thought about letting my father know he had a grandson. He had always wanted to have sons and he only had daughters. I imagined he'd be happy to have a boy in the family. I also knew he wanted to have absolutely nothing to do with me. I put it off.

I had also been told by Jackie, his once favorite daughter, now living in California, that he had written her a scathing letter when he learned she was living with her boyfriend, the man she would later marry. He condemned her lifestyle "because men only want one thing" and then for sure her boyfriend would not marry her. When they did marry, seven weeks after Joshua was born, Dad did not come to her wedding.

The following January in 1977 my middle sister Naomi, who was twenty-nine, planned a small wedding ceremony in Atlanta. At this point Naomi was the only one Dad was in contact with, the daughter who desperately wanted to be a son for him. He did not come to her wedding which we believe was not to face Jackie or me—a huge disappointment for Naomi. I had brought Joshua to each of their weddings in hopes Dad would meet his grandson.

Naomi was the only one who knew where he was living, somewhere in Bayside, Queens. His office had had a fire and he lost his direct mail advertising business. Naomi had told us, however, that Dad was ill with cancer of the sinuses; but we never knew much more.

In my early mothering days, I would gaze at my son in his carriage as we walked through the main streets of Tarrytown; I would think how precious my child is to me and I would wonder, "How could a father ever disown his own child?" I could not fathom it, it was incredulous to me. These thoughts kept churning over and over in my mind.

Finally I wrote the letter introducing my son to his grandfather and enclosing a picture. I sent the letter to Naomi requesting her to please forward this to Dad as his address was unlisted and she was the only one who could do this for me. Quite a while later the letter was returned to me; unopened. He had refused to accept delivery.

It was 1978. I became pregnant again. Joshua was now two and a half. In the beginning of October, I learned my father was in Bellevue Hospital. I wanted to see him again. I needed to not have him disown me any longer. On Monday, October 3, I made the trip into NYC. I was terrified to see him. I did not know if he would order me out again as he had done a decade before.

I found his room easily. His third wife, Sandy, stopped me from entering because he was in the process of receiving pain medication. Sandy, her adult son, and I sat in the large waiting room. She explained,

"Bob has about six months to live." Then my father was wheeled into the waiting room and placed in the middle of the room.

He was physically far away. He still had thick black hair with a few white hairs at his temple; no thinning or baldness. One of his dark eyes was slightly bulged. He did not appear ill, thin or even sickly. For half an hour, we sat quietly while Dad talked the whole time. He told jokes and stories as if he were a performer on a Las Vegas stage. I imagined he had stored these in his memory from his own experiences traveling there. When he ran out of material, he was returned to his room and put into his bed.

I followed him to his room and stood by the side of his bed. I told him I was pregnant and that I had a son two and a half years old. He said to me, "If I were to see you on the street I would not recognize you." I assumed he said this because I now had short hair, a far cry from the long hair he constantly teased me about when he used to tell me my hair looked like a mop. I leaned over to kiss him on the cheek and felt his stubby black beard.

I told him, "I will come back to visit you again next Monday." My last words to him erupted from my subconscious: "I was afraid to come to see you because I thought you would . . ." And then I caught myself, tried not to degrade myself, and was able to change my language midstream from "I thought you would kick me out" to "I thought you would ask me to leave." I felt that little switch left me a little more intact.

His response to me was, "I can see you are still not remorseful for what you did."

I didn't answer him. He was still stuck on it was my fault, my mistake. It was no use to say otherwise. I left his room.

On my drive home to my family, I imagined seeing him again, bringing my son to see him when he came home from the hospital, inviting him to our home in Westchester, worrying what would happen when I did the next thing that would make him angry and he would disown me—it could be the littlest thing, something unintentional and then it would start all over again. It was on the ride home that

I realized he did not ask a single question about me. He never said, "How have you been? Are you happy? Tell me about my grandson and your husband? Tell me about your life?"

On Wednesday morning, thirty hours after I had visited Dad, I received a call from my mother. Naomi had just called her. My father, who was only sixty-three, had died during the night. No one knew what happened except he had been in some kind of distress and died. It was a mystery.

"Coming to Terms"
A surprise after death

Arlene Schofield's feelings change after her parents have passed on. Here is her story.

As I delivered the last lines of the eulogy I wrote for my father, I spoke of an imagined argument continuing in an afterlife. "Why did you leave me?!" Dad yells at Mother. "What took you so long to join me?" Mom retorts.

I didn't add "Whew," which is what I was feeling. "Whew, it's over. They're gone. I'm free. Whew, what a long, long journey."

My mother died in March of 2006, Dad three months later. Observers wondered if their longevity, eighty-eight and eighty-nine respectively, was in part due to the intensity of the anger and hatred they expressed toward each other. Whatever the bond, Dad couldn't live without Mom and I suspect if he had died first, she would have followed as quickly as he followed her.

Sometime before her death, my mother asked me if I, a psychotherapist, would tell her which of them was really crazy. I replied they were both crazy. "For sixty-five years you've been trying to change Dad. You've screamed at him, tried to manipulate him, bargained with him. If it's not crazy to keep doing the same thing that doesn't work for sixty-five years, I don't know what is."

There was a brief silence while, I hoped, she was considering what I said. When at last she spoke, she said, "Sixty-six years, sixty-six."

I learned to deal with my parents' intransigence with humor.

I regaled friends with stories like the one above and laughed along with them. However, I was often unable to laugh. I would become too enraged or frustrated by their demands, their neediness. Toward the end of their lives I felt suffocated by their unwillingness to take any positive steps, combined with their endless calls asking me to fix their lives. I remember being grateful when they moved to Florida twenty-eight years ago. I was mistaken. Distance neither made the heart grow fonder nor lessened my responsibilities.

My parents were limited, unhappy souls. For much of my life I was bound to them by pity. After much work I came to understand the price I was paying in my attempts to bring them some joy, some respite.

It wasn't until shortly after their deaths that painful memories began to surface and profound insights were born. It was as if while they lived I could only let myself know fragments of who they were, but when they died, I allowed myself to remember and see a fuller picture. Family members helped by telling stories which triggered memories and clarified old confusions.

As I understood my parents more, I became less angry with them. Rather than pity, I now feel compassion; instead of frustration, I feel peace.

But I still wish I'd had parents I could truly miss.

"A Journey to Death"
Waiting

Audrey's story vividly describes the experience of being with a loved one who is wanting to die. (Originally published in the St. Petersburg Times, September 26, 2006)

The first time Mother wants to end her life, she fails. Given a prognosis of "a few months" by the oncologist, this spirited, independent woman decides that is not fast enough. She stops eating and taking medications—and waits.

But after two weeks she is still sitting up in the Scandinavian side chair, entertaining visitors who come to offer melancholy good-byes, and she is marveling at the glorious sunshine outside her bedroom window.

Sick enough to be miserable, says the Hospice nurse, but not sick enough to die.

So Mother starts to eat again. And this is the beginning of the end, the long, slow downhill crawl to death.

"How are you, Ma?" I ask on my daily visit.

"Time goes. Not fast. Not slow. It just goes."

"How do you feel?"

"I'm ready. I'm waiting. My job is done. The sooner the better. Everything is in order, the money, the jewelry. I have nothing to worry about."

Another time she says hopefully, "It's almost over now," as the wheels of her metal walker screech and grind across the black and white tiled hallway of her apartment. "I can hardly walk anymore."

A surreal calm settles on us. I am jolted by the realization that we are consciously waiting for her to die and actually talking about the prospect.

"Do you think I got sicker?" she asks early one morning.

"A drop."

"Can you make it two drops?"

I respond with a sorrowful grimace.

The pain isn't bad, but the emotional anguish cuts like a knife.

"My whole life I was independent," she says during one visit, "and now I depend on everyone for everything. I stay in bed. I can't get up. I can't go out. This is no life. It's terrible. Do you think there are other people suffering like me?"

"Yes, Ma, millions."

"It shouldn't be like this. There must be another way. Isn't there anyone who can do anything for me?"

She writes a letter to Dr. Kenneth Adler, an oncologist who is a close relative:

Dear Kenny:

I am sick now for a few weeks. There is no way for me to get better. How much longer must I suffer?

My mind is clear. Therefore I am asking about "assisted suicide." I know you as a doctor and here to save lives. But my quality of life is nonexistent. I want the end, God willing soon.

Give it a thought. People in my condition would sign any paper to be relieved.

Much love from Anita

The second time Mother desires to end her life, she fails again. The large kitchen knife lay on the pale sheet next to the pillow when I came to check on her.

"Ma!" I screamed, "What are you doing?"

No answer, only grief stricken eyes.

Now we are in the middle of the end.

Death is not pretty even if the sky is blue. It is sad and final, like a bird flying hard into a glass-wall reflection of trees.

I pull myself together. My modus operandi is rote attention. Eternal patience knotted with burdensome obligation.

I can practically not bear to see her anymore.

"Death be not proud," wrote John Gunther in 1949, about the courageous but losing fight his teenage son waged against a brain tumor. Please come soon.

I force myself to remember that my mother was once Mrs. Lickety-Split, Madame Posthaste, gallivanting across town to see a new film or to the concert hall to hear Viennese music or to the fabric store to buy some green thread.

Never home when I called.

Up later than me on New Year's Eve.

Even now there are opera tickets on her desk and a calendar filled with appointments. Yet on this bright afternoon, she can't make her way from the bedroom to the living room. A decrepit bundle of illness and old age. I love her. I hate what she has become.

I cope with animal-like detachment. I don't think about the future. No plans in my head, no thoughts. Work for clients stops.

I move in robotic fashion, with darting movements in and out of the car, up and down the sidewalk, a scribbled list of things to do in my hand: Wait in line at the post office. Drop off shirts at the cleaners. Buy milk and juice and bread. Do the laundry, Mother's and mine.

Visit again. Hope for the best. Make it over soon, please.

And when it is, when the end finally comes, it is merciful. Mother passes away on a Sunday morning in her sleep, after leaving me with a final note:

"Do all you can with what you have in the time you have in the place you are."

"Mom?"

A voice out of the blue?

Sometimes the unexplainable happens. Here is Dr. Judi Musaro Lichter's story.

Today I went to buy bricks for a project in my yard. It's been on my mind to level a pathway (it's a complete mess) outside of a big shed in the backyard. I often work for hours in the garden. Big projects; heavy lifting, clearing, planting, pruning. That's me. And more than ever, labor-intensive projects are appealing, liberating, exhausting—producing a unique sense of accomplishment and calm. Just after finding the bricks I needed, I was off to find a pot of lobelia. As I searched intently amidst racks and racks of flowers, throngs of people with loaded garden carts careening by (I had to stay alert so as not to be run over), I heard a woman's voice call out, "JUDI!" It was loud, clear, and had a certain familiar lilt.

I stop—it is chilling, odd, and haunting, all at the same time. It was a voice of the past, clearly sounding so much like my Mom once sounded—a strong full voice, an inflection *just* like the way she called my name. I actually looked up, and although I instantly knew it wasn't Mom, for just a millisecond before conscious thought of any kind, tears filled my eyes. At another time, it *could* have been her.

Knowing full well that it wasn't, I shook it off; but I registered that it had really caught me by surprise. In seconds I processed: Mom is not here, I know that and she no longer sounds like the voice that called out—a full, vibrant, clear tone projecting through the din in the nursery. Not anymore. The self-sufficient, clear, connected, and certain voice that I realize I haven't heard for so long. Although it once was hers, that voice is gone and has been replaced by a weak, little, sort of "mouse voice," a tiny little "judi?" that now often sounds more plaintive than certain.

Most recently the now "little" voice of my mother is largely quiet. Little to say. One-word answers. No elaborations. No stories. Little involvement, thought, or initiative.

She was the family member who could speak to anyone—social and gregarious, the key person for her parents, sisters, brothers, and many nieces and nephews. Memory of my social, engaged, active Mom brought tears to my eyes today, and caught me off guard because I thought I had been slowly dealing with her decline, and gradually accommodating it.

She has, after all, been slipping away slowly. Even though I sometimes look into her eyes when she has finished her painstaking morning routine of washing, dressing, and starting the day—replete with rosy cheeks and lipstick—and I wish for her essence to return. I hope to see her vitality, interest, and engagement in life—hers and mine. Then I return from my wish state and my rational mind registers once again that the process of ageing has taken its toll, as it is wont to do, and that she has had a great ride.

It is now at 93½ years of age that the progressive loss of memory and function are so markedly and starkly present. Yes, the decline is upsetting, I can admit; but the rush of sadness and pain at the loss of who I knew her to have been is really always, I can see, lurking just beneath the surface. I no longer have a "Mom." Not my Mom, that is.

But today for just a fraction of a second in the nursery—all time and sense suspended—it was like she was "back" and called out to me, and I fleetingly thought "Mom?" . . . impossible though I knew it to be.

Feeling exhausted and saddened by her loss is compounded by the toll exacted by encountering dispassionate systems of elder care services, attorneys, bureaucracies, and doctors. It is also complicated by facing my own mortality, of course, but that's not my focus right now. It's hard to see the frail, little person who no longer can tell me what she did or thought or said a moment ago, or remember what I might have said or done either. Still, I try to connect. But she has little energy, no spunk, and no drive. Further twisting feelings and draining energy resulting from Mom's decline and need for caretaking is the experience of trying to work on arrangements with my sister, a myriad of agencies, health care systems, and attorneys. Get me out of here, I need air. This time period is very draining. But, I must work "with" so many others on behalf of my now little, vulnerable, dependent, and frail Mom.

I hope she is treated well, that no one screams at Mom. Listen! Mom can't answer your questions. She can't tell you what she did, where things are, what happened a minute ago; she's not being difficult. Mom is really quite placid, affable, and easy. She is trying to preserve what little presence she still has. She's trying to maintain herself. She's just got fewer and fewer resources to call up. Very little, really. Mom is just not there in any way that she once was. The vitality is gone; she's gone. I feel sad for her and am sad for myself. She was so different.

I miss Mom (this is the final thought that I'll put down here) because she was pretty much always there for me in a most essential way. She often didn't know the right words or even helpful words, she didn't know how to support or encourage, but she wanted to. She just couldn't relate; life was different for her, it was quite hard. But she stood alongside me through both very good and some very difficult times. I knew that I could count on her. Not necessarily for providing guidance or understanding that spoke directly to me—she didn't have the resources to do this but I knew she wanted to. She wasn't given the gift of mothering herself until she was eighteen years old and her father remarried long after her own Mother had died when she was three. She was a powerhouse, she was talented, she was creative, and she was resourceful.

I know I won't forget the voice I heard today, calling "Judi!" . . . my split-second disorientation, and the pain of knowing it was not Mom.

Section 3

Alzheimer's: Lost and Sometimes Found

Alzheimer's deserves a separate category because it is so prevalent in this stage of life and demands so much from caregivers. It is one of the most challenging situations because the elder can turn into a completely different person, for better or for worse, confounding the emotions of the caregiver. Many times the elder has no recognition of who you are one moment and in the next moment acts as though nothing has changed.

"The Bonding Bloom"
A common interest becomes a lifeline for an elder with Alzheimer's

Kathleen Picarelli's story poignantly describes how she finds a way to cultivate a connection with her mother who has Alzheimer's.

On June mornings the summer sun skirts the oak canopy in my parents' front yard, striking their cement and red brick porch and the pots of annuals that line the periphery. It is a good place to be a plant: the sun strong, the water and nourishment plenty. Between my mother and me they get a great deal of attention; I am their propagator, she their admirer. Despite all my on-the-ground efforts, I think they mature more because of her love for them. Their roots pierce the packed soil and their petals reach skyward in order to please her. I know this to be true.

***

I returned home a few years ago at the age of forty-one to convalesce from an illness that I've had since 1994. I remained to help my parents. My father, a wiry ex-carpenter in his mid-eighties, is blessed with a stalwart constitution and a sharp mind. My mother has been less fortunate. Her body has been in a state of rebellion for forty years, attempting to overthrow all her systems. The result: a continual onslaught of afflictions including early onset osteoarthritis, coronary artery disease, osteoporosis, renal insufficiency, and the most insidious of all—Alzheimer's. In addition to these conditions, she broke her hip three years ago after a jarring fall out of the bathtub.

I awoke that morning to the sound of her screams and the sight of her sprawled out helplessly on the bathroom floor. Post replacement surgery she developed a limp so pronounced that she is required to ambulate with a walker for the rest of her life.

Nowadays, mostly sedentary, she spends the majority of time in the living room, which is cocoon-like, furnished in earth tones: avocado walls and carpet, evergreen and brown tweedy upholstery. Heavy golden drapes frame the spacious picture window facing the luxuriant front yard.

It is the morning after Father's Day and we three have ended up in the living room. Mom is watching Regis on TV, dad is milling about, I just passing through. I was curious how my father enjoyed his celebration.

"We had a really nice Father's Day, didn't we, Dad?" I go through the list of everything his kids and grandkids did for him. It is as if I want to show him how much he matters.

His face lights up. "Oh yeah, it was really nice," he proclaims, proud of his family as always.

Mom chimes in plaintively, "I don't remember any of it."

I quickly fill her in so she won't feel so badly. It saddens me that she has no recollection of such a special day. It is as if she had been somewhere else entirely.

"The family got together for a barbeque, Mom."

I watch her to see how she will respond. I already know. Her lips pout and start to quiver. A pained expression follows. Rivulets meander down her plump cheeks. Like a forlorn child unable to find her mother, she is completely lost.

Dad says to let her be when she cries; just give her space, he insists, and she will eventually stop. Sometimes I agree, sometimes not. I sit beside her on the couch and hold her hand under the blanket so my dad won't see and think I'm coddling her. I've noticed that when children are shown attention while crying, they sometimes cry even more. Distraction is a favored ploy to calm them down, and it often works with my mother as well.

"Mom, we get a good view of the zinnias on the porch railing from here, don't we?"

She turns to admire them.

"Yes, we do. Aren't they beautiful?"

"I put them there so you can see them when you sit on the couch." The tears subside. She is more animated. I continue on.

"And the vegetable garden is doing really well. We've got three tiny cucumbers growing."

"We do?" she asks, delighted. My mother responds to home-grown vegetables with the enthusiasm one displays toward cute little babies. "What else do we have growing?"

"We've got eggplants—you should see them—they have jumbo leaves. And we've got peppers, basil, and plenty of parsley. You should look at them later."

"I look at my garden several times a day," she reports proudly. "I stick my head out the kitchen window."

Her garden. Her flowers. Like a flock of orphaned children she has adopted every one. But as dearly as she loves them, she can not remember their names. During our garden visits she will ask, "What's that one called? And how about that one?"

"That's a zinnia," I'll say. You used to grow them every summer." I remember their hot pink petals bursting outward from their pom-pom heads—so bright and showy, just as vibrant as my mother herself. If mom had a signature flower, it would be a zinnia.

One by one, I identify every commonly known plant: "The bright yellows are day lilies. The coral pink, begonias. The viney ones, zucchini, the unruly staked-up ones, tomatoes." Nowadays they are all strangers to her; but every time they meet she is very glad to make their acquaintance.

After the introductions she'll survey the whole lot with wonderment, and then reiterate, "What is this one, what is that one?"

"It's a tomato. It's a zucchini. It's a petunia . . ." I'll repeat their names as if trying to teach a child language. But unlike a young person eager and able to acquire knowledge, she cannot retain any of it.

What matters is the joy she feels upon gazing at her lovely floral friends. I watch her as she studies their bold colors, their varied forms and textures: crepe trumpets, satin wings, velvety hearts. Even their foliage catches her eye; no detail escapes her. To the casual observer a leaf's a leaf. But not to my mother. She notices their intricacies, such as whether they are toothed or smooth, broad or lacy. Once in a while she'll even give one a little feel. "Oooh, this one's kind of hairy," she'll say, as if handling the creepy leg of a spider.

What pleases her most are the tender young buds, perhaps because they are vulnerable and filled with promise—hinting at a burst of color or tiny fruit. She can nurture them as she did my brothers and me. Indeed, husbanding her children was my mother's most gratifying endeavor. "Nobody's were more beautiful than mine," she likes to say. But while we left home decades ago, she still needs to feel needed. For our mother was the perennial parent, appearing on schedule under all conditions, eager to provide for our enjoyment and well-being.

Kalani Pruet, a tropical flower farmer with whom I am acquainted, told me that he equates parenting with garden tending. In an Eden-like setting on a Hawaiian island, he conceives a splendid array of exotic flora with vibrant colors and fantastical forms, like the spiky heads of prehistoric birds. In exchange for his continued care, he is amply rewarded. "Nature embodies the values we want for our families. That is why I really enjoy the farm. I'm conscious that there is a bigger picture. When I put a little nurturing energy or spirit into it, I get it back."

During her gardening years, my mother treated her seedlings like children, checking their growth and making sure that they were fed and watered properly, delighting as they reached for the sun. Her interest extends back a long way—from the time my parents and brothers moved from Brooklyn to Long Island in 1956. She developed such a passion for horticulture that her small plot of tilled land became a sanctuary. Every morning she would tend to and commune with her plant companions. In their realm she was the only human invitee. She has described her morning ritual countless times: "I couldn't wait to finish spring cleaning so when I got up I could go outside and sit down with my garden and sip my cup of tea. I loved to take a peek underneath the leaves to see what was growing. When I'd see the little plants springing up, I'd feel a little like God—like I helped create them. It was truly amazing."

I remember as a child, sitting in a patch of clover or sometimes beside her, watching her tend her botanic brood. She would dig a hole with a trowel, sprinkle in 5-10-5, add back some dirt, and then carefully plant miniature verdure, so as not to damage its filamentous tangle of roots. She'd fill in the rest of the hole with dirt, pat the earth around the gangly stem and foliage, and give it a little drink. She was organized and methodical and proficient at her plant craft. Even as a child I sensed she was in her element.

My mother relished her hobby for over twenty-five years, stopping only because the gnawing pain of arthritis afflicted her back. She continued to plant bright red salvia in the front yard, but gone were the prolific vegetable garden and beds of annuals in the back. As she got older and the pain in her back worsened, as pain often does, even the salvia disappeared. All the planting came to a halt about twenty years ago.

A few years back it occurred to me that I should resume vegetable production. Not only would it provide nutritious edibles, I reasoned, but it would be a source of enjoyment for my mother. I never had a yard of my own, so this gave me the opportunity to connect with the land—digging, scraping, smashing weeds against shovels, and freeing rootlets from stubborn clumps. I like when dirt gets underneath my nails and caked on my knees; it makes me feel strong and basic, like a farmer at day's end.

Knowing that a flower assortment would bring joy to my mother and me, I decided to resurrect the front yard flower bed and regale the porch with numerous pots. She always says, "Give me my flowers when I'm alive, not dead." So that is what I set out to do. Each year the arrangements are different but the intent is the same: to place a variety of showy, colorful blooms—hanging baskets of purple petunias, ceramic pots of salmon impatiens and crimson dahlias—within view of the room where she roosts.

The undertaking has proven a success. "The gardens are really good for her," my father has told me.

I have the sense that as the Alzheimer's progresses, she will still be stimulated by these jewels of the summer's earth: the border beauties and trailing trumpets, the stalks of pillowy multi-colored clusters. Yet, I often wonder how she sees them. Are they larger than life, like the provocative close-up flower portraits of Georgia O'Keefe? Can she see deep into them like a butterfly, and even beyond, like a tiny insect that has strolled inside? Is she awash in nectar and protected by a petaled cocoon? At times I have found myself wishing to be swallowed by a snapdragon, or better yet a gardenia, and be intoxicated by its scent. Surrounded by softness, I can hide from the world and whatever ails me, and can absorb a botanical balm, a kind of earth essence. My mother and I can experience a horticultural healing, and be transported to a place where only beauty and tenderness reside.

There is so much I will never know, except this: Gardening is a way to reach her and a hobby to share. Looking back, I wish we had had more of that. As adults, my mother and I have led very different lives, always several states apart, and sometimes at opposite ends of the country.

During my high school years, I yearned to live in the wilderness, to be out in the open and immersed in exquisite beauty. A poster in the guidance counselor's office depicted a female forester, with her long hair and plaid shirt, a specimen pouch tied around the waist of her jeans. It suddenly became clear to me that conservation was the type of work I wanted to do. After college, I moved to the Southwest to work as a national park ranger in some of the most untrammeled, pristine landscapes in the country.

My new lifestyle greatly disappointed my family, particularly my mother, as it was an uncharacteristic path for a young woman in a clannish Italian-American family. "How can you move to Utah?"

she once asked in disbelief. "The family doesn't live in Utah." But I desired in the strongest way to feel free, and my adventures—rafting the Colorado, horseback riding on windswept mesas, working in the depths of the Grand Canyon, and traveling through Latin America and Europe with a backpack—all reflected that need.

Interestingly, I did a considerable amount of my exploring alone. I remember hiking to the top of a two-thousand-foot sandstone escarpment and dangling my legs off the edge, marveling at the magnificent chasm before me. I had spent several hours backpacking to that point through steep, rugged terrain and it was almost nightfall. My sleeping bag was laid out under a dome of stars. There was not a soul in sight, but I was neither scared nor lonely. I felt the kind of peace experienced when one is exactly where they belong. During my twenties I experienced many such moments such as that.

Therein lay the dilemma: reside in landscapes that made my spirit soar but were distant from home, or live near my family in a place I disliked—but I could never do both. This conflict remains a source of sadness for me. Surely there had to be some way to bridge that divide.

Family-wise, I never had one of my own. My brothers and their wives did. Born to fawn, our mother would exclaim, "Cuanda bella!" every time she saw her grandchildren's beautiful faces. She would have treasured mine too, had I given her that pleasure.

My mother, on the other hand, stayed closer to home and was the consummate homemaker, tending to our family as she did her garden: with the conscious care one gives a prized rosebush or delicate orchid. Because of my mother's skillful hands and loving heart, we thrived; she derived a great deal of contentment from watching this.

In grade school, I would arrive home each afternoon to find a Hostess Twinkie and glass of milk waiting for me on the kitchen table. While I ate my snack, my mother would sit across from me at the table and listen to my oddball stories. She heard me tell me about the teacher we tormented until he had a panic attack; my classmate Adam Sargent, who introduced us to a strange and naughty word;

and Frankie the bully, whom I pushed into the bushes for making fun of my last name. Whatever experiences we had, whatever joys and sorrows we felt, my mother bore witness to them. She watched our lives take shape, change course, falter, and flourish.

She recently confided that she plans to be my witness after she passes too. "I'm still going to be with you when I go," she said recently, out of the blue.

Stunned by this unexpected remark (and the thought of my mother following me around for the rest of my life), I teased: "You mean you're going to come back to haunt me?"

"No silly," she replied, very matter-of-fact. "I'm going to help you."

A few years ago, I decided to make a video montage of my parents' life together. While the camera was running, my mother expressed her gratitude toward her children: "I cherish you, Kath, my only daughter. Cherish you like your brothers. You all made my life quite lovely."

She also adored the verdant suburban enclave that had been her home for decades. Compared to Brooklyn, Long Island was country. The broad-leaf trees and manicured yards were enough for her. And understandably so. But not for me.

Because of our different lifestyles, my mother and I never went on as many outings as either of us would have liked. Now that I'm home, I realize we have more in common than I had thought; and fortunately we have more time to spend. While the types of activities we can do now are limited, we can at least garden. My mom, the virtual gardener; me, the laborer; and both of us, observers. A simple glance out the window and we become wide-eyed and exhilarated; we turn to each other and smile. After the many growing seasons, we have realized it is never too late to cultivate compassion. As our charges bloom and flourish, we experience tremendous satisfaction. Along with them we bloom and bond.

My mother recently told me she always wanted to have a daughter. "Why?" I asked.

"To have someone that would take after me."

I've come to realize that in many ways I do. She thinks so too. Whenever I recite a poem I've written or sing a melody for my parents, she will proclaim, "I was always good at composition and music. You've got a lot of me in you, Kathy. Doesn't she have a lot of me in her?"

My father and I agree.

***

Life has changed considerably since my rangering days, and so has the view from home. Gone are the unimpaired vistas, the canyons that fan in all directions and mountains that reach for the sky. Nowadays, I experience a subtler, time-honored beauty—familiar, familial. I take solace in the sameness and charm of our easy breezy block, where each home and garden is well-cared for, decade after decade.

It is a streetscape of oaks, gnarled and sheltering, and lawns, green and pervasive as caterpillars; of dogwoods, whose blossoms grace the springtime, and maples whose leaves ignite the fall. The clover smells sweet here, like angels, and the air is never still: Butterflies duet, bumbles vibrate, and jays flit nervously about. I've grown especially fond of the beings that seem to clamor for attention: the fireflies that dance across evening, the robins, whose song sweeten the air, and even the rabbits that nibble on our garden.

There are places to which I am much better suited, but for now, this is where I'll remain. And while a small, cultivated plot is no match for the spacious scenery of the West, it at least provides some relief—the soft greenery summoning fragments of spirit that had been left behind.

***

Early this morning, before breakfast, my mother and I walk into our garden. We are surrounded by a plethora of herbage, notably the zucchini leaves, which resemble vegetation from a time prehistoric. Amidst the floppy foliage is the largest squash blossom we've ever

208

seen, its petals the size of batwings, its color margarine. Six fuzzy tongues emanate from its center, supported by a network of green veins—stunning and sunning in all its morning glory.

By midday, it has shriveled, its petals collapsed and entwined. How sad that something so striking could fade so fast.

Drawn inward, we peer through the umbrella of leaves, into the dense tangle of stems leading to the heart. Relief comes, for in the protective shadow, a pale green finger, withered blossom at its tip—a projection from source and soul—grows. A promise is kept and carried forward, then gently, lovingly released.

"Finding Dad"

A bright moment in the sea of Alzheimer's

*Often people are afraid of joining their elder
who is hallucinating or on a trip into the land of
Alzheimer's. Here Joan Campagna shows us how she
joined her father in a far-off land and the healing
that came out of it for her.*

Dad has dementia. He's in and out now. Here now and there now, wherever there is. He walks into the dining room and I say, "Hi, Dad."

His face twists almost snarly and he answers, "Who are you?" He's not teasing. His face is angry, his voice is challenging. He doesn't know me.

Everything inside me stops and then catapults. I feel like crying, yet I have no tears. I'm in fear and devastating sadness all at once. The little girl in me feels like she's dying.

Months later . . .

I enter my dad's room at the rehab center. He's had a stroke, one of several. He's sitting in his wheelchair, looking far away. I approach him and call out gently, "Dad?" He looks right through me. "Dad," I call again. No response. I get in his face and look for him in his eyes. "Dad, dad, it's me, Joanie, where are you?"

His face, his eyes reveal some response. "Hi, Dad, I say," still softly. His return is slow as if coming out of a stupor. Very gently, still, "Hi, Dad, it's me, Joanie." The beginnings of a smile. He seems to be looking at me. The beginnings of recognition. Then the twinkle of his playful eyes lights up and now he's beaming. He knows me.

"Where did you go?" I ask him.

"Arabia," he answers, still smiling and twinkling. I'm ready to play along.

"Arabia?" I say. "What were you doing in Arabia? He begins to tell me and I'm an excited little girl again playing with dad. This time in a very different way than we ever did before. And, this time the adult woman sitting with her father in complete delight is awed and grateful for the gift of revelation he gives me of a whole other side of him. I have met and delight in the storyteller for the first time.

"Long Time Gone"
Understanding Mom

At the end of her mother's life, Virginia Flanagan makes a discovery and an awakening occurs.

Both my mother and father were forty years old when I was born, unusually old for first-time parents in 1936. In third grade I lived for a week at the home of a classmate whose parents were nearly twenty years younger than mine. She called them "Ruth" and "Mal," and they drank beer and played guitars. Forever after, my parents seemed disappointingly outdated. I don't recall, however, considering they would someday die.

One night when I was twenty-seven, I got a barely coherent call from my mother telling me my father was in the hospital. She was increasingly forgetful and confused and didn't remember why she called an ambulance. She thought he might be dead. I reserved a plane ticket for the next morning for the short flight from New York City to Harrisburg, Pennsylvania, then spoke to the hospital and learned he was still alive and would possibly recover.

I called a friend and told her, sobbing, "He's dying and he never knew I loved him." Yes he did, she assured me. Several years before, she was present during a minor squabble between the two of us and when I stalked out of the room, my friend told him, "She does love you, you know." My father smiled. "I never doubted that," he said. She saved the story, she explained, for a time I really needed it.

My father lived another five months, but he was slowed down and his thoughts were foggy and disorganized. Having been a salesman all of his life, he was able to maintain a social façade intact enough to fool almost everyone. The banker in charge of his accounts presided over my acquiring power of attorney as my father nodded agreement to all questions. Although he had no idea what he was signing that day, he did have occasional clear moments. Sitting in his favorite chair on one of my mother's particularly bad days, he looked at me with a worried frown. "I don't understand," he said slowly. Is she more crazy than I am . . . or am I more crazy than she is?"

After it became obvious my mother couldn't manage the household, and I declined to move back home, my father's sister invited them to stay with her in Fort Lauderdale. A couple months later, my father suffered a series of strokes that left him paralyzed, speechless, and eventually non-responsive. I went down to Florida and sat daily by his bedside, telling him I loved him. Finally relieved of fending off the intensity of his rage, affection, and demands, I was surprised by the immensity of my sadness. I pretended he knew I was there. Unable to deal with ambiguity, my mother alternately insisted that he was dead and that he was almost well again.

I spent many of the hours sitting under a tree in my aunt's backyard, twisting and pounding clay into tortured, human-like shapes. For the first time in my life, I couldn't concentrate on a book. After a week I flew back to New York.

I was with a psychotherapy patient when the call came from my aunt. "Your father died about half an hour ago."

"OK," I said, "I'll call you in a little while." I finished the session, returned the call, and flew to Florida for the funeral and burial. Numbness was my only protection against overwhelming emotion. It served as a massive door shutting away my grief, my imagined shortcomings as a daughter, and the fear of being fully responsible for my mother.

She wanted to return to their house in Harrisburg, but it was now obvious she couldn't live alone. Although my mother had been declining for years, her dementia was suddenly inescapable. She stayed with me for only a few days, complaining when I arrived home each evening that men were trying to get in the back door of the apartment. There were, of course, no back door and no men.

By the time I got her settled in an assisted living complex, she was much too confused and fearful to maintain herself. I was called out of a conference in midtown Manhattan by an urgent message: My mother was getting lost in the halls, unable to find the dining room, and in her frustration had hit one of the attendants. I had nightmares of the two of us running frantically through an endless series of corridors.

With my reluctant consent, the facility placed her in a state hospital. I visited her many times in the first weeks and was amazed to find her once again quiet and content. The attention and structure calmed her, and she told me with pleasure of her daily visits with Vivian, her favorite cousin, dead for ten years. Eventually she was transferred to a smaller residence where she continued to be well cared for. I visited less often as she lost awareness and stopped when she no longer showed any sign of recognition.

I was forty-two years old when I got a call telling me my mother had died in her sleep. I flew once again to Fort Lauderdale, where she was buried next to my father; but for me she had died years before.

Alzheimer's was a rare diagnosis back then, and only after her death did I speculate that it began to claim her even before I left for college at seventeen. Her illness was prolonged and unnamed; it seemed merely an exaggeration of my mother's vulnerabilities; it was part of her for more than half my lifetime. Some years after her death I was able to resurrect my mother's truer self and to recall the sweetness and playfulness of the mother of my childhood.

"This Is Not My Dad"
Dr. Jekyll and Mr. Hyde

Alzheimer's can turn our elders into completely different people, confounding the caregiver and leaving unfinished business. —Anonymous.

My father, a conservative, middle-class professional who had been a moral person and active in his community throughout his life, was living on his own in a house in another state. When he was around seventy-five we started to get ideas that he was making friends with people who needed help to start a church, to get to a funeral, to have surgery, and so on. We tried to tell him these people may not have legitimate problems but he wouldn't hear it. We saw some signs of dementia in conversation, but he seemed to be functioning fine when we visited.

Then one Christmas we saw signs that someone was living with him, a young woman. He told us there was a program where senior citizens help former drug addicts get back on their feet. There are a lot of details about how it spun downhill as we tried to help him and he refused, and we tried to get a judge to give us permission to get him into assisted living but his doctor refused to call it dementia. It ended with him having a houseful of drug addicts clean out all valuables and incur debts of around $80,000.

They used him to drive and watch as they conducted what appeared to be illegal activities. For instance they'd come out of a house with a television. We worked daily for about a year with social workers and lawyers and the police to resolve this.

It finally ended with the police going undercover into his house, making a drug buy, and then returning for a dramatic drug bust during which they broke down the door sending broken glass into my father's eye. We finally got restraining orders on everyone and somehow legally got permission to have another doctor evaluate him and then got a judge to let us be his guardians. He was very difficult, resisting the whole way, and the police had to physically move him sometimes in handcuffs because he resisted.

My frame of mind at the time was disbelief. This was made more challenging because his lucid moments came and went at first. It was so hard to judge just how much of a problem he really was having. It emerged so slowly over a number of years. Once he became involved with prostitution, drugs, and other crimes, I was scared that he was involved in crime himself and could get put in jail, injured, or killed. Because the prostitute drug addicts living with him slept with him, I also worried about sexually transmitted diseases and his possibly fathering a child with them, a child who would be exposed to drugs in the womb.

The change in our relationship was very difficult. He was always a powerful, self-confident, strong, and moral man. He became a weak, scared, gullible, and to some extent amoral victim. I was embarrassed to talk to him. I still feared his powerful, angry, my-life-is-none-of-your-business attitude—an attitude that did not succumb to Alzheimer's. If anything, it became stronger. I had a simultaneous personal crisis with my daughter that took much of my time, so I often felt guilty that I couldn't just fly there and move in with him and try to spend more time reasoning with him.

I was so angry at the people who stole so much from him and trashed his house. I heard from someone that they treated him "worse than a dog," making him do their laundry, for example. I felt helpless when he refused our help and authorities were so slow to help. It was just plain difficult in so many ways.

A judge finally put him in a nursing home instead of in jail for continuing to associate with the drug addicts. We tried him in a couple of settings. Assisted living did not work out at first. He finally had a stay in a psych ward for a week, where meds helped get his physical aggression under control. He is now settled in an assisted living home in an Alzheimer's section, and he no longer knows us.

One of the big shocks for me was how little the legal system was willing to interfere. They took the position that he did not have a diagnosis of dementia, and so he had a legal right to let these people move in and take his money. They would not consider that dementia is a slowly progressive disease and that those who prey on slowly increasing cognitive impairment take advantage of that fact.

One thing that frustrated us was that he had refused our help, stubbornly holding onto his independence—and yet would take help from these people who were taking advantage of him. They were able to do it by making him feel that he was helping them. In hindsight, I wonder what would have happened if I had told him that I really needed him and made up some crises that would help him feel useful during this transition period.

Instead, with my brother and sister, I kept thinking that if I just provided one more piece of data, surely the system would arrest these people. But it never happened. There were never any charges against them for what they did to my father. And we are left with the debt and trying to figure out how to come up with the money to keep him in the assisted living facility.

I can tell you about amazing sacrifices my sister made to help my father. Because she was not employed full-time, she took on much of the long hours spent daily in communication with the lawyer, the social worker, and the police, as well as my father. She helped my mother take legal steps to protect her financial assets (our parents had been separated for years but not divorced). She moved to a city closer to my brother so that they could both visit my father regularly in the home. She is still so harassed by the bill collectors going after my father's debt that she never answers the phone.

It has been wonderful to watch her tender caring for him as she takes him out regularly for meals in restaurants or for ice cream, and how she just adapts to each stage of the disease and still maintains some form of communication with him. As his prefrontal cortex became riddled with a combination of mini-strokes and Alzheimer's and his moral compass disappeared, he put her through hell. But she holds no bitterness toward him about this and has been devoted throughout. I live in another state and am so grateful that she is there close to my father looking out for him.

Section 4

Waking up to the Mystical: The Caregiver's Call to Higher Consciousness

Our personal attitudes surrounding Death and beyond are buried in the deepest part of our nature, intrinsically linked to our spiritual (including atheist) and religious beliefs. They are prickly like cactus, not wanting to be tampered with by anyone or anything. Most of us experience an archetypal fear of Death and there is usually great resistance to talking about this subject.

When our elder is close to Death's door, however, something awesome, almost numinous (divine) in nature often takes place. These experiences can shake the foundation of our known world, confronting us with overwhelming emotions and unusual experiences that defy our ordinary sense of reality. The stories in this section offer a variety of experiences in which Death parts the veils to other worlds and non-ordinary realities, opening us up to a higher realm of consciousness, leaving much for us to ponder about the nature of reality.

For those who have reached beyond the veil, life will never be the same.

"Cutting the Cord"
Kali, the Hindu goddess, gives aid in the dying process

Kathy Taylor gives an amazing account of another reality she experienced when her father was at Death's door.

My father died in 1992. He'd been ill for five years with kidney failure (on dialysis) and some heart complications. He wound up in hospital for exploratory surgery (throat to groin incision) and they found inoperable cancer. He decided to go home to die. My mother was not able to cope, so my younger brother and my sister-in-law and I arranged to be at my mother's house on the Oregon coast, to take care of her and to take care of my father twenty-four hours a day.

I was forty-eight at the time (am now sixty-six). I've worked with my dreams for thirty years (my husband Jeremy Taylor has written four books on the subject and we work our dreams every day) and am familiar with archetypes and mythology in general.

On the ninth day of caring for my father he asked how long he'd been at home. I told him and he said he had no idea it would take so long and he apologized. He spent his days moving in and out of consciousness, drugged heavily with morphine, sometimes able to get up for a moment or two.

Daily care was physically and emotionally demanding. The surgeons had not been able to put back all the "pieces" so he'd had a colostomy and was left with an enormous incision we had to care for, lest it become infected and increase his discomfort. The three of us were "just plain folks" when it comes to nursing care, so caring for him physically was challenging. Hospice came once a week and checked the incision and gave much comfort and compassion.

Emotionally, all three of us coped as best we could. My way of handling my time with him was to simply "meet" him where he was at that moment. If he was in the midst of hallucination I went there with him. At one point, for example, he said firmly that there was a huge, warm pizza sitting on his stomach and would I cut him a piece because it smelled so good. I said sure, and he said he knew it wasn't really there but it was tasty nonetheless. When he was more or less present and aware we reminisced and I told him stories. It was immensely draining to "dolphin" in and out of the waves of consciousness with him.

By the ninth day we were all exhausted. When we weren't sitting with him we were caring for our mother and keeping the household running. We were sleeping in shifts, to make sure someone was with him every moment—we couldn't stand the idea of him dying alone—and we all became increasingly tired since something always interfered with the ability to catch up with lost sleep.

That evening I fell into bed, sure I'd sleep soundly for my four hours of time off. But I lay there wide awake wondering how I would get through the next day without emotionally breaking down. I loved my father dearly, and I was having a slow, nine-day realization that there was no turning back, no getting better, no more father in my life after this.

I wanted everything: to understand him, to be understood, to say everything I'd left out in forty-eight years, to apologize for hurts, to be witness to his passing, to hold him as he crossed over and to keep him safe from any harm. And I wanted him to die and move on to whatever came next for him. My "monkey" brain just reeled. And being one to somatize pain to my heart, I found my heart literally aching.

Suddenly I saw (and I cannot bring myself to put quotes around the word because the experience was so utterly real) a thick bundle of white fibers arching out of my chest and through the wall between the bedroom and his hospital bed in the living room. I was stunned. Was I looking at that thing psychics are always talking about? Was I somehow holding my father here? The wrongness of this really overwhelmed me. He wanted to die and I wanted him to be done with this body. But I couldn't deny what I was seeing and what it seemed to mean.

I couldn't think of what to do. Then I had one of those epiphanies that just come out of nowhere. I had to cut the cord and who better to help with that than the goddess Kali, she of Indian myth who wears the human skulls around her neck and carries a sword.

Suddenly I see her standing next to the bed, a fiery sword in hand, holding it out to me. I find myself panicking, but a little portion of my brain is thinking Good Lord, the archetypes are absolutely real! I know I'm supposed to take the sword and use it and I try to reach for it, but my hand is shaking and I miss it. Then she's in my head—or so it seems—saying Take it but if you do you have to be willing to die. My sense of her in my mind is of a vastness, not at all human, no feelings; she doesn't care if I live or die or if my father dies. She just came when called.

Everything inside me comes together in that moment and I decide: I will take it and will cut this cord. I grab the sword and slash it down through the cord. Kali disappears and I fall asleep and am awakened a few minutes later by my brother telling me my father has died.

After this happened the only way I could explain it was to think of it as a dream, but that's truly a rationalization. I remember the smells in the room, the light, the sound of voices in the other room, all happening while I'm encountering Kali. His death right after I cut the cord? Coincidence? I don't know. This remains one of the most profound moments in my life.

"Uncle Duane"
A dream imparting wisdom

Dreams of those who have crossed over can be
powerful and healing. Many native cultures believe
that dreams are a place where those who have
passed on communicate with the living. Laura Deal
describes the wisdom she gleaned from her uncle on
the other side.

In April of 2001, I woke from a dream about my paternal grandfather and uncle, neither of whom had ever entered my dreams before that I remember. Within twenty-four hours, my uncle, who lived more than a thousand miles away, suffered a massive stroke from which he would not recover, and which led to his death less than two months later at the age of seventy-seven. My grandfather passed away when I was four, also of a stroke at the age of seventy-seven. Here is the dream:

> *"Granddad gives me seed corn while Dad and Uncle*
> *Duane talk of childhood"*
>
> *I'm visiting with Granddad, and he has a big barn*
> *full of bundles of dried cornstalks with the seeds still*
> *on them. They're every color—orange, blue, golden. I*
> *ask him if I can have some kernels to take home, and*
> *he's delighted to be sharing them. He shows me his*
> *notebook where he keeps his notes on all of it.*

> *Dad and Uncle Duane are there, reminiscing about*
> *childhood and how their brother had a friend, a girl*
> *his age, who lived next door. They called her Raggedy*
> *Ann because her name started with those initials.*

Thinking about the dream, the first thing that came to mind was that the seed corn represents the genetic and learned traits that are passed from one generation to another. Though my grandfather was not a farmer, he came from a farming community. He was the first in his family to go to college, and continued on to earn his Ph.D., spending his adult life in academia in Nebraska. So, too, my uncle and father became professors, and at the time of the dream I had earned a Ph.D. and taught for a while at a university.

The uncle in this dream was the one I was closest to of my father's three brothers. He used to come visit us every year at Christmas, the jolly bachelor uncle who made us all laugh. The fact that he and my dad are discussing their childhood in this dream, and that my favorite toy as a child was my Raggedy Ann doll, suggests that the patterns I lived by, to some extent anyway, were those learned in childhood, in the same way that my father and uncle learned their patterns of living as children.

I see this as a hopeful dream. My grandfather offers me seeds—seeds that contain the potential to grow into something nourishing, seeds that contain his passion for learning about the larger world, seeds that are a range of colors. The seeds represent the possibility of changing the path of my offspring; as my grandfather left his family's path to become a professor and I left academia to pursue creative writing. In this dream, I think, I receive my grandfather's blessing to choose my own path.

I also see the dream as a warning, since it came almost simultaneously with my uncle's stroke, that I should take care to reduce the risks in my life (perhaps changing patterns I learned as a child) that could lead to my having a stroke at the age of seventy-seven.

"Accompanied: A Journey towards Inner and Outer Relationship"
Midwiving the soul

The power of the bond between Adela Windsor and her dying mother takes one right into being with the dying and the birthing of the soul of her mother to the other side.

To Joy Nevin, my mother, whom I accompanied on her journey towards death and relationship, and who catalyzed my parallel journey. Our experience together gave me a peace and understanding that later guided me through the dying of my husband, Clyde.

The night after my mother died, I hunched over her table, Chinese food lumped on my plate untouched, her wineglass in my hand, crying, despairing, wondering if all that had passed between us on her last night was constructed by my imagination in an attempt to soothe my loss. I split the fortune cookie open and found my answer. I felt her eyes lock onto mine again, as naked as they had been in the moment before death, as I read: "Love comes singly and leaves accompanied."

Seven years earlier, as mom's illness began, I'd had this dream:

I go upstairs in our house to have a baby. A little girl slides out. I bundle and dry her, attempt to hold her to me but she grows each moment, lively and alert.

> *She begins to crawl around the floor, heading for the*
> *stairs leading down. I grab her, turn her around,*
> *and show her how to go safely down the stairs*
> *backwards. I say, "Backwards," and she repeats,*
> *"Backwards." It is night. I wonder whether I should*
> *call my mother then or wait till morning.*

Backwards. One word. A prime example of how many layers of meaning can lie in one image or one word within a dream. Have you ever tried to crawl head-first down stairs? We would love to keep our consciousness in charge, eyes to the fore. But to keep our balance, we must turn and feel our way blindly. So, the descent to the deeper realms of the inner, where all transformation occurs, must be done backwards, as blindly as we come down the birth canal. We cannot see our path in advance, we must feel it one step at a time, with instinctual toes.

There is also an occult tradition which teaches that, after our body dies, our soul moves backwards through our life until we pass through birth, but this time into death, assimilating our life's significance as we go. I have observed that this method of assimilation is not restricted to physical death, but also is the psyche's method of moving us through loss, upheaval, and change. Again, backwards has as much to do with a stance of blindness and trust as it does with chronology.

In this dream, the part of my feminine self that will midwife my mother and myself through her death passage has been born, and will go through its own passage, necessarily backwards. Whether in a man or a woman, it is the feminine aspect of the psyche that gives birth, and death.

4 October, 1998
The call from my husband Clyde

I am at work, just shortly after report, when Debbie calls me to the nurse's station. "You'd better phone your mother right away."

My hands shake as I dial, my stomach shrinking to an acorn. I hear her voice, so slow and thick, but with a vulnerability that reaches out for me like the arms of a child. *"I'm real sick, Dee."*

Off the phone, I melt with the acid wind of approaching loss, cry and shake in Debbie's arms. I know at that moment, though I choose to forget in order to focus my eyes on the road and drive the familiar five-hour drive.

When I arrive, the nurse in me goes into assessment mode, though the little girl in me wants to wail and cling to her mother. Odd, the cool psychotherapist in me comments, since you know wailing and clinging has never brought a positive response from her. The nurse proceeds: voice stronger than this morning, breathing labored and wet but passing, weak, pale, no angina since 10:00. I persuade her to return to a schedule of all three inhalers and breathing treatments, and scribble an itinerary of puffs for the day. I bring her lemonade. I empty ashtrays piled with frothy Kleenex.

I watch a calm settle over her that spreads to me, so that at last I can drop the doing, to simply be with her. The afternoon drifts into evening. I shut the curtain. We close further into our own world, where she drifts in and out of sleep in her recliner. I wake her for breathing treatments or to puff on an inhaler; she wakes herself to make sure I'm there, to ask what my son Mick's doing in school, to ask whether my pet llama is still resisting hugs. Two old friends enveloped in each other's presence, adrift in a palpable fluid of trust and well-worn love.

I remember thinking how complete I felt. I avoided the realization that this sense of completion radiated from her. A settling into the basket of death, just as a baby drops into the pelvis a day or so before birth. Now, I'm reassured by that memory. This woman, who struggled through all stages of her life to achieve enough, to be good enough, was able to drop the struggle and rest in the arms of a force that some would call God. I might call it grace. If she were here now, after letting it have its effect on her, I think she would call it love.

While she finishes her last breathing treatment, I flip on the TV and channel-surf. She signals for me to stop as Tutankhamen's tomb appears on the screen. We listen to Egyptian beliefs on the afterlife as the steam from the treatment rises before her face like incense.

Shuffling to the kitchen to take her nightly medications is slow, laborious for her. The snake of oxygen tubing writhes behind her. I stand at her side as she washes up, I pull her up from the toilet where she is marooned, I hold her arm as she walks. She has never allowed these intimate cares before. But I never once think in terms of dying, until she refuses to take the Metamucil she has taken religiously for five years. *"Not tonight, not tonight."* Even then, I push aside the knowing, as I had done that morning at work.

As she settles into bed, I bring her the old cowbell from the mantle. "Ring this if you need me."

She gives it a trial shake, and manages a tiny grin. *"Jeesus, that's enough to wake the dead."*

I wander the hall for a while, peeking in and listening to her breathing until it comes evenly, still labored but coated with the rhythm of sleep. I am anxious, restless. Although my room is less than five feet from hers, a sort of separation anxiety plagues me. I am split between this anxiety that sucks me back towards her room and an urge to fold myself inwards, into black peace. I wait to hear her bell.

I must have fallen asleep, and deeply, because I wake suddenly, as if from far away. No dream recall. Certain that it is morning. The magic with which sleep can erase the events of the previous day has worked upon me. I imagine how we would talk about how well we'd slept after all, and how we'd passed through the crisis. Then I realize what has actually woken me. Groaning. As I run to her room, I check the clock: 2:00 a.m.

She is on the pot chair, an antique family relic that had decorated the porch throughout my life, only within this last month returning to its original mission. Her head hangs forward, her back lunges up and down with each groan.

"Mom?"

"My nitro."

I shake the tablets into the cap, press them into her mouth, check the clock, and wait. Touching her shoulder gingerly, aware that she's not soothed by touch when she's in pain, but knowing that I need it. Two minutes, no change, more nitro.

"Help me to the bed."

She can't lie down. Breathing comes too hard. I lift her hospital bed to nearly upright, shove pillows behind her back. Two minutes, no change, more nitro. Two minutes, no change; I can't give more. I call her doctor, Frank. When I hear that he's coming, something in me releases. I crawl onto the bed next to her, enfold her in my arms, sob. "I'd do anything, anything, to make this pain go away."

She does not resist my hold, but leans into me. *"Oh, God, Dee. Oh, God, Dee."*

Suddenly Frank leans above us. As taciturn as usual, but with the soft, wet eyes of an old friend, he examines her quickly.

"I'm sorry, Frank," she whispers, as if to apologize for needlessly waking him.

"Hush, Joy." He darts a hypodermic needle into her rump. "This should let her sleep now." Knowing I'm a nurse, he adds, "I'll leave some extra Stadol here. If she needs more after four hours, give it."

Her breathing softens. I watch her sleep. I slip out to the bathroom, and return to find her groaning again. Only ten minutes have passed. More nitro. No change. I call Frank. Please let me give extra Stadol. Yes. I alternate Stadol and nitro through the night. There is very little, perhaps no, relief of pain. No sleep.

"Why can't I just die? . . . Poor Frank."

"I love you so much, Mama."

"I love you too, Dee dear."

In the morning, I call Frank again. I hear myself pull a concise nurse's report out of some recess of my overwrought brain. My motivation is sharp: I want pain relief for her. "Give her an extra shot of Stadol; I'll order morphine."

I choose the buttock with fewer jab marks and once again inject the body that gave birth to me. The incongruity of the roles of daughter and nurse still sandpapers against me, but the roles are blurring as the hours go by, so that it seems that there has never been any other purpose for one or the other than to converge at this crucial moment. This is the breath and the meaning for life.

After the extra Stadol, she sleeps for nearly fifteen minutes. I feel like a lost child. I wander to the bathroom, staring at my face, as if trying to find an identity of my own. Poem images begin to swirl, a momentary anchor for my mind:

The Survivor

After long days of watching you fade,
your skin a lace curtain
through which light bleeds shyly into my heart,
I cling to the mirror, frantic
to know myself, hook myself with eyes
that store the sharp edges of my life,
so that when you are torn from me,
dissolved into shoreless silence,
I will remain, bones against your sky.

Awake again. In pain again. Within the hour, the morphine arrives from the pharmacy in the hands of her trusted neighbor. For the first time in eight hours, the heart pain is gone. Still, her breathing is thick and labored. It won't let her lie down. It focuses all her energy on the act of sucking air past the ponds of accumulating fluid in her lungs.

She hasn't peed for eight hours. I call Frank and ask for an IV and something to help her breathe and pee. He agrees, avoiding the unspoken question: "Can't you persuade her to go to the hospital?"

When I return to the bedroom, she is pretzeled over, elbows on knees, unable to lie back in the bed, respirations thicker and more rapid. A wave of helplessness passes into me, jellos my stomach. "Mom, I can't do anything to help. If you were in the hospital, they could help you breathe better."

"Goddammit, no. I wanna be in my own home."

I sit beside her. Hands on her knees. She holds my hands, with an undulating force that echoes her breathing. I wipe her forehead with a damp facecloth. I touch her back. Although she has never been one for touch, it's different now. How do I say it? We are together. I am her companion, her succor. Layers are ripped away. We are down beyond bone, down to the marrow of our love. Our love surrounds and leaks into her pain, and into my different sort of pain, changing its color and texture.

"I love you so very much, Mama."

"I know, darling, I know. I'm so tired."

At one point, she lifts her face to touch eyes, *"WHEN is this baby going to be born??"* She's fully aware that she is dying; she is fully aware that she is in labor, moving towards another kind of birth. As much as the pain and medication may be dulling her outer perceptions, her inner perceptions are being subtly refined.

I phone Clyde, say simply, "Please come?" I have no way of verbalizing what's occurring. But he hears my need, and arrives in less than five hours.

Lana, the home health nurse, appears at the door before 1:00 p.m., hauling IV equipment. In the midst of my nurse's report to her, I succumb to sobs: "I don't know what else to do." She reassures me that I'm doing all that can be done in the home, and that I'm respecting my mother's wishes to die naturally, to die at home. Her words scrape away my helplessness like mold from cheese, leaving me strangely refreshed to continue. It has been eleven hours.

Mom's breathing comes harder and harder, wetter and wetter. The pharmacy in this little town is as yet unable to find IV Lasix, so she hasn't peed. As her heart becomes less able to pump, the fluids rise in her lungs. Her nausea increases—*"I'm gonna throw up, Dee, I'm gonna throw up,"* throughout the day until Frank sends me an anti-nausea suppository.

Another taboo to break. I thought it would be a jolt to push a suppository into my own mother, but all touch to her body now feels like love. Like washing your baby's body, brushing your lover's hair.

231

Ice chips soothe her dry mouth and nausea. I leave the room long enough to pound cubes to slivers with my grandfather's antique ice cracker.

Her neighbor, Catherine, offers to sit with her to give me time with Clyde. As I cling to him, cry into his shirt, I stretch the bond with Mom to a distance from which I can see more clearly. It's time to let go. I don't want to see her suffer any more. When I go back to her room, I carry a shift in my heart.

"Mom, I love you so much, but I don't want you to suffer any more. You can go now and be free." I gently brush back her hair, hold her against my chest.

At 5:00, Frank delivers Lasix and more reassurance. Or at least a sense of camaraderie: We are all helpless, riding on waves of fate much bigger than our human capabilities. He says very little, mutters that I can up the morphine.

"Dee, I messed myself."

I send next door for Catherine, to help me clean and change her. To preserve her dignity, we lift her onto the pot chair, where I change her pajama bottoms while Catherine changes her bed.

"Let me sit," she puffs, exhausted from the move. I wash her face, then her bottom, a kind of last rite, a sacred ablution.

Back in bed, she must sit upright to get air into her lungs. I kneel on the floor, she pushes her head against my left shoulder with more force than I had imagined possible. She mantras, *"Mamamamamama."* We rock back and forth with her breathing.

"This is the hardest part, Momma, but it won't last forever. I love you so much." Twice she stops to lean back and stare into my eyes. It's as if she looks at me from a faraway place, and at the same time is the closest she has ever been. Her soul locks into mine, with none of the years of protective barriers left. The words of the "Charge of the Goddess" chant in my mind: ". . . and as a sign that ye be really free, ye shall be naked in your rites." For twenty-five years I have recited them, but now I understand their deeper meaning. We are naked of soul. It is absolutely freeing.

The atmosphere in the room changes. A calm fills it. Another line from the sacred books whispers in it: "There is a peace that passeth understanding . . . It abides in the hearts of those who know the Self as One."

It is at this point that I ask her, "Do you want to lie back now?"

"*Yes.*"

I ease her onto the pillow, half turned towards me. Our eyes stay locked together. My hands stay cradling her shoulders. I tell her everything, with eyes, with voice, with presence. I feel possessed by a force larger and brighter than my own.

Clyde has come to the doorway: he later tells me that I looked like an ancient priestess. She and I are priestesses together. I watch her breathing ease and slow. Peace rises in our bodies, like a gentle wave, visible and palpable. Her breathing stops. Her eyes stay on me until her eyelids flutter shut.

She is gone. So is the force that filled us both. I cry in grief and in joy. "Oh, Momma, I'm so glad you're free. I'm going to cry something awful now, but it doesn't mean I want you to come back, but I miss you so much. Did I ever tell you how beautiful I thought you were when I was little? I thought you were the Goddess. You had such beautiful hands. I'll never forget your hands."

Clyde helps me to adjust her body, untilt her head. I kiss her, smooth her hair, stroke her hands. How can something look so much like her, but she is not there?

We do the ritual I've been taught for the dispersing of the elements from the body. This ritual is, in part, a psychological tool to help loved ones let go of the form once the soul has left. I know this, but never knew before how hard it is to let go of form. I sit on a stool, clutching the heart pillow I made her thirty years before, and stare at her. After an hour, Clyde calls Frank.

His face is without expression. He doesn't look at me. He listens for her heart. He feels for her pulse. He pulls the IV from her arm. I join in this new ritual. I pull the electrodes from her abdomen—the electrodes which sent signals from her spinal implant to her left hand, mutilated twenty years before by a blast of buckshot, so that the pain could remain endurable.

"You'll never need this again. You'll never be in pain again. No more pain, Momma, no more pain." I pace, and shake uncontrollably, my teeth clicking together like some strange insect wings.

They, strange men dressed like bankers, come to take her body away. This is the last giving up. No longer will I be able to look at her, touch her. There is no priestess in me now, only an orphaned child. The child who had felt it her duty to save her mother, each time she was sick, each time she was loaded into the ambulance by strangers. I scream and cling to her. Her dog screams with me, high-pitched yikes of pain.

Clyde has to pull me away, hold me in the kitchen. Catherine holds the dog. I see the eyes of Frank, of Catherine, and of her husband Harvey staring at me. Their eyes are not naked, their eyes are not the soul touch. I am utterly alone.

Only Clyde and I remain in the house. I pace, I shake, I click my teeth. Then a familiar voice in my head: *"Oh, for God's sake, Dee, just sit down and have a glass of wine."* I giggle. She's there. I drink the wine, seated where I had so many glasses with her. The hurt is dulled a little, the shaking softer.

That night, in the short time in which I do sleep, I see a fireplace. On it is an amethyst crystal. This image is somehow soothing. I know it to be Mom's stone. I know her to be soothing my soul and reaffirming the eternal. The woman who did not believe in either symbols or the afterlife is using the former to assure me of the latter. It's a way of telling me, *"I understand now."*

"Loving Buddha Mama"
A dream/vision gives instruction

Hazel Weiser gives an account of how a dream / vision instructed her to help her mother to the light. This is a powerful story for trust in oneself, especially in those realms that often can bewilder or frighten.

No men are born into my family. We are a family of mothers and daughters, and of sisters who disappoint each other as friends. Boy babies are not conceived or fail within the first weeks of pregnancy. The men who marry into this family either work themselves to death, literally, or while at home at least, they remain as undercurrent.

We are Jewish. According to the Old Testament, we are the chosen people, special in God's eye, tested for our devotion, never spoiled, but brutally punished when we fail. Our family has adapted this legacy of choosing. Without boys the mothers choose one daughter, the special daughter, into whom they place their hopes and dreams.

My maternal grandmother, we called her Nana, told me about the chosen. Not my mother. Nana had just moved in with her sister so I must have been seven years old. It was the first time she showed me the box of sepia photographs. One I recall: all five sisters when they were young women—Sarah, Fanny, Rose, Lena, and Anna—dressed as prosperous eligible wives. Nana was my favorite old person, a woman whose emotional distance and dignity drew me to her. I found her reserve enticing. She gave me opportunities to be myself in her presence.

"Nana, were you the chosen daughter?" She didn't answer.

My mother was not chosen. I knew she favored me. Was it that I wanted to make her smile? I worked hard; I was earnest in my comedic performances and little dances. I made up elaborate fantasies to keep her amused. Was it that my older sister Adele was already moody and changeable, dark like my father's family, tainted by having been almost lost to polio just weeks after I was born? I was cheerful and uncomplaining. Later my mother would confess that as a child I was independent in a way that allowed her to almost forget that I needed her. Was it that I insisted she hold me and touch me even though she was not inclined to mother that way?

My mother never spoke those words to me; she never told me I was chosen. But I knew. My sister knew, too. I didn't fully understand what it meant, not until my mother began to die.

* * *

My mother is suffering. I look at her, gray with a tinge of yellow. How old she has gotten! She has a lace face like her mother. Tiny lines subdivide her skin into an intricate pattern of threads that tie together the episodes of her life. Her face has made sense out of her life. I will have a lace face, too. Now everything on my mother's face is sagging. Her back demands all of her attention. She can hardly walk. She lies in bed, trying to adjust pillows, her legs, her arms, anything. But nothing takes away the pain in her back.

Rage fills me, pinning me to the doorway of her bedroom. I am just standing there unable to walk to the bed where she is lying in a position complexly convoluted with pillows under here and there. I had practiced all through the pre-dawn plane ride from New York to Florida how I would just walk into her home empty of my own feelings, ready to receive hers, and know exactly what she needed. I would care for her, this frail and diminutive woman who never asks for anything, whose demands are silent but unrelenting.

Instead I am a raging teenager, fury enveloping me as an impenetrable shield and as I look behind me, he is standing there. My father. This feels too familiar, old, long grown out of; but it is real and it is now. Every argument we've ever had lines up in my memory as a retrospective of this failed father-daughter relationship. Because that's how it's been with him. All I feel is blame.

There was a time when it wasn't like this. When my mother dressed Adele and me in sister dresses, and sometimes she wore the mother version: gray polka dots on the top, a gray full skirt with its own crinoline, a red belt at the waist. We went to the Statue of Liberty, all of us, Ted and his girls, in our gray polka dot polished cotton dresses.

It was 1955 during the "duck and cover" days of air raid drills in the hallways of elementary school. Ike was president. We still wore gloves in springtime and stiff patent leather shoes that gave us blisters on the backs of our heels. Our mother's chidings echoed about us whenever we left home: Everything we did reflected on our father's status and her good bearing, even among strangers. She threatened my sister and me with a stern look. By my teens I would mock her and call it her hawk look.

"Mama, what can I do for you?" I break the silence because of the longing in her eyes. Nothing could prepare me for this moment of seeing her. I want to make everything better, but I can't. She is beyond my magic.

"I just want to hear the sound of your voice." I still can't move towards her, believing I will damage her with my slightest touch.

How could he let her suffer? How could he, armed as he is with a law degree, a masters in medical jurisprudence, a lifetime of cross-examining doctors under oath beneath the American flag? How could he let her pretend that it didn't hurt that much long enough to reduce her, as she is reduced, to something less than my mother? She's emanating pure pain, pain that I can see, feel coursing through my own body, pain I can smell as each cell dies from the onslaught of whatever it is inside her still undiagnosed. She can no longer pretend that it isn't so bad, that she can cope.

I cannot move. I am stunned by the sight of her, by my reaction to him, by my own impotence, because I know I will not be able to distract her. I will not be able to make her laugh. I can only force the issue and surrender her reluctantly into the hands of doctors who will not see her as my mother, but as a problem that, because of her age, may or may not be solved.

* * *

My mother is dying. No one will say that. But that is the truth and the truth is pounding inside my ears, reminding me with each heartbeat that she is dying.

My father placed a conference call to my sister and me at 9:30 on Tuesday night. "Mom's back broke because she has bone cancer that most probably started in the lung." Tears, sobs, I could imagine this old man collapsed alone at the kitchen table, crying without relief.

"Dad, it's OK," my sister says. I say nothing.

"She has agreed to radiation, but no chemotherapy."

My mother is dying. That isn't what my father says. Instead, between sobs, he gives us the list of tests: CAT scans and MRIs in search of other hot spots in her body. There is nothing in the upper gastrointestinal system; her esophagus is clean. My sister sighs relief; I feign it. But my mother refuses a colonoscopy. Gasp from my sister. She is afraid of the pain and humiliation of that procedure.

There are two small enhancements, that's what they are calling them, in the inner sections of the brain. Her brain. Enhancements. I've never heard that word before, and I know if I ask for a definition here, I will break a rule.

"Dad, what's an enhancement?"

"Something is showing up on the films," his voice quivers, "but they don't know what it is exactly. It could be dust."

Of course, they know. Of course, it isn't dust.

My mother is dying. I cannot imagine the world without her. I cannot imagine the world without this woman who has loved me, feared me, preened me, disapproved of me, wanted me so much that entire decades of my life were spent getting disconnected from her.

The telephone conference call ends. I am lying in bed with my husband Jordan by my side. He has placed his competent hands around me as the tone of the conversation and my own tears betray its content. He hangs up the receiver for me. I sob. I shake. I howl. I weep. Jordan just holds me and lets me cry. I have to stop occasionally to blow my nose, to get my bearings, to catch my breath. But he never tells me that I must stop. He never tells me that everything will be all right. I cannot see an end to my tears. Somehow I fall asleep and stay asleep until morning.

I am crying on the toilet. I am wildly abandoned to convulsive shudders; my entire body is reeling from sorrow. Even I can smell the terror that my mother is slipping away slowly, painfully.

"Mommy," Lena rushes to me and folds her newly-turned-nine-year-old arms around me, patting my back in a rhythm that tries to interrupt the rhythm of my sobs. "Mommy." And she begins to cry, too, because she cannot protect herself from my sadness, not yet. Still I cannot stop crying.

Should I allow her to care for me?

Years back when I was just five, I recall finding my mother sobbing in the bathroom, because her sister was dying. I recall holding her and realizing that I could soothe her, calm her, that I had this power to make her feel better. That's when I curiously extended cords into her heart, not knowing, of course, that I was, or the consequences. These cords snaked their way into her body, so that I could feel her heart breaking. These cords told me how to love her. These cords let me listen to her inner conversations. And now I feel Lena extending her cords into me. I am hesitant. Do I want her to know me like this? Will she have any protection against my sorrow? I feel them enter me; these are my daughter's roots, taking hold of my heart.

Now she knows and that takes away my sadness long enough to stand, flush the toilet, wash my face, and hold Lena so that I, too, can get my strength from being a mother, so that she, too, can understand the courage of being a daughter.

* * *

"I decided against chemotherapy," she begins the telephone call.

We are a family of pauses and silences, a family of implied and too often wrongly assumed responses. I want to tell her: I don't want you to die. Instead I stir a pot of winter soup.

"That's your decision, Mama." This is what finally comes out. I don't recall formulating the words. I can anticipate my father's disappointment if I don't use my favored position to convince her to go ahead with chemotherapy. I cannot say that to her. As yet, I don't know why. I add wine to the soup stock and take a sip to taste.

"This is no one's decision but yours, Mom."

"Your father wants me to take the chemo." Her voice wavers, because we aren't talking about her getting well, and we both know that. We're talking about inevitabilities. We're talking about her leaving her family, abdicating her marriage, of never seeing her granddaughters married, or having children themselves.

I just stir the soup.

"I want you to understand," she continues. "I need you to understand." I can't remember my mother ever being this determined. Once she married my father against her mother's better wishes, she seemed unable to stand up to him, except when she was protecting me. She did it quietly and privately. Now she's letting me see that she is willing to disagree with him. She needs my allegiance. I stir the pot although the soup does not require such diligence.

"I understand." I add more salt; I put in a chipotle pepper. The soup is now too spicy for my mother's palate. I understand that she wants something out of this conversation. She has practiced her lines, I'm sure. She wants one thing as she looks ahead, and she needs me to help her: She wants to preserve her dignity. That is now my imperative. She hasn't told me, of course. I know from the cords that extend to wherever she may be. My tears fall into the soup. I press a piece of squash to see if it's soft enough. It isn't.

From the silence, I believe she's crying, too.

* * *

I'm home again wearing another new bracelet, another gift from Jordan. The kitchen, bedroom, and my office, each has a vase filled with flowers, in the middle of February. Jordan's offering to me: roses, lilies that smell, lilies that don't smell, irises, tuberoses, my own personal springtime. Lena is in her room listening to a teenage boy group sing about first heartbreaks on a new stereo, her birthday present. Her girlfriends are over, and their chatter and laughter, only the sounds of which are audible, not the words, provide me with the courage to push the "on" button to begin my computer.

I've been outside. It's barely ten degrees. I ran to the oldest tree in the back yard and wrapped my arms around it. It's over a hundred years old, a tall proud maple, the last to lose its leaves every fall once they turn a shocking yellow. I love this tree and watch it often from the kitchen window. I want to know what this tree has seen. I want its wisdom. I want the confidence to accept the natural cycle of life: growth, bloom, fade, and bare.

I wish I could put my hands into the earth, but it's frozen. I opt instead for watering the plants in my bedroom. I mist the leaves while the computer flashes icons for each of its software programs.

I type the phrase "lung cancer" into a search engine. The response is enormous, thousands of entries list instantaneously. I really want to type in "Hilda S. Weiser—a pleasant lady," but there won't be an exact match; there cannot be a clear path to knowing what and when and how the end will come. Still I need to know as much as I can.

Lung cancer likes to spread to bone. Once it disperses, there is no treatment. A little radiation might ease the pain, but only minutely. And the brain enhancements: One text says that brain tumors originating from the lung carry "a poor prognosis and high morbidity." Despite the cold, clinical terms, I translate this into my language. My mother is going to die.

My mother has stage four adenocarcinoma lung cancer—the worst kind, because it has spread beyond the lung, through the lymph system into distant sites. Surgery is not an option. Radiation is merely palliative. Chemotherapy doesn't work. My mother has a 0% survival rate after five years. No one lives for very long with what she has.

Now I'm sitting in the living room with little girls dancing wildly in costumes that don't want to stay put. Sometimes they are singing along, sometimes they are laughing so hard they can't do anything but look at each other and laugh some more. Sometimes they are working hard to mouth the words of teenage pathos, practicing for what will come in just a few more years. I cannot resist them; I laugh.

Their joyfulness and intention flood through my body, traveling with the words I have just read into the deepest reaches of my consciousness. Now I know there's nothing to do. I feel lightened and relieved. My mother knows what's happening inside her. I can trust her intuition and not fight her.

Yet perhaps this information seems so blunt and unambiguous because I don't have any context. I don't know how cells divide, how mutant cells gobble up healthy ones. I don't know the secret language of oncology.

* * *

I see now what is killing my mother. I am looking at a blown-up photograph of a cancer cell, actually adenocarcinoma from someone else's lung. It is beautiful, stained blue to contrast against the red normal cells. Instead of distinct cells, like the red ones, the blue cells are all connected, hundreds of cells merged together and monstrously larger than the normal ones. The image is so big, filling most of the computer screen, that it becomes abstract art, quite modern, although still adhering to traditional concepts of beauty: the colors, the placement of the cells that makes the observing eye return again and again to the near center of the photograph, to the blue stained amoebic cancer. I am mesmerized by my enemy.

The telephone rings. It's my father speaking from the portable phone, and my mother is in the kitchen. She has been home now for five days. This joint telephone call seems ordinary. "Girls, quiet down a bit. I can't hear."

My mother has a taste for melon and is eating cantaloupe, watermelon, and honeydew for lunch now, in addition to a bowl of pasta with butter and a scattering of cheese at night. Her only complaint is that the daytime attendant who comes for just six hours a day doesn't remember to store the fruits separately once they are cut. My mother is annoyed at having to tell her daily.

She isn't eating any protein.

"Yes, I am." In the mornings, she likes a little peanut butter on a single cracker, along with a cup of tea. She actually has two breakfasts, one before the Medicare aide comes to bathe her and the other after the morning nap she takes when the Medicare aide leaves. She has the peanut butter at the second breakfast.

I stare at these mutant cells while we speak. I think I know a lot about cancer now. I think I know what she feels inside her.

"We have something to tell you, Hazel." My mother's voice is faintly jovial although I can't imagine what good news they could possibly have.

I'm staring at the cell, wondering how it got to be so beautiful, different, deadly.

"Your mother fell the other afternoon after the attendant left." My father gives a little laugh as he tells the story. "She was coming back from . . ."

"Mom, you didn't have your walker with you?"

"I was in a hurry. I didn't want to have another accident."

I hear the word "another."

"I fell and called for your father."

"Were you wearing the back brace?"

There is a long silence. I stare back at the cell on the computer screen: Its story is very complicated and perhaps its genetic tale, just thinking about it, will distract me from nagging my parents to reconsider how they are caring for my mother at home with less than twenty-four-hour care. My mother's safety doesn't seem to be their top priority.

". . . climbed up Daddy's leg . . ." That's all I hear. In my imagination, despite the seductive blue and red image before me, I see a long, slow crawl by my mother with weakened hands, trying to get enough of a grip on my father's pants leg to stand.

"The x-ray for a broken hip was negative."

This beautiful blue evil creature is killing my mother.

* * *

I'm staring at my foot. I don't ordinarily look at my foot; but today, perhaps because this is my first day home after six days in Florida, I need to make sure I'm all here, that I haven't left anything behind. And of course, because of the nightly foot massages I gave my mother, now I know her feet so I can make the comparison. People have often commented that we look like mother and daughter. My mother was always pleased because she never considered herself a pretty woman, and looked at me with my taller stature, fuller hair, less Semitic features as being handsome. I have her coloring, at least before she turned gray. I have light brown hair that was once blonde, and like her I have not turned gray even edging onto fifty. We each have fair eyes; mine are gray-green that turn darker when I cry. Hers are gray-blue that go pale when she does. Now I notice that I have her feet.

Do I have her flawed genes, too? Someday will I wake up with a pain or a twitch, feel something, or have a lump discovered that will reduce my world to the words in medical dictionaries and journals? Lost, at least for now, among the thousands of genes that make me Hazel, is there that same combination of flawed genes that soon will allow damaged cells to reproduce over and over and over again? I don't want to think about this. I need a distraction, something to prevent this from becoming an obsession, because in just four days, I'll be back in Florida.

I don't want to go. I don't want to see my father's sad and defeated face. I don't want to see my mother's creeping disregard for her loss of self. I don't want to see their friends, the aging couples beset with their own miseries who look at me as if I were a saint, because they know how hard this has been, living two lives, in two different states. I don't want to respond to their appreciation, their knowing recognition that some children, perhaps even their own, would not sacrifice as Adele and I are sacrificing. I don't want to pretend that this is a normal, ordinary family.

I don't want to go back to Florida to play perfect daughter so my mother can show me off. I don't want to be her possession. I resent being her daughter. I gasp, trying to blot out these last thoughts, because suddenly I remember, once again, that there will be a last opportunity she has to display me.

It is close, so close to the end. I want to wear sackcloth and ashes, but it's too early. It will only get worse. I am so tired. I don't know if I'm ready, but the end will come quickly no matter how I feel, no matter what I do or don't do. None of this is about me. This is about a disease that is consuming my mother.

* * *

We are stuck in traffic on the Northern Parkway, bumper to bumper, on Sunday evening. It's 7:00. At 7:40 the last plane leaves for Palm Beach International, and I might not be on it. Lena is in the back seat. Jordan is driving. We got here, just another car in an unceasing line of stalled cars, with little more than half an hour to get to the airport, because Jordan didn't want me to call my sister back until after dinner. I understand. He was being protective.

We are driving on the Northern Parkway so slowly that the arm on the speedometer doesn't register. It stays in its resting-place. My heart is pumping loudly, consuming most of my attention. It feels like it's growing in size with each beat, so large that there's no room for a breath even. My chest might explode. My heart might be too scarred and damaged to sustain any bravery when courage is really what I need.

When I finally called my sister back after dinner, she started to cry. "Mommy can't get out of bed. I arrived this morning, and she can't get out of bed. I'm sorry, Hazel, I'm sorry, but . . ." She weeps. My sister has not shown herself to me in so many years that I had

245

Take Me Home

come to believe that she can't cry, that she had hardened herself into a rigid mold of obligation. But now she's crying: fear, sadness, worry, confusion, insecurity, all the same emotions that are bleeding out of me.

"I'm coming down."

I hang up the phone. I calmly give orders. "Jordan, get me on a plane as soon as possible. Tonight. It has to be tonight. Lena, go into my bedroom and pack my bag. Put in cosmetics, deodorant, toothbrush, underwear for at least five days. I will choose the clothing." The first thing I grab is the black ensemble.

We're ready to leave the house in less than fifteen minutes. Jordan has purchased the last ticket, and it happens to be first class, on a Delta flight leaving LaGuardia at 7:40. I call Adele back and tell her what time I'm supposed to land.

"I'll pick you up at the airport."

"No, don't leave Daddy alone. You shouldn't drive. Call a cab for me."

I don't think about what I'm saying before the words come out. I don't know where my authority is coming from. I sense someone is whispering in my ear, telling me what to do, what to think, what to say. I am not as wise as my instructions.

"Mommy," Lena calls out from the back seat, "what happens if you don't make the plane?"

"Nowhere to go, nothing to do," I respond. Now I know what this mantra means. My friend Anna had given it to me weeks ago, and I didn't understand it, or why it might come in handy. Now I know. "There's nothing I can do, Lena. If I get to the airport, I get there. If I don't, I will have to wait until the morning. It's not up to me."

My heartbeats betray me. I must make that plane tonight. I have to see my mother. I have to watch her take that last breath or else how will I ever believe that she is really gone? I can't think about that. I must not drown in that sorrow, not yet. I must stay in the present tense. My heartbeat pulls me back. I am here, utterly here, now.

Jordan gets off the Northern Parkway and turns onto the Cross Island, hoping that traffic will lighten, but he forgets that people come to Long Island beaches, in early June, from Westchester and the Bronx, so this roadway is clogged, too; but the speedometer arm lifts a bit. Not much.

Nowhere to go, nothing to do. I repeat that phrase silently, and it syncopates with my pounding heartbeat. I am mesmerized by the rhythms of my heart and how the mantra has counterbalanced the drumming in my chest, all resounding inside my head: a song with a lyric. I am consumed by this song.

Jordan has his hand over mine. He feels guilty for not having me call my sister back sooner. I don't blame him. His entire life has been taken away from him since January, and he has never complained. It's his busiest time of year, yet he has come home early from work to supervise Lena's homework, her test preparation, and to make dinner for the two of them. They watch science fiction snuggled together at night, communicating better physically than with words. With words they fight. I can feel his calm enter my hand, move up my arm, but nothing can stop the pounding of my heart. Nowhere to go, nothing to do.

It is 7:17. We are stopped, caught solidly in traffic. Nothing is moving. We haven't even passed a sign for LaGuardia Airport. That's how far away we are.

"Lena, see that dark cloud over there?" The voice just comes up and out of me.

"Yeah," she eagerly responds.

"Move that cloud over the airport. Delay the plane." I'm shocked at how nonchalantly this request spills out from me. I look in the rear view mirror and see Lena concentrating, staring at the cloud, piercing it with all of her naïve attention. Seconds pass, minutes evolve. One, two, five. I count the raindrops as they splatter on the windshield.

"I did it, Mommy, I did it!" Lena cries out in triumph.

"Thank you, my little witch," I smile, but the heartbeats are so loud that I shout. Jordan looks at me concerned at this crack in my veneer.

Suddenly the traffic speeds up around Shea Stadium. Jordan guns the engine. He moves way beyond the legal speed limit, weaving in and out of lanes, passing every vehicle with precise and predetermined turns of the wheel. He has well-honed warrior skills, and they are useful now.

"Go, Daddy!" Lena squeals from the back seat.

It is 7:30, and I run inside the Delta Terminal, breathless as I go through security and with some luck, oh I need some luck, the departing gate is Gate One, and Gate One is the first beyond security. I run up to the counter.

"You can't buy the ticket here," a young insolent woman informs me when I hand her my credit card.

"That's not what the man told us on the telephone. He said I could pay at the gate."

"That's not possible." I look at this woman. She is just plain nasty, that's all, tired and fed up with travelers all wanting something special from her.

"My mother is dying. I must get to Florida to be with her. Here is her doctor's telephone number. Call him, if you want, but you must let me pay for the ticket here. I must get on this plane." That whisper's in my ear again. It's a woman's voice telling me what to say, preventing me from shouting or crying. There are tears in my eyes, and my face is more vulnerable than angry.

She takes my credit card. Jordan and Lena will drive around the airport to make sure I get on the plane. I can call his cell and have him pick me up if there's been a failure of time. The woman calls the plane and tells the flight attendant on board that a last passenger is coming. "Don't close the door yet." She hands me the ticket. I look her in the eyes. I let her see my pain.

"Thank you."

* * *

At 11:30 I get to my parents' home. My father opens the door, but I push past him, dropping my bag at his feet. I don't stop for anyone. My sister is coming in from the kitchen. I don't acknowledge her. I must get to my mother's bedroom. I must see for myself. Has she? Is she? Yes, she's breathing, shallowly. She's alive. As I touch her hand, her fingers are icy, she opens her eyes.

"Oh, my Hazel." And she begins to cry. I see what looks like ecstasy radiating from her. I pause startled. How can she possibly still feel joy?

I lean over to kiss her so she cannot see the tears pouring out of my eyes. Some new reservoir fed by unceasing sadness has been discovered near my heart. I thought I had already cried forever. Now, once again, I cannot stop myself. My lips touch her cheek. I can smell the perfume of last days coming up from her skin, her breath, her hair. Molecules of my mother are spinning off. I want to breathe her in so that tiny parts of her will be forever lodged near my soul.

"*Mama sheyn, Mama sheyn.*" Where do these old Yiddish words come from?

She lifts my face and touches its stream of tears, my hair, my own tired skin, all the while taking me in, taking in her last breaths of me. I fold her cold, bony hands into my heated ones, and steadily look in her eyes, and see through my tears and hers that yes, she is dying. The blue has faded from her eyes; they are mostly gray now. I see no fear. I see incredible pain, drowning pain, pain that makes life impossible. I forgive her for no longer trying.

Now that her daughters are here together, she will die. This has been the unspoken throughout these months.

* * *

We are alone together, my mother and I, in the dimming light of afternoon. She has not moved or spoken since she fell asleep exhausted after her good-byes, to Adele and me together, to our father alone. I sit vigilantly by her side, watching her, wondering if I will see the moment when life leaves her and frees her from this suffering. Her body is on fire, every cell of her body is calling out, claiming her last attention, then dying off into a cold that cannot be re-ignited. She no longer wants to be here.

"You're going to help me, aren't you?" She opens her eyes and speaks immediately, in a casual tone of voice, matter-of-factly. I hear those words thunder through the room, surround my body, rattle around in there, touching every memory, every hope and dream, every part of me that will ever be. Her pain is mine. Her love is mine. Her desire to return to God, not pleading, but with dignity, well, that's mine, too.

I cannot avoid her eyes. She knows me. She knows my daring. She knows my convictions. She knows my love. She inadvertently taught me how to stand up to her authority, to my father, to teachers, to judges, to jailers and police. I feel no fear, no reluctance, no hesitation. That voice comes up again.

"Yes." And I kiss my mother's fevered forehead. I know what to do. I know what to do so that she might just slip away, so that she will not feel the fire and the cold anymore, that she will not feel that very moment when her body and soul are freed from the bond that keeps them together. She will return to God without cursing him.

This is the task for which I was chosen.

She falls back asleep. This last request. This only time she has ever asked for anything.

I take her hand, and we are locked together once again; our eyes, hers gray, mine green, tell all. I want her to know before she closes her eyes, that I love her, that I forgive her, that I am hoping, beseeching whatever spirit there is in the world that she will never open her eyes again.

I lie down on the bed next to her. She's falling into ash, not quite ready to blow away. Her lace face is no longer becoming.

Now I am about to lose my mother. Forever. That much I know about death. I will never see her again. I will never hear her voice. I will never have another casual conversation with her. I will never be able to bring a smile to her face or make her laugh.

She's no longer dreaming. I wonder what she's thinking. She hasn't shared any of what she thinks about dying with me. I don't know how she feels about death except that she's not afraid.

* * *

I see my mother lying there, and then I see her getting up, carefully, first her head rising, then she swings her legs over the side of the bed. She uses her hands to boost herself up, and now she is walking away. She starts off doubled over as I have grown accustomed to seeing her. She is walking slowly and confidently without her walker. The farther she gets from the bed, the more she is straightening her back, yes, the younger she's getting. She is once again how I remember her when I was a little girl and might catch her in repose, sad and distant, when I would climb into her lap and tell her stories just so I could get her to smile. So she would hold me.

I jump out of bed. It is indeed evening. The guest room where I have been napping for just a few minutes, maybe a half-hour, is black with night. I run toward my mother's bedroom.

"Mama, Mama, I can help you." I'm running down the hallway, dark, oh it seems too long and so dark. I'm not sure whether I have spoken out loud. This imperative that I tell my mother what I know, she must be alive still, is vibrating inside my head so loudly that I assume I have spoken. I don't know. So I slow down as I enter her room. I try to walk, but I arrive in her bedroom like a streak of madness. There are no lights on in the bedroom; it is silent except for the death rattle. My father and sister are seated in chairs by the side of the bed. They are staring at me. I am out of breath. I look away. I look over at her, at my mother. She's still lying there near dead, less there than she was just hours before.

There's no more time. I must tell her now. I lean close to her ear, and a longing startles me, a longing for what I know I am losing. I want to stop time, but I know I must not. "Get out of bed, Mama." I am commanding, slowly, carefully, enunciating my words so there is no misunderstanding. "You can do it. Get up and walk away from us. Mama, you won't hurt anymore. You won't hurt anymore if you just walk away."

My father and sister look at me astonished and distressed. I have been speaking out loud all along. But they can't stop me.

"Does Mommy ever use a metaphor?" I ask him urgently, still wild from my dream, not caring what he thinks or my sister thinks, only knowing that I must tell my mother what she needs to know.

"Your mother didn't use figures of speech," he finally says. "She was a very literal woman." He has used the past tense and the room fills with the echo of "didn't" and "was."

"We will let you go, Mama." Adele's eyes fill up with tears. "You are free to go." My father puts his face into his hands.

* * *

Every part of me now, every part that has ever been her daughter wants to touch her hand, to feel the softness of her skin, to stroke her lace face, just one more time. But I cannot. I must not bring her back to me. I must not divert her from her journey. I must not cry. I must not let even a tear distract her as she nears departure. I pause. I breathe in the last of her breaths.

Her skin is mostly gray and blue with just a tad of pink left, like twilight as it nears darkness.

Silently I release her from being my mother. And then the cords that extend between my heart and my mother's fall away. I am startled. Once again, I'm separate from her. I cannot feel her heartbeat, her pain. She has no more desire.

We wait without speaking. We are each in our own separate meditation, dream, memory, desire, dread. The last of his wife, the last of her mother, the last of my mother. I am watching each breath, how weak the inhale is; the exhale barely perceptible. I am watching life leave my mother's body and realize that nothing in my life except for my life could have prepared me for this.

I am hoping now, as close as I can come to praying that each breath will be her last. We sit silently. Silently. Time is marked by waiting for the next breath. There is no time. We are here, all waiting, all wishing finally for the end to come. Then there is eternity between a breath and the breath that never comes.

"Mother Mary"
Miracles happen

*Megan Burt's story takes us into the powerful realm
of prayer and a transformation that happens on the
'deathbed'.*

It was Mother's Day. I was driving to the hospital to see my mother, who was dying of ovarian cancer. I was thirty-three. She was fifty-five. The prognosis left my mother angry and afraid and withdrawn. I remember how hard it was for me to see her so frightened. I recall the profound feeling of powerlessness as I drove to the hospital on that Mother's Day. As I neared the hospital I began very automatically to say: *Mother be with my Mother on Mother's Day*. This became a mantra, a prayer. I repeated it again and again and again.

I arrived there to discover my mother alone in an ancillary room. It was very large. Probably used for treatments of some sort. She appeared very small and alone in this large cold room. In my mind I kept repeating: *Mother be with my Mother on Mother's Day*.

Moments after my arrival a nurse came in to say she would be moved into another room. Once settled in the room my mother wanted the privacy curtain shut. She was withdrawing and closing off from life and she didn't want to have to engage anybody.

The woman in the next bed, however, was hard to ignore. To the degree that my mother was afraid, angry, and closed off, this woman was open, happy, and engaging. I couldn't ignore her. She was sitting in a hospital bed and she was radiant. As I greeted her, my father walked into the room. I could see on his face despair. I began to repeat my mantra, it becoming: *Mother, Mother, Mother ...*

The woman in the next bed was a persistent conversationalist. She began to talk to me, sharing the circumstances of why she was there—a minor medical issue. She then told me that she recently returned from a most extraordinary spiritual pilgrimage to Medjugorje, Yugoslavia, the site of recent Marian apparitions to a group of young children ... Mother Mary!

I stood at the foot of both beds—my mother on one, this stranger on the other, the privacy curtain drawn between them. I slowly began to recognize that my prayer/mantra, *Mother be with my Mother on Mother's Day,* was manifesting. Synchronistically, just that week prior I had seen a program about this phenomenon in Yugoslavia. I had found it quite striking and it had awakened my own memory of being that ten-year-old child gazing up at Holy Mother Mary in the grotto.

Gently I began to bring my parents into the conversation. I could see them begin to transform. They became open and curious.

I had to leave the hospital to go to work. I felt infused with grace. I had a knowing that all will be well. I felt that I had been given an extraordinary gift of universal support.

I called my mother later that night. She too was transformed. She continued to talk with her roommate and was given a gift of a photograph. This photograph was taken of a tree in the village of Medjugorje. There was an apparition on it: the face of Jesus Christ. My mother told me that she placed it on her abdomen and felt tremendous warmth and energy.

She left the hospital and lived another year—a year longer than predicted by her surgeon and oncologists. In that time she became a spiritual seeker of sorts. She was less frightened and much more peaceful. My father experienced a deepening of this faith. I had the memory of being loved and safe and felt great universal support as I went through the caring of my dying mother.

"My Rose"
Afterlife happening

*Linda Moseley's story portrays the tragic
unexpected death of her mother and a mystical
afterlife happening.*

My mom's name is Rose. She was born and raised in Little Italy in
New York City. She was tall, warm, and loving, with the most beautiful
smile that would light up a room. During WWII, mom worked in a
small sewing company. She was great at sewing and making things.
One day the boss's son (Edwin, my dad), came home after the war
and met my mom. Six months later, they got married.

In 1950, my parents had my sister Patricia and then they had
me in 1959. In the early 1960s, children still received the smallpox
vaccine. I received it when I was six months old and had a severe
reaction that left me with permanent neurological damage. By the
time I was three years old a secondary condition called scoliosis was
rapidly developing.

The reason I mention this is because of the overall effect my
impairments had on my family. We became completely connected to
each other. My mom gave me my strength to keep trying. She gave
me the encouragement and support with everything I did. But I knew
that she continuously worried. She was always there protecting me
and my sister.

When I was a teenager we liked to go to the mall together, or
the beach, or watch late night TV. Often because of my neuropathy, I
would get tired walking and lose my balance. I always held my mom's
left arm as we walked together shopping or sightseeing on family

vacations. I held her left arm up until I met my husband. Then I started to hold his arm, but mom always (even in my forties) held out her arm to me for support.

The last day that I held my mom's arm was March 23, 2004. I was forty-four years old and we were walking together towards the front door of the hospital where she died three days later, something that we did not expect. My dad and my sister were there, too. We were all together.

This hospital procedure was supposed to be routine. Mom should be home the next day. She was very nervous but still making jokes and as always establishing relationships with the hospital staff. My mom had such a great personality, that no matter where she was, people really liked her.

The next day was the "procedure." I was there first. My sister was going to pick up my dad. He had broken his hip three months before and was recuperating. After the procedure was finished, the doctor told me that everything was fine. Mom was okay and in a recovery area. When I went to see her, she looked great.

"Hey, Mom. The doctor said that everything is fine. Isn't that great?" She was happy, but she still had a worried look on her face. She knew that something didn't feel right. But the doctor said that everything was fine—"She's fine," he said.

I went back to my mom's hospital room. The nurses told me that they would bring her down to the room in an hour. So while I waited there I called my sister, my dad, my husband, and my mother-in-law to say that she was okay. My dad and my sister came to the hospital a short time later.

One hour went by. Then two hours. I asked the nurses on the floor why it was taking so long, but they had no answer. After three hours I went back up to recovery. My mom was not in the place where I saw her before.

In another area of this large room, I saw four or five nurses working quickly and anxiously on a person behind a drawn curtain. I kept asking, "Where is my mother? Where is she?" I then heard my mom's voice say, ". . . my daughter. That's my daughter." I then heard a nurse say, "Your daughter went home."

I ran to the person behind the drawn curtains: "MOM!" To my horror this gravely ill person was my mom. I ran to her side with the shocking realization that she was dying. I knew it. She knew it. All of her vitals were dropping. I remember hearing them say that they were trying to stabilize her. This shock I think prevented me from remembering exactly what I said or what my mom had said to me.

I remember looking at her whole body in despair. What is happening? I remember that she told me she was praying; praying that she will see all of us again because she knew she was dying. I remember leaving her bedside to let the nurses continue to work on her. They closed the curtain again in front of me. I became overwhelmed. My mom was dying. What happened? What happened!

I started to cry uncontrollably. I knew that my dad and my sister were waiting downstairs and they had no idea how gravely ill mom was. How can I tell them? I have to go downstairs to see them, but how do I tell them? Daddy was just recuperating; just starting to venture out with his cane. He didn't need his wheelchair or walker anymore. Things were just starting to get back the way they were. We were all feeling so much better. Oh, I had to go downstairs.

A nurse sat me in a chair and gave me some water. I pulled myself together and went down to them. I don't remember what I said, but my sister knew what was happening. I'm not sure what my dad thought; if he realized just how serious this was becoming. He's an optimist. Everything will be alright. It was heartbreaking later when he realized that this was not so, when hope was gone.

When the three of us were around my mom's bed in recovery, she was so happy to see our faces again and said she prayed for it to happen; to see us again. Her doctor came over and said again that she would be fine. She was stabilized and she should be going home in a few days.

He left the room and about twenty minutes later I cannot describe to you the horrific episode my mom went through. Just writing this now is filling my heart with so much pain. I watched helplessly as my sister, my father, and all the nurses were desperately trying to help save her. I stood and watched. My sister was trying to hold her. My dad was saying, "Rose, hold still. Don't move!" What was happening?

The nurses told us to leave the room and go into the hall. While standing in the hall, mom's doctor came back and said to my amazement, "Hey, how's mom?" He didn't know what was going on in the room. The nurses didn't call him? He looked at my horrified face and then ran in to see my mom.

For hours and hours of going in and out of surgery, of hope and then despair, we waited and my mom's condition worsened. Her blood pressure dropped so much that they pumped large amounts of fluids into her body to keep the pressure up. This caused excessive swelling in her body and face. It was heart-wrenching to watch her beautiful face swell and change so much in a short period of time.

I slept over at the hospital that night. My sister took my dad home to take care of him and let him rest. I sat next to mom's bed during the night. I think she was aware that I was there, but when I spoke to her she seemed to look distressed and would move. I wanted her to stay calm, so I tried to say little. She seemed to stay calm and sleep when the room was quiet. I slept in a waiting room for a few hours.

By morning, matters seemed to have gotten worse. Mom's blood pressure was so very low, her organs were dying. More surgery was scheduled and again we were all together—my dad, sister, my husband, and my sister's husband. At one point, the doctors started to give us some hope again, but by late that evening the hope was quickly disappearing.

Then the next day, on March 26, 2004, the doctor explained to us that hope was gone. Machines were now keeping my mom alive temporarily. To keep her on the machines would "prolong her death" as he explained it. What a horrifying thought.

Then the decision was made to turn the machines off. How horrifying and unthinkable. This can't be true.

Now the doctor tells us that we have to go up the elevator and go to a specific room to see mom to say good-bye. A special bereavement nurse will meet us there. I remember the three of us standing up, "Which elevator? Oh, what floor? Nineteen? Okay. Dad, be careful. Take your time. What room number is mommy in?" We were walking and moving, but we were stunned. How do you process this? I still don't know.

The nurse assured me that my mom was comfortable. She had not been conscious for about two days now. My sister and I stayed in the room with her. I don't remember how long we stayed. We couldn't talk to her. She was hooked up to all kinds of machines. Was it one hour? Two hours? I don't know, but it seemed that there had to be a time when we needed to say good-bye.

I don't know when, but I gave my mom a hug. At that moment I suddenly felt a surge of hysteria come up. It was overwhelming. I was going to scream out and lose all control. I feared this was going to cause great distress to everyone. I CANNOT STAY IN THIS ROOM WHEN THEY TURN THESE MACHINES OFF. I CAN'T WATCH THIS! I had to leave. I went into the hallway.

How can I watch her die? I couldn't let this scream out. I knew it wouldn't stop. The nurse said it was okay to stay in the hallway. She assured me that mom was very comfortable and completely unconscious and unaware, which I MUST believe to this day.

But when it was too late, I suddenly regretted not being next to her—a regret that I carry each day. My heart, my mind, my whole physical and mental body was overwhelmed and straining to stay in control. But I should have been in that room.

Realizing and understanding that I suddenly was shocked and horrified, unable to face what was going to happen, has helped me to accept it better. In addition, I understand that this was the beginning of a lifelong process of becoming devastated by the loss of a parent. It is a process that will be different for everyone. For me, it helps to know that this is a continuous process of feelings and emotions which I am going through.

The very beginning of this process started with the horror of losing my mother, then the need to stay in control, suppress my hysteria, and now take care of daddy. Only after my mother's doctor (on his knees) held my hand and expressed his condolences, did I begin to focus my complete attention on the well-being of my father. My sister and I pulled all of our energy and our emotional control to stay focused on helping dad. He sat so quietly in the waiting room; so thin, so pale, holding onto his cane.

A nurse was talking to him. He looked at us and said, "I don't want to cry. I can't start. The nurse is making me feel worse. Tell her to stop talking to me." Dad needed his own time to process what just happened. The bereavement nurse "expert" couldn't understand this.

She continued to tell him to cry and let it out. Dad needed time. His Rose was gone. He needed time. Not a stranger pressing him to start crying "now." That moment came later, at home.

It is so important to respect and understand that everyone is different in how they are going to feel, act, and respond to this type of devastating situation. Everyone is different.

The first year I put much energy into making sure dad was okay emotionally. Holidays and birthdays my sister and I worked so hard on making these moments positive; and they were. Support from my husband and my sister's husband was so wonderful. Emotional breakdowns, for me, came during private moments.

It was a surprise to me, however, that the very beginning of the second year I felt worse. I felt so angry and sad. Then I began to realize that when you experience a loss, this process has stages. This understanding helped me. I also realized that dad was doing well by the second year and my focus on him wasn't as intense, which allowed me to feel and grieve more.

A different aspect has helped me as well. This aspect is more spiritual or mystical in nature. It started right away. Mom was gone about two or three days when I was sitting in my living room and a strong perfume scent came to me. I asked my husband if he smelled it too and he asked me what I was talking about. This happened to me few times in different locations during the week. Then my aunt called and said, "Do you smell mommy yet? Her perfume? Mommy will be around you for a little while."

I couldn't believe what she said. My aunt told me about her own similar experiences and that I needed to be "open" to them. Mom's pretty perfume scent came to me in various locations for more than a year, and then they faded away. I felt her with me. Other experiences were happening as well.

One month after my mom died, my dad wanted to go see her grave at the cemetery. We hadn't been there since the funeral. We took my dad's big old white Cadillac and my sister was going to drive. My dad sat in the front and I sat in the back with my mother-in-law. We of course knew where the huge cemetery was located, but we had no idea where mom's grave was. During the funeral we didn't pay attention at the cemetery.

There are miles and miles of gravestones, curving roads, traffic circles, and mausoleums here and there. We had no idea where to go. Someone said to turn left at the stop sign. No, we need to go straight. My dad said to go this way and then turn right. For about half an hour around and around we went.

Then my sister became so frustrated that she told us that she is pulling over, "now." She turned the car off and got out. She looked at us and said, "Stay in the car." If you knew my sister, you would know that this is highly unusual behavior. My sister is calm, patient and would NEVER, NEVER walk through all the different gravestones, and NEVER alone, as she was now doing. I could not believe what I was seeing. She came back a few moments later and said, "No. I just felt it was here, but it's not."

Suddenly a family name popped into my head. A family that were friends with my parents many years before and they had relatives buried near my mom. I said the name and my sister looked at me with surprise. She just saw that family name on a headstone. My sister and I jumped out of the car and quickly walked down the line of graves, reading names. Then I saw it. The flowers. Right in front of me. The cemetery staff didn't remove them. They were dried up and brown, but the same ones we brought for my mom the day of the funeral. We found our mom.

I truly believe mom helped us find her that day. I think it was for our well-being. To help us accept what happened and to feel calm. In the past my mom was not able to come to the cemetery after she lost her mother. Her reaction to the cemetery was highly emotional and strongly resistant. My sister had similar reactions as well, until now. Today my sister and I can go to the cemetery and actually feel calm. Only my mom could help us with that.

Then came Mother's Day, about two months after my mom passed away. My sister brought daffodils and I brought roses to the cemetery. The next day at school (I am a preschool teacher), two little four-year-old girls came up to me (not my students) and one said, "I love daffodils" and the other girl said, "I love roses." Then they walked away.

I was stunned. I heard that children and animals are very sensitive to spiritual messages. It really might be true. And if it's true, then I believe that my mom wants us to feel happy and calm.

I had felt for years prior to my mom's passing that my connection with her was so strong that losing her would have caused a significant breakdown in my life. The thought of losing her had always sent panic butterflies inside me. She was my strength and support. Yet, it has been three years and now I seem to be okay. I am so very sad, but I think okay. Could it be that my mom is helping and supporting me?

I know that she never wanted us to feel pain and despair in our lives. She knew the pain of losing her mother suddenly (in a hospital under similar conditions). She never wanted us to feel that pain.

Perhaps I am stronger than I thought I would be; perhaps with mom's help, I found my own strength. I don't know the answer, but I am realizing the importance of continuing to allow happiness, love, and laughter into our lives when we are ready and to also expect the moments of despair and pain because of our broken hearts. My mom lost her mother under similar circumstances, but strived to make our lives filled with happiness and love. She continued to be creative and fulfilled her goals. My mom is my inspiration. My dad is my inspiration. At eighty-nine years old, dad continues to teach us how to enjoy life, to enjoy humor, art, nature, and love.

Yes, our hearts are broken. We miss her so much. But we found inspiration and with help and family support, we are finding our strength.

"My Blue Heaven"
A deal for an afterlife experience

Roberta Rachel Omin's mother leaves her signs after
she passes on.

"I love you, Mom. I wish you a comfortable and safe passage. Thank you for giving birth to me." These, my last words to my mother, pulled from my inner reservoir, were in response to Jackie's urgent call from Seattle: "Mom's dying right now; this is your last chance to talk with her. I'm putting the phone to her ear."

Jackie came back on the phone. "She just died. I think she heard you."

It was late Sunday morning, November 9, 1997. The Hospice nurse and Jackie had been supporting our mother through the final stages of dying. Before reaching me, Jackie called our sister Naomi in Sarasota.

Mom's death was peaceful, dignified, just the way she wanted it—no heroics and no being kept alive mechanically. She was intensely fearful about suffering and pain. This last cancer, her third, was lymphoma, discovered when she had exploratory surgery a month earlier. It was inoperable, yet ironically a colostomy bag was necessary.

Naomi and I had planned to visit Mom the weekend of her birthday, November 6, for our last time all together. Then Jackie called at the end of October. She was emphatic, "Mom is going faster than we expected. Can you come this weekend?" That was Wednesday night. On Friday morning I was on the plane headed for

Seattle. Naomi was doing the same. We arrived to find the downstairs of Jackie's home converted to provide Mom all the comforts she could possibly have. Her hospital bed faced the windows with the striking views of autumn.

There had been a huge shift in Mom when she came to New York in the middle of the summer to spend time with me. It was as if she knew she would never make the trip east again. She was slower, not her peppy brisk self. She gave me ideas for places to donate books and items I no longer wanted as I prepared to move from the house to a condo. Her pace set the course for the weekend. Terry, my future husband, and she had a chance to meet.

This, the last weekend in October, would be spent with my mother. She was drawn, weak, pale white; and for a woman who was always thin, she was now very fragile. Her grey, blue, green eyes were sunken and surrounded with darkness.

Strangely enough, I did not experience the familiar needy pull I had disliked intensely, particularly whenever she was ill. She seemed to be in her own body instead of reaching out to grab mine. I used to say, "My mother wants to nurse from my breast." I had reflexively always pulled away from her whenever I felt this emotional tugging, the opposite of what she wanted. I noticed, as well, that she did not speak in her sugary sweet tones meant to mask her real feelings I associated with her anger or depression. This voice would make me cringe and shrink inside, it was so saccharine.

Jackie asked if I would sleep in the extra bed in the room with Mom. Ever since Mom had come home from the hospital, Jackie had been sleeping next to her. Now Jackie wanted a break so she could be upstairs with her husband and daughters. Although I was worried about the ways my mother might need me, namely emptying her colostomy bag, I knew I had to do this. "Yes" was the only answer.

What became a key figure for me in this Hospice set-up was the hardcover copy of Elisabeth Kubler Ross's last book, *The Wheel of Life: A Memoir of Living and Dying*. Because of my work with people who were dying, I had read Kubler Ross's books. She had broken the taboo, talking openly and sensitively with people who had terminal illnesses about their impending death. With a sense of immediacy and excitement, Mom told me, "I have to finish this book before I die. Will you read it to me? I can only hear a little at a time."

"Of course, we'll do that." This became our project together. We read one chapter at a time spread out over the weekend.

During one of our reading sessions, Elisabeth, herself dying from an extended illness when she wrote the book, referred to a conversation with her ex-husband before his death. She asked if he would send her a signal after he died. Indeed he did. She found dozens of roses in the snow the day of his funeral—something that had had meaning for them. I looked at Mom and inquired, "Would you send me a sign, too?" She agreed. This was a chancy question at best, as my mother was not spiritual and did not believe that you exist in any way after death. I did not question her willingness to do this.

Naomi, Jackie, and I stopped at Mom's nearby apartment to look through her things. While I had not been there previously, what I saw was totally predictable. Living there about two years, she had not bothered to put anything on the walls. This was part of her divesting instead of acquiring. The portraits of "Marilyn" and "Monroe" that were a part of our growing up, along with the framed family photographs we had each given her over the years, were neatly bubble-wrapped and placed under her twin beds. As we expected, her kitchen was sparse and her refrigerator was empty except for the jug of cold water that was always there.

Never liking to cook, especially for herself, she would regularly have breakfast at Shari's Restaurant. Arriving at 6:30 in the morning, she ate the same thing—lightly buttered toast with marmalade and coffee with half and half. If the toast wasn't just right, it was sent back and she did not want her coffee until she asked for it. The wait staff became quite fond of Mom, as she took a keen interest in their lives. They have since placed a plaque near her spot at the counter, honoring Mom: "In memory of Louise Fontaine—a loyal friend and guest—a well done toast."

Mom's desk, except for the dust, was immaculate and unencumbered with uncompleted projects. Her file cabinet was fully in order as she had long been preparing for her death. There was a file for each of us girls with every card and every letter we had ever sent her along with typed carbon copies of hers to us. It was a record of each of our mother-daughter relationships. Without planning, we found ourselves settling on her bedroom floor as we began to go through our personal file.

As I reread a few of the birthday and Mother's Day cards I sent her, I recalled what I felt when I searched the store racks. They were carefully chosen for not conveying too much sentimentality and trying to stay true to my feelings. Intuiting my mother well, I always knew she wanted more from me—testaments of "I love you" and "You are the best mother ever." I could not authentically give her that.

Our mother-daughter relationship was fraught with difficulties. On one hand it was riddled with anger—me trying to fend off her emotional intrusiveness and neediness—and likewise, filled with hurt and resentment because of her inability and sometimes resistance to connect with me in meaningful ways. I had long since erected a wall around me, trying to protect my body and emotional boundary, to not let her take more from me than I could or wanted to give.

Now, pausing over the contents of my file, I felt guilty, while my younger sisters were deep into theirs. I imagined they were relishing their memories. I decided it was better to go on to other files. There was one file of cards sent between her and her mother, especially the ones my grandmother Jennie sent after the car accident when Mom had to remain hospitalized in Maryland for two weeks following emergency surgery. I suspect those cards and others between them were a mere micro-reflection and could not possibly bear witness to their mother-daughter bond. The silvery gray box was filled with air mail letters from her father, Marc, who lived in Israel. This exchange covered all of Mom's adult life until her father died in 1971. I decided to put off reading these letters until a later time.

Something else caught my attention—a batch of correspondence between my mother and her attorney along with letters to her husband, my father. Included were some handwritten notes from the mid 1960s, the time she was working out their divorce. Her terror, how she would manage financially and get a binding agreement, came through the pages.

Historically, my father repeatedly backed out of his commitments. I was surprised to discover that Mom had made an attempt to get some money from him for my college education. That never came to pass. In those moments, when I felt some emotional space, I could feel her, not as my mother, but as a suppressed woman struggling to combat her fright and anxiety.

I'd had a partial taste of what she experienced as I, too, went through my divorce with some similar feelings. The difference was that my father was emotionally abusive in his cruelty, intimidation, and control and she knew it. He eventually did bail on her at the closing of the house, when he refused to sign over half the check to her. For all her attempts to cover each base, she was left with no money and homeless.

In the end, her resilience won as she gained her freedom. As I read these letters, I felt an understanding of her and admired her courage. I asked my sisters if I could have this file when everything was dispersed. It was agreed.

In the bathroom, there was as always Mom's enema bag, hoisted on the shower rod ready for its daily ritual. Each of us was very familiar with its long-standing presence in our family. Wherever Mom went so did her enema bag, which included visits to our homes. We knew Mom could not go to the bathroom without it. We had heard her stories of 'not being able to clean herself out,' so after a lifelong close companionship with it her intestines were no longer functional. On more than one occasion as a child I had been subjected to its use. Jackie was the first to joyfully declare, "When Mom dies I am throwing this thing out." We all burst into laughter, thrilled it would finally meet its demise.

That night at dinner, Mom was carried to the table by Martin, Jackie's husband, where she spent a few minutes with all of us. She nibbled and returned to bed. At one point when Mom was not at the table, Martin decided to share his view that Mom only had a short time left to take Jesus into her life and she was still refusing. Naomi and I were silent and we let the conversation die out. Jackie and Martin had become born-again Christians and were, as well, politically in the far right. It had always been quite clear where Mom stood and that she was a liberal. However, wanting to keep peace with her daughter and son-in-law, she had long since abandoned any religious or political discussions with them in this arena of dissention. The "taking in of Jesus" did not come up again as far as I knew.

Over this weekend Mom's female minister paid a visit to go over plans for the cremation and memorial service. With this attended to, Mom was satisfied and pleased. She had nothing left to do except easily let go of her life. I was struck with how her dying was dignified. The Hospice team came regularly and anytime they were needed. Jackie and I were grateful to Evergreen Hospice; they made her ending days physically and emotionally comfortable.

During one of our reading sessions, Mom commented to me, "You learn from books, not from experience." This was one of her insults, the only one she gave me over the weekend. I let it go, but it did sting. I felt she wanted to hurt me and at the same time I told myself she doesn't really know me.

We took last pictures together. Most of all, Mom had her deepest and dearest wish granted—to have her three daughters with her. Naomi and I were able to get along unusually well and we all decided to have sisters' reunions with some of the money Mom was leaving us.

A conversation amongst us sisters concerned Mom's upcoming eighty-first birthday on November 6th less than a week away. We knew a birthday cake and celebration was not in order. Then I thought about my niece's birthdays: Sara's on November 8th and Kristyn's on November 13th. I mentioned, "Mom will not be thinking about their birthdays and she could easily die on one of them." Jackie confided she did not want the happiness of her daughters' birthdays complicated with their grandmother's death. Not feeling in the least way uncomfortable, I assured Jackie I would speak with Mom.

Sitting next to my mother on her bed, I placed my hand over her parchment-skin forearm as I broached the subject: "Mom, Sara and Kristyn's birthdays are coming up soon. If you have any choice in when you die, could you do your best not to do it on their birthdays?" She appeared fuzzy and unaware of the dates, so bringing this up jogged her to think about it.

At the end of the weekend, Naomi returned to Sarasota. Monday morning Mom and I awoke early. We completed the last chapter in *The Wheel of Life* and said our last good-byes. At the airport, Jackie grabbed me and cried. I held her as long as I could and told her that I would be with her in spirit and we'd speak every day.

Each day, Mom faded more. She was never in pain. By her birthday on Thursday, she could barely whisper. On my daily call I said, "It's your birthday today." I felt her nod through the phone. On Friday Mom moved into less consciousness; Jackie held the phone to her ear as I let her know I was thinking about her. Early Saturday morning Jackie went to Mom's bedside and whispered, "Today is Sara's birthday." Mom waited.

Sunday November 9th Terry and I were spending the weekend at his cozy cottage on Long Island. It was our first anniversary together—a bright sunny and cold day. When the phone rang, Terry immediately handed it to me. It was Jackie telling me Mom was taking her last breaths.

Terry held me at various times during the day but the tears couldn't come. When I reached Dave at college, I sobbed before any words were spoken. Dave patiently held the space and stayed on the phone.

That night, Terry and I went to bed in the loft. Just before awakening I had a dream. I saw Mom's face; she was much younger, she looked beautiful and serene. I remembered she always teasingly said, "Don't bury me until you are sure I am dead." She looked so good I had to catch myself that she had really died. I then knew my mother and her spirit were all right. She had sent me her sign.

271

Postscript: A year later, on the same weekend, Terry and I spent our second anniversary in Northampton, Massachusetts. On the drive I mentioned that I realize how much I am like my mother. Then I musingly added, "I wish she would send me another sign. I just want to know she's okay."

When we arrived at the bed and breakfast, I decided to check my office answering machine. The guest phone was located in a little converted closet. On the floor was a wooden magazine rack with sheet music; on the top was my mother's favorite song, "My Blue Heaven." Because she loved it so much, Uncle Charlie had taught me the motions to this song, which I performed at our family gatherings.

The following day as we walked through the town browsing the shops a street accordionist played the same song. I commented to Terry, "Do you realize that the likelihood of "My Blue Heaven" being in my presence twice this weekend is highly unusual?"

Terry simply replied, "Your mother sent you two signs."

It was true. My mother was well. I could feel at ease.

Part Three

The Inner Home:

A Guide to Conscious Care Giving

Centuries ago, the ancients discovered that the human being is capable of transforming negative, threatening, and compulsive states of mind into landscapes of inner peace, rejuvenation, and illumination.

1: Discovery of the Inner Home

There is much wisdom to be gained in accompanying our elders into the last stage of their lives. Death, known through the ages as the Great Awakener, is the teacher of this wisdom. Death summons us to awaken—to our mortality, to our imperfections, to matters of the heart, to the preciousness of life. We caregivers are exposed to new and demanding experiences within and around us that are terrifying, challenging, haunting, and profound. Our hearts are exposed to all kinds of suffering.

The concept of an Inner Home grew and developed in me as a natural response to my struggles with the challenges I faced caring for Mom. I was overwhelmed and anxious much of the time, and the intensity of these feelings literally forced me to find a way to calm down so that I could cope with her situation and function in my life. I began to make time to reach inward by closing my eyes as though I were closing the door to the outside world and opening a door within that led to a soft, cave-like shelter.

Often I created a place in my house where I could retreat into a simple environment of candlelight and a blanket. Sitting quietly in this atmosphere, listening to my breath or the silence in the room, I discovered a warm retreat. I began to look forward to these private moments that carried me into another realm of peace.

Eventually I discovered that this retreat which I eventually called my Inner Home was not just a place for refuge. I began to experiment with this inner space and found that often a sense of timelessness and a particular quality of stillness would come over me. A door seemed to open to another realm where everything felt more vibrant and I would become infused with gratitude and a sense of the sacred.

This atmosphere caused a vibrancy of mind that helped me think more objectively. I used this state of mind to work on difficult issues and interactions with Mom, to inform decisions regarding her care, and to work on dreams that had pertinent meaning. One thing began to lead to another and I realized I was on a path of discovery.

Coincidences, inspirational books, dreams, and intuitions appeared like little jeweled helpers guiding me deeper into a world of light and meaning amidst the agonies of witnessing Mom's sufferings.

Sometimes I created a ritual to enter and exit my Inner Home to intensify the quality of stillness. I found that candles and meaningful objects added to this intensification, as well as an inspirational book. I usually would turn to *In Tune with the Infinite,* by Ralph Waldo Trine, or an oracle like the Tarot or the I Ching for input. When stillness arrived, I would open the book randomly or pick a card and allow the message to circulate. Sometimes an insight would come or an instructive memory or image. Many times I heard a voice speak to me. As I grew familiar with the feeling of stillness, it would come over me especially in nature. I would actually feel my heart open, transporting me to greater sources of wisdom, compassion, and reverence.

These discoveries and practices turned the task of caring for Mom into a journey that depended on and was enriched by my own psychological and spiritual work. A connection to something bigger and wiser within and around me was born as Mom was leaving this world.

So on the basis of this learning I will share with you more specifically how to create the Inner Home.

2: The Inner Home

The Inner Home is a well-spring of unfathomable riches within each and every one of us. It is a multi-faceted jewel of potential that consists of five rooms. Note the word potential! Some rooms require the creation of an atmosphere that will unlock its potential.

The following section describes the purpose and atmosphere, as well as exercises for each room for rejuvenation, personal growth, and wisdom. I used an experiential technique to show you how to create the atmosphere that will open up certain rooms where this is required.

If my imagery does not fit with yours you may want to explore this method your own way, with your own imagery. Go through the exercises at the end of each room to help you identify which room you want to enter.

You may, for example, want to put some meditative music on and light some candles. Tune your mind to your breathing and the rise and fall of your chest. Become aware of your environment around you. After you have done this, turn your attention inward and notice your inner atmosphere. Bring attention to your body and how it feels. If there is a place that needs energy, breathe into it or readjust your position. Once you're settled in, become aware of what you need. There may be a particular question or exercise that comes to mind. Focus on this for a few minutes and then let it go. Keep in mind that you are on a journey to your inner self, where wisdom abides and connection to higher realms of intelligence is available. Listen for images, intuitions, or any other type of information. Focusing your attention on connecting with your innermost self will awaken it from sleep. Answers and help will come to you.

Spend at least fifteen minutes in silence in each room in order to open to its mystery. Allow yourself to slow everything down in your thoughts and imagery, as though in slow motion, so that all of your senses can become finely tuned. When you get distracted come back to your breath.

The Five Rooms of the Inner Home

The Sanctuary

The Sanctuary is often the most needed room for caregivers. The task of care giving requires so much energy and time that thoughts about caring for oneself often slip by the wayside. Thankfully you can enter The Sanctuary anytime or anywhere: at the doctor's office, in an elevator, during a difficult interaction, a morning run or a walk in nature. No one will even notice that you have turned your awareness inward—to The Sanctuary.

The Purpose of this room:

The Sanctuary offers comfort and a sense of well-being, but most of all entitlement to respite from life. It provides an invisible barrier between you and the outside world granting permission for self-care, which is especially necessary for caregivers. Like sanctuaries for wildlife, this place exists for your protection. There is a guard dog at the entrance.

The Atmosphere of this room:

A quiet, peaceful, and protective quality, infused with the feeling of being entitled to care for oneself.

Entry (how to enter this room):

The wish to have a place that is totally yours comes over you as the light of your awareness turns inward. Your focus intensifies the idea that somewhere in your psyche there is a room called The Sanctuary. And suddenly, out of the darkness of your mind, the felt sense of this sanctuary and of being entitled to take care of yourself begins to appear and circulate through your being for several minutes.

The impression of The Sanctuary becomes more real as you

explore it, move around in it, and absorb the feeling of it. You can suddenly experience the sensation of relaxing into the shelter of this space. You notice the colors, the quality of light, the textures, the smells, the movements, and whatever else is present to you.

After a while a particularly soothing quality of The Sanctuary becomes apparent. You begin to focus in on it and amplify the sensation of its presence until you get slightly lost and absorbed by it. Slowly this sensation shifts into an atmosphere that instills peace and protection both within you and around you at the same time. You feel cared about and that your well-being matters.

You can have the thought/feeling:

'Sanctuary Consciousness' is now flowing throughout my entire being and surrounding me with its invisible shield.

Abiding with the presence of this feeling, you can do any or all of the following that has an appeal for you:

1. Read a page from a book of meditations or any inspiring book that moves you. Read it several times until you can feel into its effect on you or its message to you. Write down your experience if you wish.

2. Play a CD that is soothing and wrap up in something comfortable. (Sounds True Catalog has a great selection worth looking into.) Feel all of your tension begin to flow out of you as the vibration of the music comes into you.

3. Paint, draw, color, or mold clay from your imagination, allowing total freedom to your feelings. It is important to know that what you do is not art but rather an expression of an inner voice or feeling that will lighten the burden of intense emotions. It can be helpful and enlightening to see, for example, a drawing of one's anger or love or guilt. Give a name to your work and keep it in a safe place, or you can burn it or frame it. Does this activity bring any new insight into your relationship with your elder?

4. Write an affirmation of commitment to care for your body, mind, spirit every day.

5. Write about your experience in a journal.

6. Move in slow motion to a peaceful CD. Get absorbed by the rhythm.

Here are examples of some images of Sanctuary (it is most important to go with your own):

a walled garden

a cave

a cabin

a sound

light

a scent or perfume

an atmosphere of color

sensation of rocking or being surrounded by a soft blanket

moonlight.

These examples cover a wide range of sensory experience because not everyone is visual. Some people "visualize" through sound, light, smell, or sensation.

The Room of "Little Jeweled Helpers"

It has been revealed to me on this journey with Mom that there are sources of wisdom I call "little jeweled helpers" that will appear when beckoned. These helpers are mysterious and come from the compassionate side of the universe. They appear through dreams, intuitions, body symptoms, oracles, prayer, coincidences, psychic phenomena, a voice, chance meetings, epiphanies, whisperings, and in many other subtle modes. Their presence evokes feelings of awe, of being accompanied, a sense of the sacred, bliss, stillness, compassion, and gratitude to name just a few of the ways I came to experience them. If you are willing to imagine that they exist, you will have access to the room of Little Jeweled Helpers and engage them to take part in your journey.

The Purpose:

When you open to the existence of these helpers you will begin to feel accompanied and those 'strange, mystifying or weird experiences' will be understood as messages of wisdom from these jeweled helpers.

The Atmosphere:

An open mind and attuned observation to one's inner and outer environment.

Entry:

You can enter into the "space" of these helpers by doing as many of the following things as appeal to you:

1. Keep track of coincidences, synchronicities, big dreams, chance meetings, and whisperings. When you make a request for help, pay special attention for signs from these helpers.

2. If it feels right, follow the message of this wisdom. For example, if you get a message that tells you to call your parent right now, do so. Or if you have a sense to go another way home, try it. Record how these helpers show up and guide you.

3. Work with oracles such as the Tarot Cards or the I Ching: Think of what you would like help with or what you would like to know more about in a situation with your elder or just for yourself. When you formulate your request, ask the Sage that resides within the oracle for his/her help. Imagine what this Sage might look like and really feel her/his presence. And then toss the coins (I Ching) or pick a card (Tarot or other card oracles) and work with the message given. Let it circulate in you throughout the day and digest it slowly. How does it bring a broader understanding to your situation? Write about it, paint it, or talk about your experience with a friend.

4. Write a prayer to the little jeweled helpers and put it under your pillow at night. Believe that some form of help will appear. What did you dream? Did any image or memory come to you in the early dawn or wake you up in the wee hours of the night? Did anything unusual happen during the day, the week?

5. If you dream about an interesting, compelling, or helpful figure, animal, bird, stone, tree, etc., make an object to represent it and then place that object where you can see it easily and often. Begin to form a relationship with it through dialog so that you can receive its wisdom.

Intuitions are like a soft knocking on the door trying to get your attention. Did I hear something or not? Sharpen your senses and pay attention.

A friend of mine, for example, knew that there was something she needed to do for her mother but she could not recall what it was. Her mother, even though she was in a coma, appeared to be experiencing pain and discomfort. Intuitively, she closed her eyes. Suddenly she leaped up and remembered what her mother had said to her earlier in the week that would help her when she was dying.

The Room of Sacred Ground

The Room of Sacred Ground is the place to connect with your heart. Sacred means that which we greatly honor and hold reverent, "close to the bone." When we enter into the Room of Sacred Ground we come into a consciousness of deep compassion and connection to all that is around us. In this room we open to the unknown and can experience vision that is not limited by barriers of judgment, logic, and belief systems. Our hearts are fearless and can help us take risks in matters of the heart, especially important for us caregivers dealing with our elders.

The Purpose:

An experience of reverence and sacredness has a therapeutic effect on the mind/body. This room is stress free and can help us shift out of ordinary ego consciousness into the realm of golden light and warmth, to recover a sense of something larger and more comprehensive watching over us. There is an awareness in this room of belonging more to the world than to ourselves.

This consciousness awakens the place of higher wisdom within us, often referred to as the Higher Self. The Higher Self can perceive the Divine Web that I refer to in my memoir section of this book. The Divine Web is an experience of illumination where you can actually feel an energetic connection to everything around: the trees, a stranger, the wind, the birds, insects, etc. You can actually sense consciousness in everything and realize that these things are also conscious of you. How might this affect your actions? Your thoughts? Your intentions? This is the hallmark of the Room of Sacred Ground.

The Atmosphere:

A felt sense of sacredness, compassion, and illumination.

Entry:

You have just found a comfortable and quiet place to sit for a while, free from all distractions of your daily life. You slowly turn your awareness inward to the sensation of air coming in through your nose. You notice the soft motion of the rise and fall of your chest. Consciously you focus the "light" of your attention toward your heart, touching it with a soft warm glow, in recognition, in invitation. As this happens, a prayer for your heart to open comes to you. You take time to formulate this prayer and after a while you can hear it. You become aware of the energy and light within each word and your heart slowly opens. Out of darkness a small dim light emerges and slowly expands into a golden glow, illuminating The Room of Sacred Ground.

Enveloped in this golden atmosphere, you become aware of where you are right now. All of your senses suddenly become keener: your sight; hearing; smell; and sensation to temperature. Your awareness moves down and your heart becomes the source of perception; illumination is all around and within you. Every detail intensifies. You can feel into the shapes of things, the color of things and textures. A deeper appreciation for the uniqueness of everything around you, including yourself, comes over you. There is a feeling that everything is here now in this moment and has a right to be here now in this moment. Time slows down and an awareness of stillness sets in. The felt sense of the "preciousness of life" comes over you.

You may have the thought/feeling:

I am now in Sacred Ground Consciousness.

Ways to deepen your awareness of being in this consciousness include:

1. Read some "heart" poetry by Mary Oliver, Rumi, or any other inspired poet of your choosing.

2. Imagine that a holy being has made you a cup of ambrosia. It has a magical power to produce a feeling of lightness of being. You are offered this drink in a beautiful tea cup. You consciously drink the potion and feel it glide down your throat, immediately lighting up your interior.

3. Imagine that you are sitting in the center of a circle of healers who all want to help you. Open to this experience and look around for what in you needs healing. They begin to perform a ceremony for you. Let your imagination go and take your time to experience what happens. Feel what it is like to be in the center of their medicine energy and their intention to give you healing and rejuvenation. How do they work with you?

4. Experiment with ways to open your heart: Focus on thoughts of gratitude, meditate on some object of beauty, create an altar, during the week perform some acts of kindness or generosity. What kinds of things open your heart?

5. Prepare a mantra, prayer, or affirmation that speaks to your heart. Repeat it until it gets into you. Try using this mantra the next time you are in a difficult interaction with your elder or experiencing an intense anxiety or rage. What happens?

6. Set up a place in your living space where you can be alone. Create an altar on which you place objects that are sacred to you at this time in your life. Set some time aside where you can sit in quiet for a while. Make an offering to your altar. Spend some time with it during the week so that you can call it to mind when needed. Is there a particular essence or spirit that your altar emanates?

7. For five minutes perform a tedious activity as though you are doing it for a holy being.

The Room of Alchemy

The Room of Alchemy is a workroom for personal growth and wisdom. This is the room where you can work on difficult issues and feelings that arise in the process of caring for your elder. I use the word alchemy because it was an ancient science of transforming lower states of mind/matter into higher realms of consciousness. Achieving the consciousness of Stillness, or vibrancy of mind, is an atmosphere that opens the door to the Room of Alchemy. Coming into the present moment facilitates access to the atmosphere of stillness that is especially conducive for inner work and expanding consciousness. The key is learning the art of embodiment. Embodiment induces a "present moment consciousness." There is an aliveness in the present moment similar to a magnetic field: New ideas begin to take shape in the mind; images appear containing important information; there is a vibrancy of mind and a sharpening of the senses. This is the atmosphere that is most conducive for inner work.

The Purpose:

This room is a place to increase understanding and get help dealing with the difficult issues and emotions that caring for our elders presents. It is also a place where we can learn to perceive through a refined consciousness that can help us become more objective.

The Atmosphere:

A sense of vibrant stillness, mental alertness, and inner spaciousness.

Entry:

The Room of Alchemy is the top floor of the Inner Home. The archway to this higher level is constructed of all different kinds of stones and crystals. Over the archway is an ancient alchemical picture. Through the archway you can see a stone hallway leading to a staircase to the higher level. Windows of various shapes line the hallway. The staircase is made of worn smooth stones and crystals and sconces of light line the walls. Just above the stairs in ancient text appear the words, "To Awaken the Room of Alchemy, ascend each of these ten stairs in slow motion and observe every stone and crystal along the way."

There is a sense of luminosity and curiosity in the air. Slowly you ascend the stairs. This is a "secret" place that seekers, scholars, and mystics have known about for hundreds of years. Take some time to breathe this in.

As you step onto the landing at the top of the stairs, a large room with windows and huge stone fireplaces opens before you. Taking your time you slowly walk around the room, noticing all of the objects, tinctures, and other elements. A feeling of awe begins to come over you as you realize that this is the place where alchemists first discovered how to refine and transform lower states of mind into gold, a symbol of illuminated consciousness.

As you look around, you find a comfortable place to sit down. There are candles to light as well as incense. There are blankets to wrap up in and a stone cup filled with spring water. You light the candles and incense and then settle down into the comfortable chair with a blanket ready to do some inner work. The smell of incense and the flickering lights of candles lull you into an atmosphere of lightness of being.

You now turn the light of your mind inward to your breath. Your attention takes in the rise and fall of your chest, the archetypal movement of great eternal rhythms of the world: the waves coming and going into shore; the sun rising and sun setting; the tides ebbing and flowing. Everything begins to slow down as you sink deeper into yourself, deeper into this mystical rhythm of life unique to planet earth. You have the sense of being in two places at once—here now and ancient eternity.

Your senses become sharper and time seems to slow down as though you could almost touch the air around you. The atmosphere is shifting into stillness and spaciousness. Your mind becomes vibrant and you can see and feel everything more clearly.

You are now in 'present moment consciousness' . . . the Room of Alchemy.

In this consciousness:

1. Bring back the memory of a troubling situation or interaction with your elder with as much clarity as possible.

   Notice what is going on: Where are you in this memory? Where is your elder? Spend some time with each of the following questions: What is the atmosphere of the room—the colors, the textures, the lighting, the time of day? What are you feeling, thinking, or knowing? Take some time to pinpoint this. What is your posture? What are your expectations? Your desires? Your fears? Allow yourself some time to go deeper into your experience.

   Now focus on the thought, feeling, or action that troubles you. Notice when and where this situation occurred. Was there something you couldn't say or do? Is there something you can't admit or face? Bring it to your awareness.

   What got in your way? What was avoided?

   Now visualize your desired outcome. Slowly re-do the situation in your mind. For example, if you were afraid to say something, imagine saying it. How might this affect your relationship? What are you aware of as you experience the memory through this new lens?

2. Bring an image to mind in slow motion of an interaction

between you and your elder. What is your body posture? What does it feel like and what does it convey? Is there a posture that would make you feel better? If so, try it in your imagination and see what happens.

To take this alchemy a step further, try on this posture the next time you actually are with your elder. What do you experience?

The Room of the Great Mystery

The Room of The Great Mystery is an unknowable place within all of us. It is a reminder that there are parts of ourselves that we will never know. Like outer space, beyond the Milky Way, we too contain a Great Mystery.

The Purpose:

This room can bring into awareness that we know only part of ourselves. This knowledge can help us accept that we cannot do everything perfectly. This is especially important for us caregivers because there is always a feeling we could have done or should be doing more. This room also brings to light that our knowledge of ourselves and the world is shaped by our personal history and therefore, limited. Tuning into this room can inspire us to push the envelope of the way in which we live and relate so that more and more rooms can open before us.

The Atmosphere:

An open mind to "not knowing" and awe of the unconscious that is an endless unknowable space, remarkable like outer space with no beginning and no end.

Entry:

Imagine that you have a place in your psyche that is way beyond your reach, yet it is joined in this mysterious universe where all are one. Put on some meditative music and let this thought circulate through you for at least fifteen minutes.

You may find it helpful to think:

I, and all that is around me, are part of The Great Mystery.

Ralph Waldo Trine formed the thought this way, in his book, *In Tune with the Infinite*:

I stay my haste, I make delays,
For what avails this eager pace?
I stand amid eternal ways,
And what is mine shall know my face.

Asleep, awake by night or day,
The friends I seek are seeking me;
No wind can drive my bark astray
Nor change the tide of destiny.

The waters know their own, and draw
The brooks that spring in yonder height,
So flows the good with equal law

Unto the soul of pure delight.
The stars come nightly to the sky;
The tidal wave unto the sea;
Nor time, nor space, nor deep, nor high,
Can keep my own away from me.

Contributors: the Storytellers of Part Two

(in order of the appearance of their stories)

Enid Ikeda ("September Weekend") grew up on a farm in North Dakota in the midst of the Depression. She worked as a junior high school counselor and as a high school counselor, and served as dean of students in the Great Falls, Montana, high school. Of her childhood she says, "I did not ever feel deprived, because no one in the community had any "discretionary funds," as the saying goes. No running water, no electricity, no telephone . . . only a loving, safe home and a mother who was always there. She made the most remarkable meals on a wood-burning stove, and without a refrigerator. And I do not ever remember her uttering a complaint. In one of her letters, she wrote: 'How extra lucky we are," and that summarized her attitude. She is the beacon who gave a light to my path, and does to this day."

Marsha Benoff ("Yesterday's Road") has had several short pieces published, including excerpts from her first book *Today Is for Tomorrow*, which is now being readied for publication. Currently she is working on a second book, also a memoir, that picks up where her first left off. Marsha is also a painter whose work has been exhibited at a number of juried shows. She also creates beaded jewelry.

Marsha is a longtime member of Herstory Writers Workshop, for which she facilitated workshops for adolescents on Long Island. Additionally she is a member of the Oakstreet Writer's Workshop in Southampton, NY.

Her first book is told entirely in the voice of the child and through the overheard voices of her mentally ill mother and the equally unreliable voice of her angry older sister. The young Marsha is able to escape the restrictions of her mother's madness by connecting with the outside world through books, teachers, and friends. bmarsha3@ optonline.net

Ruby Anastasia Sturcey, R.N., M.A. ("Let Me Die at Home") is a former midwife and registered nurse with a wide variety of nursing experience. She has most recently spent several years working for Hospice in her local community, and currently works as a psychiatric nurse as well as having a private practice as an Embodied Imagery Psychotherapist. She received her Master of Arts degree from Lesley University, Cambridge MA, and is certified as an Embodied Imagery Psychotherapist through The International Society of Embodied Imagination. Her work includes focusing on living with serious illness and end of life issues, as well as exploring new dimensions of one's sexuality and erotic life. She is the devoted and proud mother and grandmother of a beautiful family, and lives with her many four-legged family members in upstate New York. She can be reached at rsturcey@gmail.com.

Emmelien Brouwers, M.A., M.P.S. ("Invisible Loyalties") was born in The Hague, Netherlands, in 1955, where she obtained a Master of Arts Degree from the Royal Academy of Fine Arts. She moved to New York in 1979 where she received a Master of Professional Studies in Art Therapy and Creative Development from Pratt Institute and Psychoanalytic Certification from the Institute for Contemporary Psychotherapy and Psychoanalysis. She studied Psychodrama and Sociometry at the Psychodrama Institute of New York and Embodied Dreaming at the Embodied Imagination Institute. Prior to starting her private practice she worked as an art therapist at Interfaith Medical Center, Brooklyn, New York. She is an artist and licensed psychoanalyst practicing in New York City. She can be reached at emmelienbrouwers@earthlink.net

Colleen Donahue ("Finding Love"), a woman of many facets, was born in New York City and grew up on Long Island. She has worked in the music field under many hats as a professional traditional Irish & Scottish musician, tunesmith, and multi-instrumentalist. She operates her own company, Big Grey, for which she provides sound engineering and concert production, and was the creator and producer of Big Grey Concerts, Long Island's first and only dedicated Irish and Scottish concert series.

Colleen is also a light worker, a traditional Usui Reiki Master and Teacher, and a Heart Based Energetic Healer and Shamanic practitioner. By day, she is an international freight forwarder and U.S. Compliance Manager in the import and export industry. Colleen resides in Suffolk County, New York, with her four feline companions.

Roberta Rachel Omin, L.C.S.W. ("Liar!" and "My Blue Heaven") was born in New York City. She is a mind/body psychotherapist in Westchester County, New York. Roberta has written many memoir pieces and has published articles in various magazines.

Arlene Schofield, L.C.S.W. ("Coming to Terms") is a member of NASW (National Association of Social Workers) and has been in private practice for more than thirty years. She feels grateful for the wisdom re how not to live she gleaned from her parents.

Audrey Hoffer ("A Journey to Death") is a communications specialist with the U.S. Environmental Protection Agency in Washington, DC, and a freelance writer.

Judith Musaro Lichter Ph.D., L.C.S.W. ("Mom?") was interested in the visual arts and psychology from a young age. Early on she demonstrated remarkable ability as an artist and studied painting at the High School of Music and Art, The Cooper Union, and Bradley

University, earning Bachelor and Master of Fine Arts degrees. Judith creates lush, vibrant landscapes and figurative abstractions in oils and pastels. An invitation to use art mediums with terminally ill children and adult psychiatric inpatients led her to pursue Masters, Postmasters, and Ph.D. degrees in Clinical Social Work. Her work as a child and adult psychotherapist and adjunct professor of Clinical Social Work at NYU utilizes her knowledge, creativity, and deep appreciation for the uniqueness of individual lives. The journey through her mother's latter years focuses attention on the exquisite balance of human frailty and strength.

Kathleen Picarelli ("The Bonding Bloom") is an essayist and poet whose work explores health and healing, spirituality, nature, and the inspiring accomplishments of ordinary people in diverse cultures. Her stories are designed to be uplifting, especially for those souls who are most in need. Ms. Picarelli is currently working on two memoirs. The first explores her evolving relationship with her mother, an Alzheimer's patient, since becoming her caregiver. Through heartfelt prose and poems, the book will show how illness can be a vehicle for restoring relationships, and provide novel ways to connect with Alzheimer's patients. The second memoir is about the author's efforts to recover from two life-changing disabilities, and to find clarity and hope amidst chronic loss and hardship.

Joan Campagna, L.C.S.W. ("Finding Dad") has thirty years in private practice with adults. She specializes in Life Transitions & Self-Empowerment and Esoteric Studies and is a certified Gestalt therapist and faculty member of the Gestalt Center of Long Island. 516-674-8035

Virginia Flanagan ("Long Time Gone") has "had a great life so far"—listening to people's stories for fifty years as a psychotherapist and is "not tired yet." She is also writing stories of her own, and taking countless photos, mostly in exotic places.

Kathryn Taylor ("Cutting the Cord") is a Northern California artist particularly interested in the role the unconscious plays in creativity. She is a longtime dream worker and author of *Generations of Denial: 75 Short Biographies of Women in History* (1971, Times Change Press).

Laura K. Deal ("Uncle Duane") is a writer, teacher, and dream interpreter. She holds a certificate as a Dream Work Facilitator from the Marin Institute for Projective Dream Work, a Ph.D. in History from the University of Colorado at Boulder, and has published fiction and poetry for children and adults. You can find her online at www.lauradeal.com

Adela Windsor ("Accompanied: A Journey towards Inner and Outer Relationship") worked as both a psychiatric nurse and a psychotherapist in Colorado at the time of her mother's death. Shortly afterwards, she and her husband moved to central Mexico. They had two more precious years together before she accompanied him through dying from leukemia. She has written a bilingual book of poems, *Skinless: Sin Piel*, as part of her healing process from his death.

Hazel Weiser ("Loving Buddha Mama") was part of that first wave of women to graduate from law school in the mid-1970s. She practiced law in San Francisco, then became a law professor. She married late, just a month before her thirty-ninth birthday, and had a child at the age of forty. This chapter comes from a longer book that she wrote while a member of the Herstory Writers Workshop. She is the executive director of a national organization of law faculty, loves to garden, and is hoping to grow old in a city where there are museums, public transportation, and lots of young people.

Megan Burt, M.S., R.N., P.M.H.N.-B.C., C.A.R.N. ("Mother Mary") has witnessed and tended to multiple dimensions of human suffering as a professional nurse with more than thirty-five years of experience. Her personal journey was greatly influenced by nursing her mother through her illness and death and the transpersonal moments that redefined life, death, and love for her.

Linda Moseley, M.S.Ed. ("My Rose") has worked with special needs children for twenty-five years as a special education teacher and supervisor at a school on Long Island. She has her bachelor's degree in art therapy. She is a life-long sailor and is a member of a Long Island yacht club.

About the Author

Liza C. Johnson is a Licensed Marriage Family Therapist in private practice in Huntington, New York. She is a certified Gestalt therapist and a graduate of the International Institute for Embodied Imagery and Dream Work. Liza traveled to Iceland, France, Brazil, and South Africa to study dreams. She is also a certified Clinical Meditation Teacher. Liza discovered that writing her story brought deeper meaning to her experience. She plans to write a sequel and invites caregivers to send her their stories. She can be reached at liza@lizajohnson.com. Her Web site is www.lizajohnson.com.

Additional Products by Liza C. Johnson

1. An Inner Home Workbook and Journal—$15.00
2. CD of The Inner Home and the Five Rooms—$20.00
3. CD's for each room...$5 Each...specify which room you would like:
   The Sanctuary

   The Room of Little Jeweled Helpers

   The Room of Sacred Ground

   The Room of Alchemy

   The Room of the Great Mystery
4. CD's of Individual Chapters 1-55 of Part One...$5.00

Purchase via Pay Pal through Liza's web site www.lizajohnson.com